DEEP BLUE

STORIES OF SHIPWRECK, SUNKEN TREASURE AND SURVIVAL

DEEP BLUE

STORIES OF SHIPWRECK, SUNKEN TREASURE AND SURVIVAL

EDITED BY NATE HARDCASTLE
ADRENALINE SERIES EDITOR CLINT WILLIS

**Thunder's Mouth Press and
Balliett & Fitzgerald Inc.**

New York

Adrenaline ® and the Adrenaline® logo are trademarks of
Balliett & Fitzgerald Inc. New York, NY.

An Adrenaline Book®

Published by
Thunder's Mouth Press/Balliett & Fitzgerald Inc.
An Imprint of Avalon Publishing Group Incorporated
841 Broadway, 4th Floor
New York, NY 10003

Distributed by Publishers Group West

Book design: Sue Canavan

frontispiece photo: © Sean Sexton Collection/Corbis

Manufactured in the United States of America

ISBN: 1-56025-313-4

Library of Congress Cataloging-in-Publication Data

Deep blue: stories of shipwreck, sunken treasure and survival/edited by Nate
Hardcastle.
    p. cm.
"Adrenaline."
Contents: From The Nutmeg of Consolation/by Patrick O'Brian— Everest at
the bottom of the sea/by Buck McMahon—From North to the night/by Alvah
Simon—From The boat who wouldn't float/by Farley Mowat—From Treasure
Island/by Robert Louis Stevenson—From Philip Ashton's Own account/by
Philip Ashton—From Run silent, run deep/by Edward L. Beach—From
Pincher Martin/by William Golding—From N by E/by Rockwell Kent—From
Moby Dick/by Herman Melville—From In the heart of the sea/by Nathaniel
Philbrick—The open boat/by Stephen Crane—From Every man for
himself/by Beryl Bainbridge.
ISBN 1-56025-313-4
1. Sea stories, American. 2. Survival after airplane accidents, shipwrecks, etc.
—Fiction. 3. Treasur-trove—Fiction. 4. Shipwrecks—Fiction. 5. Sea stories,
English. I. Hardcastle. Nate.

PS648.S4 D44 2001
813'.010832162—dc21   20011027056

For Y.F. Hardcastle, Jr.,
who loved the sea and its stories.

contents

photographs

introduction

Natural selection long ago should have weeded out the tug that draws us to the sea. The sea is dangerous. It is magnificently and absurdly strong. Worse, it doesn't care about us; we are insignificant to it.

Friends of mine have a vacation house on Long Beach Island, one of the barrier islands that line the New Jersey shore and protect it from the open ocean. The islands are little more than sandbars; they migrate continuously, arranged and rearranged by the constant pounding of waves and by the hurricanes and Nor'easters that batter the Atlantic coast. For decades New York City's wealthy have built massive, garish houses, some now worth tens of millions of dollars, on Long Beach Island's beachfronts. My friends have a book about the island's history; most of the photographs show residents trying to keep their houses from falling into the water.

The ocean can be deadly even when it is calm. It has the power to isolate us and strip away everything we need: fresh water, food, shelter, clothing, companionship. Boon Island, a chunk of granite just 12 miles off the Maine coast, in 1710 was the scene of an episode of cannibalism following a shipwreck. The sailors trapped on the rock could see the mainland.

And then there are the ocean's cold, the crushing pressure it exerts on divers, the beasts it harbors, its very salinity. Christopher Martin finds himself underwater in William Golding's *Pincher Martin*: "When the air had gone with the shriek, water came in to fill its place—burning water, hard in the throat and mouth as stones that hurt."

I live near the sea. If I were to get up from my desk right now and walk south for five minutes, I would find myself staring across the Harraseeket River's tidal mud flats to the tip of the Wolfe's Neck peninsula, where the river bends around Pound of Tea Island and enters Casco Bay. My family came to this area every year when I was a child, and I think I knew from the time I was very young—six, maybe eight years old—that the Maine coast would be my home. And indeed the desire to be in this place near the ocean has shaped my adult life. The sea comforts me—yet it terrifies me.

I once lived on a small island—about two acres of dirt, stone and trees—in the middle of a salt marsh in Georgetown, Maine, near the mouth of the Kennebec River. Tidal flows had carved inlets through the muck and grass surrounding the island. I sometimes have nightmares in which I'm tromping through that marsh, the mud sucking at my boots and nearly pulling them off, when I sense the presence of massive reptilian creatures waiting patiently to rip me apart. The dream isn't about crocodiles—the most dangerous things in the water around here are mercury and dioxin. I think the dream is about the unknown, about threats that lie below the surface of my comprehension.

It's no accident that my dreams draw upon images I associate with the sea to represent things I don't understand: coldness, chaos, mindless violence. What in our everyday lives do we understand less than the ocean? What feels less familiar than the impassive stare of a fish or the wriggling, primordial legs of a horseshoe crab? My dream betrays my fear that the world I inhabit is, like the ocean, a world I can't understand.

So why does the ocean attract us? Ishmael in *Moby Dick* wonders the same thing:

> Were Niagara but a cataract of sand, would you travel your thousand miles to see it? . . . Why is almost every robust healthy boy with a robust healthy soul in him, at some time or other crazy to go to sea? Why upon your first voyage as a passenger, did you yourself feel such a mystical vibration, when first told that you and your ship were now out of sight of land? Why did the old Persians hold the sea holy? Why did the Greeks give it a separate deity, and own brother of Jove? Surely all this is not without meaning.

Some of us go to sea to escape. Water covers 70 percent of the earth's surface. That's a lot of space—about 140 million square miles—where pirates, smugglers, convicts and other outcasts can leave behind society and its power over them. That space means freedom for people like the fictional buccaneers in *Treasure Island* or the all-too-real pirate Ned Low, described in Philip Ashton's 1722 account.

Sometimes, like Ishmael, we want to escape to sea not because we're in trouble, but because we're sick of other people:

> Whenever my hypos get such an upper hand of me, that it requires a strong moral principle to prevent me from deliberately stepping into the street, and methodically knocking people's hats off—then, I account it high time to get to sea as soon as I can.

George Carlin put it differently, but his reason for living on the seashore is related: "You've only got assholes on three sides of you, and if they come the other way you can hear 'em splash."

Other people go to sea to show off. Bucky McMahon imagines diving 180 feet to the *Andrea Doria* and returning with a China plate. He dreams of earning "the merit badge of big-boy diving, the artifact that says it best:

I fuckin' did it—I dove da *Doria!*" Rockwell Kent in 1929 sailed his 33-foot boat from New York to Greenland. Approaching his destination, Kent began to imagine how the island's inhabitants would receive him and his men:

> They'd come aboard to see the ship and marvel at it. How small, how strong, how clean and neat and beautiful! How brave you are! And the men—even the hardy Danes—would admire and envy us; and the girls—sweet, gentle, blue-eyed Danish girls—they'd *love* us!

There is more to the ocean's allure, however, than the chance to escape or show off. I feel comforted when I'm near the sea. Why? There is the notion that at some level it reminds me of my mother's womb: the salty water, the rhythm of the waves approximating the rhythm of her heartbeat. I wonder too if something deep in our genes is nostalgic for the time before our ancestors dragged themselves from the brine onto dry land.

At any rate, the ocean reminds me that I am a part, however small, of something indescribably large. The ocean is permanent, unfathomable, all-powerful and mysterious, in the way I was taught as a child that God is those things. It is immortal—and it reminds me that in some way I am too.

Alvah Simon spent a winter on an icebound sailboat in Canada's arctic Tay Bay. After initially panicking at his isolation and powerlessness, he began to grow calmer:

> . . . I found myself feeling less alone, more purposeful, and deeply grateful just to be alive. Daily, that gratitude escaped my lips with an audible "Thank you." Then, as now, I had no earthly idea who I was thanking. But I think I know what I was thankful for: the privilege of being a small, frail, faulted, but integral part of the magic and mystery of life on earth.

Maybe we are drawn to the ocean because it reminds us that we are alive: It offers us freedom; it harks back to the origins of each our lives and the life of our species; it shows us that our world is larger than ourselves; it can kill us. Here is E.B. White as an old man, writing about sailing:

> And with the tiller in my hand, I'll feel again the wind imparting life to a boat, will smell again the old menace, the one that imparts life to me: the cruel beauty of the salt world, the barnacle's tiny knives, the sharp spine of the urchin, the stinger of the sun jelly, the claw of the crab.

Rockwell Kent did not get to welcome the Greenlanders aboard his boat; high seas smashed the vessel to pieces against the rocks of Greenland's shore. Kent and the boat's crew scrambled ashore cold and bruised. The next day they saw an extraordinary sunset, and one of the men had this to say: "It's right that we should pay for beautiful things."

—Nate Hardcastle

from The Nutmeg of Consolation
by Patrick O'Brian

Patrick O'Brian's (1914–2000) 20 novels about Jack Aubrey and Stephen Maturin paint a convincing picture of life at sea two centuries ago. This selection from the 14th book in the series finds Aubrey's crew shipwrecked on an island in the South China Sea. They have just met some of the region's natives, including a facinating but devious woman named Kesegaran. The sailors are trying to repair their boat—but the locals have other ideas.

Another misery of human life,' remarked Stephen to the morning darkness, 'is having a contubernal that snores like ten.'

'I was not snoring,' said Jack. 'I was wide awake. What is a contubernal?'

'You are a contubernal.'

'And you are another. I was wide awake; and I was thinking about Sunday. If Raffles' stores come in, we shall rig church by way of thanksgiving, eat a full ration of plum-duff, and observe the rest of the day as a holiday. Then on Monday we shall set to . . .'

'What was that noise? Not thunder, Heaven preserve?'

'It was only Chips and the bosun stealing away without a sound: they and their party mean to lay out the work early and start the tar-kettle a-going well in advance, and Joe Gower is taking his fishgig in the hope of some of those well-tasting stingrays that lie in the shallows by night. You will smell the smoke and the tar presently, if you pay attention.'

They lay there paying mild attention for several wholly relaxed, luxurious minutes, but it was not the smell of tar that brought Jack Aubrey leaping from his hammock. From down by the slip came a furious confused bellowing, the sound of blows, an immensely loud bubbling scream that died in agony.

It was still dark when he reached the breastwork, but lights were moving about down there and over the sea. The flames under the tar-kettle seemed to show the loom of a considerable vessel just off shore, but before he could be certain of it the first of the carpenter's party came scrambling up the hill. 'What has happened, Jenning?' he asked.

'They killed Hadley, sir. They killed Joe Gower. Black men are stealing our tools.'

'Beat to quarters,' cried Jack, and as the drum thundered several more hands came up the slope, the last half-carrying the bosun between them, pouring blood as he came.

Then first light in the east: false dawn: the red rim of the sun, and all at once full brilliant day. The largest double-hulled proa Jack had ever seen was lying a few yards off the mouth of the slip, close enough at low tide for dense lines of men to wade out, carrying tools, cordage, sailcloth, metal-work, while on the shore still others were gathered, some round their dead friends, some round their dead enemies.

'May I fire, sir?' asked Welby, whose Marines had lined the breastwork.

'At that distance, and with doubtful powder? No. How many charges do your men possess?'

'Most have two, sir; in moderate condition.'

Jack nodded. 'Mr Reade,' he called. 'My glass, if you please; and pass the word for the gunner.'

The telescope brought the shore startlingly close. They were carefully cutting off the carpenter's head: Gower and another man he could no longer identify had already lost theirs. There were two dead Malays or Dyaks and even at this juncture he was shocked to see that one was Kesegaran. Although she was now wearing Chinese trousers

and although she had been pierced through and through she was perfectly recognizable, lying there looking fiercely up at the sky.

Jennings was still at his side, still voluble from the shock. 'It was Joe
Gower that done it,' he said. 'Mr White went for to stop her taking his
broad axe; she slashed his leg out of hand, and as he lay there she slit
his throat quick as whistlejack—he screamed like a pig. So Joe served
her out with his fishgig. It came natural to him, being a quean, as they
say, and carpenter's mate.'

'Sir?' said the gunner.

'Mr White, let the carronades be drawn and reloaded with grape.
What do you say to their charges?'

'I should not like to answer for the piece forward, sir; but the nine-
pounder and the after carronade may do their duty.'

'At least change the old flannel for something dry, mix in a little
priming and let them air. Those people will be busy down there for
quite a while.' He turned to his first lieutenant and said 'Mr Fielding,
boarding-pikes and cutlasses have been served out, I am sure?'

'Oh yes, sir.'

'Then let the people go to breakfast watch by watch; and pray search
all possible sources for powder, flasks, fowling-pieces, pistols that may
have been overlooked, rockets. Ah, Doctor, there you are. You have
seen what is afoot, I dare say?'

'I have a general notion. Should you like me to go down and parley,
make peace if it is at all possible?'

'Do you know that Kesegaran was there, and has been killed?'

'I did not,' said Stephen, looking very grave.

'Take my glass. They have not carried her back to the proa yet. From
the way they are behaving I do not think any truce is possible and you
would be killed at once. In an encounter like this one side or the other
has to be beaten entirely.'

'Sure, you are in the right of it.'

Killick put a tray on the earthwork and they sat either side of it,
looking over the slip and the busy Dyaks below. 'How is the bosun?'
asked Jack, putting down his cup.

'We have sewn him up,' said Stephen, 'and unless there is infection he will do; but he will never dance again. One of his wounds was a severed hamstring.'

'He loved a hornpipe, poor fellow, and the Irish trot. Do you see they are putting on whitish jackets?'

'The Dyak guard at Prabang wore them. Wan Da told me they would turn a bullet, being padded with kapok.'

They watched in silence for the space of two coffee-pots. Most of the immediate looting had stopped and now the space round the slip was bright with spear-heads catching the sun. Finishing his cup, Captain Aubrey called 'Mr Welby, there: what do you make of the situation?'

'I believe they mean to attack, sir, and to attack in an intelligent way. I have been watching that old gentleman with a green headcloth who directs them. This last half hour he has been sending off little parties into the trees on our left. Several go, but only a few come back, waving branches and calling out so that they shall be seen. And then more men have been quietly moved under the bank this side of the slip, where we cannot see them—dead ground for us. I think his plan is to send a large body straight at us—charge right uphill, engage on the earthwork, kill as many as they can and then fall back slowly, still fighting, and then turn and run so that we shall leave our lines and pursue them, whereupon the group in the forest will take us in the flank while the people in the dead ground jump up and the first attacking party face about and between them cut us to pieces. After all, they are rather better than 300 to our 150-odd.'

'You have been there before, Mr Welby, I find,' said Jack, looking sharply into the trees on the left, where the gleam of weapons could in fact be made out quite easily.

'I have seen a good deal of service, sir,' said Mr Welby. As he spoke a swivel-gun and a gingall flashed aboard the proa. The gun's half-pound ball kicked up earth on the breast-work; the gingall's bullet—probably a rounded stone—passed overhead with a wavering howl. This seemed to be the whole of the Dyaks' artillery—no muskets were to be seen—and immediately after the discharge the white-jacketed spearmen began forming below.

After a quick, low-voiced exchange with Jack, Welby called 'Marines: one shot, one man. No one is to leave the lines. Independent fire: no one is to shoot without he is sure of killing his man. No Marine is to reload, but having fired, is to fix his bayonet. Sergeant, repeat the orders.'

The sergeant did so, adding 'having cleaned his lock and barrel if time permits.'

Now an ululation, the beating of a small shrill drum, and the spearmen came racing up the hill in groups. A first nervous musket at a hundred yards: 'Sergeant, take that man's name.' Nearer, and their panting could be heard. The last stretch: twenty or thirty musket-shots; and in a close-packed shouting mêlée they were on the earthwork: spears, pikes, swords, bayonets clashing, dust flying, clouds of dust; and then at a huge shout from some chief man they fell back, at first slowly, still facing the camp, then faster, turning their backs and fairly running away. A dozen ardent foremast jacks ran after them, bawling like hounds; but Jack, Fielding and Richardson knew each by name and roared them back to the lines—fools, half-wits, great hulking girls.

The fleeing Dyaks stopped halfway down and gathered to mock and challenge the camp with marks of scorn.

'Forward carronade,' called Jack. 'Fire into the brown.'

The flint failed at the first pull of the lanyard—a frightful anticlimax—but it fired on the second and the carronade uttered a flat poop, scattering a gentle shower of grape among the Dyaks, who howled with laughter, capered and leapt into the air. Some of them waved their penises at the English, others showed their buttocks; and the powerful reinforcement from the trees came running out to join them for a charge in deadly earnest.

'After carronade,' said Jack: and his voice was instantly followed by a great solemn crash and a cloud of orange-lined smoke. While the echoes were still going to and fro the cloud swept to leeward, showing the awful swathe the grape had cut. There was a headlong flight to the slip, and although some came back, creeping low, to

help their wounded friends back down the hill, they left at least a
score of dead.

Now there followed a long period with no action, well on into the
afternoon, but it soon became clear that the Dyaks and their Malay
friends (for they were a mixed crew) had not lost heart. There was a
great deal of movement down by the slip and between the slip and the
proa; and from time to time they fired the swivel-gun. At noon they lit
their fires for a meal: the camp did the same.

All this time Jack had been watching the enemy with the closest
attention and it was clear to him and his officers that old Green Headcloth was certainly in command down there. The Dyak chief watched
the English with equal care, often standing on the bank with shaded
eyes; and a good hand with a rifle, having an earthwork to lean on,
could certainly bring him down. Stephen could do it, he was sure; but
he knew with equal certainty that Stephen never would: in any case
both medicos were busy with the wounded—several men had been
hurt in the fighting on the breastwork. Nor would he do it himself, not
in cold blood and at a distance: although he was not displeased when
a broadside cleared an enemy quarterdeck, there was still something
illogically sacred about the person of the opposing commander, and
some perceptible but indefinable difference between killing and
murder. Query: did it apply to a man appointed as a sharpshooter?
Answer: it did not. Nor did it apply in even a very humble mêlée.

Captain Aubrey, his officers and David Edwards, the envoy's secre-
tary, ate their dinner on trestled planks laid this side of the breastwork,
which had sandbags on its top to protect their heads from the not
infrequent swivel-gun, whose layer made remarkably good practice,
hitting the embankment or skimming just over it almost every time—
such good practice that the moment they saw the flash all hands
dropped to their knees, out of direct range. Their genuflexion did not
always save them, however, and twice during the meal Dr Maturin was
called away to deal with the more sluggish.

Dinner today was informal, so much so that Richardson might
without impropriety peer between the sandbags with his telescope and

say 'It is my belief, sir, that the enemy are entirely out of water. I see three parties trying to make holes in what they take to be the water-course; and Green Headcloth is blackguarding them like a fishfag.'

'They expected to be drinking out of our well by now,' said Welby, smiling. 'Though mark you, they may do so yet,' he added as a sop to Fate.

'The odds are more even now,' observed the purser. 'And if it goes on at this rate we shall soon have the advantage.'

'If that should come about they will surely sail away and come back three times as strong,' said the master. 'Sir, would it be foolish to suggest destroying their proa out of hand? It is frail past belief—no metal in its whole construction—and a ball in either hull or better still at the junction between 'em would knock it to pieces.'

'I dare say it would, Mr Warren,' said Jack. 'But that would leave us with better than two hundred thirsty villains eating us out of house and home. The Doctor says there are barely a score of pigs left, and only a few days' ration of ring-tailed apes. No. There is nothing I should like better than seeing them weigh and set off for reinforcements. Almost all our long-sawing is done, and very fortunately poor dear Mr Hadley had left several of his most important tools up here for sharpening and resetting; working double-tides I believe we can launch the schooner and be on our way to Batavia before they come back. Their home port is certainly in Borneo.'

'Oh,' cried the purser, as though he had been struck by a new idea: but he said no more. The swivel-gun and the gingall both hit the sandbag immediately opposite, ripping it and covering both him and the table with its contents. When they picked him up he was dead. Stephen opened his shirt, put his ear to his chest and said 'Heart, I am afraid: God be with him.'

During the hot still hours that followed Jack, Fielding and the gunner overhauled the powder, all that had been found, scraped from barrels, withdrawn from flasks and bandoliers, signal cartridges and even rockets. 'We have a charge for each of the carronades and the nine-pounder, with just enough over to leave the Doctor half a flask for his rifle,' said Jack. 'Master gunner, it might be well to load them now, while the metal hardly bears touching: the heat will make the powder brisk. And let the nine-pounder ball be very carefully chipped—indeed, oiled and polished.'

'Aye aye, sir. Grape for the carronades, I do suppose?'

'Case is your real slaughter-house charge at close quarters, but I am afraid we have none?'

The gunner shook his head with a melancholy air. 'All on that fucking reef, sir, pardon me.'

'Then grape, Mr White.'

'Sir, sir,' cried Bennett, 'Captain Welby says they are sending men up through the forest.'

'Perhaps, sir,' said Welby when Jack joined him at his look-out point, 'it would be prudent not to direct your glass: they might think we had smoked them. But if you watch the open ground to the left of that great crimson-flowering tree at eleven o'clock from the flagstaff, you will see them slip across, their spearheads held low and wrapped in leaves or grass.'

'What do you think they are at?'

'I believe they are a forlorn hope, a storming-party sent to attack the camp from behind, where the silver is. They are to catch up a chest or two and run off into the broken country behind while their friends amuse us with a false attack in front.'

'They cannot know what the back of the camp is like. We can hold it with half a dozen men: there is a shocking great drop where the land-slide swept the earth away.'

'No, sir. And as the young person came in by the west gate and left by the south, she would not have seen the drop either. No doubt it is all their general's theory; but still I am sure he thought he could rely on surprise.'

'How many men did you reckon?'

'I counted twenty-nine, sir, but I may well have missed a few.'

'Well, I think we can deal with that—Mr Reade, stop that goddam fool pointing at the trees. Stop it at once, d'ye hear me there? You and Harper can pick up the biggest stones you can carry and take them to the north wall steps at the double. Mr Welby, I think we can afford a round apiece to your eight best marksmen. A quarter of your people down before you start your attack is discouraging. It will be uncommon brave men that go on, with such a rise in front of them.'

Almost at once the diversion began. The swivel-gun and the gingall fired as fast as they could; large bodies of men raced diagonally across and across the broad open slope between the camp and the building-slip, hallooing as they ran or howling like gibbons, and presently there was a furious discharge of crackers along the inner border of the forest. Jack had to shout to make himself heard. 'Mr Seymour, there is a forlorn hope about to make a dash for the silver by way of the north wall. Take Killick and Bonden and the eight Marines Mr Welby has told off together with whatever other men you need to line the wall and deal with the situation while we watch their attempt at amusing us and make sure it don't turn ugly.'

The feint, the diversion, did not turn ugly: the real attack did. The storming-party had been picked for strength and courage and in spite of a heavy loss the moment they left cover they ran straight on to the steps and the foot of the wall, where Killick, beside himself with pale hatred and fury, flung great stones down upon them, helped on either hand by the Marines, all the Captain's bargemen and his coxswain. Again and again a Dyak would make a back for another and up he would come, spear poised, only to be flung back at pike-point, pierced through with a cutlass or smashed with a fifty-pound stone. And presently there were no more to come. Seymour, nominally in command, had to beat on the men's backs to prevent them stoning the few dreadfully shattered cripples who were crawling off among the rocks. Even then Killick stood for a great while, livid and glaring, a boarding-axe in one hand and a jagged lump of basalt in the other.

The diversion soon lost all conviction. The diagonal running to and fro grew languid, the crackers spluttered away to one last pop. The sun too was tiring of the day—it had been extraordinarily hot—and sloped westward through a deeper blue.

'Yet even so, sir,' said Welby, 'I do not believe this is the end. Their general has lost a power of men and he has nothing to show for it.

They have no water—see how they dig!—and they won't find any there. So they cannot wait. The general cannot wait. As soon as they have rested a little he will launch the whole lot at us, straight at us: he is a death or glory cove, I am sure. See how he harangues them, jumping up and down. Oh my God they have fired the schooner.'

As the black smoke billowed up and away on the shifting breeze the whole camp burst out in a yell of desperate anger, frustration, plain grief. Jack raised his voice and hailed the gunner. 'Mr White, Mr White, there. Draw those carronades and reload with the very best round-shot we possess. Your mates have perhaps five minutes to chip them as smooth as ever they can: certainly not more. And Mr White, let there be slow-match at hand.'

This time there were no manoeuvres, no diversions. They came steadily up the hill, at first at a trot and lastly at a furious run. They came straight at the guns, with no sign of fear, but in no kind of formation either, so that they reached the earthwork in dispersed order, the fleetest first, in tens rather than fifties, and they never beat their way through the massed pikes and bayonets. Their chief arrived in the second wave, still running but scarcely able to see or fetch his breath: he leapt on to a body, slashing blindly at the seaman opposite him, and fell back, his head split down the middle with an axe.

It was cruel fighting, kill or be killed, all in a great roar of sound and the clash of swords and spears, grunting and dust, sometimes a shriek. For what seemed a great while the enemy never fell back except for another spring forward; but the Dyaks and Malays were fighting uphill, against an enemy in close contact with strong-voiced competent naval and military commanders and sheltered by a moderate breastwork; besides, however great their courage, they were smaller, lighter men than the English, and at a given point, when there was a general withdrawal on the right and the centre, a regrouping for a fresh assault, Jack Aubrey felt the turn of the tide. He called out 'Mr Welby, charge. Dianes follow me.'

The whole camp leapt on to the wall with a cheer. The drum beat and they hurled themselves forward. After the first frightful clash the

Marines' weight and their exact order bore all before them. It was a rout, a total, disastrous rout: the Dyaks ran for their lives.

They ran faster than the English and on reaching the sea they leapt straight in and swam fast to the proa, as nimble as otters, perhaps a hundred men left.

Jack stood gasping on the shore, his sword dangling from his wrist. He wiped the blood from his eyes—blood from some unfelt blow—looked at the blazing schooner, its ribs outlined in fire, and at the Dyaks, already hauling on their cable. 'Mr Fielding,' he said in a strong, hoarse voice, 'see what can be done to put out the fire. Mr White, gun-crews, gun-crews I say, come along with me.'

They toiled up again, those that were whole; and never before had Jack so felt the burden of his weight. The bodies lay thick half-way to the camp, thicker in front of the earthwork, but he hardly noticed as he picked his way through just by the brass nine-pounder. Bonden, the captain of the gun and a faster runner, gave him a hand over the parapet and said 'They are under way, sir.' He looked round, and there indeed was the proa luffing up, coming as close to the awkward breeze as ever she could sail; the tide had been on the ebb long enough to bare the reef and she had to get all possible offing on the unhandy starboard tack to weather the west point with its shocking tide-rip and northward-setting current.

The gunner, helped by his surviving mate, arrived a moment later. 'There is more match in my tent, sir,' he called in a voice that hardly carried over the breastwork.

'Never fret about that, Mr White,' said Jack, smiling. 'The first still has half a glass to go.' And there it was in fact, untouched, unkicked in the turmoil and confusion of battle, smouldering away in its tubs, its smoke drifting away across the empty camp.

'God love us,' whispered the gunner as they crouched there laying the forward carronade, 'I had thought the set-to was much longer. Four degrees, would you say, sir?'

'Pitch it well up, master gunner.'

'Well up it is, sir,' said the gunner, giving the screw half another turn.

For a perceptible instant the match hissed on the priming: the carronade spoke out loud and sharp, screeching back along its slide; all hands peered out and under the smoke and some caught the high curving flight of the ball. Jack watched it so intently that only his heart remembered to rejoice that the powder had proved sound, beating so hard it almost stopped his breath. The line was true: the ball short by twenty yards.

Jack ran to the nine-pounder, calling to the captain of the other carronade, 'Four and a half, Willett. Fire as she rises.'

The carronade fired an instant later: a noble crash once more. This time Jack did not see the ball, but there was its white plume in the sea, just ahead of the proa, the line as true as the last. He heaved on his handspike, shifting the lay of the gun a trifle to the right, called 'Stand by, there,' and clapped the match to the touch-hole. At the same moment the proa's helmsman put his tiller hard over to avoid the shot and sailed straight into the point of its fall. There was no splash. For an instant all hands looked blank: then the two hulls fell apart, the great sail collapsed, the entire vessel disintegrated, and the whole, already spread over twenty or thirty yards of sea, drifted fast towards the west point and its terrible overfall.

'What is the cheering?' asked Stephen, coming bloody-handed from the hospital-tent and peering molelike through spectacles he now wore for the fine-work of surgery.

'We have sunk the proa,' said Jack. 'You can see the wreckage sweeping past the cape. They will be in the tide-rip directly—Lord, how it cuts up!—and no man living can swim through that. But at least we do not have to fear any reinforcements.'

'You take your pleasures rather sadly, brother, do you not?'

'They fired the schooner, do you see; and from what little I saw there is no hope of saving a single frame.'

Fielding heaved himself wearily over the corpses and the parapet, took off his battered hat, and said 'Well, sir, I give you joy of your glorious shot: never was there such a genuine smasher. But I am very sorry to have to report that although several hands got burnt in their zeal, there is nothing, nothing we could do to save the schooner. There is not a single frame left entire—left at all. Even the keelson is gone; and of course all the planking. As well as the cutter.'

'I am heartily sorry for it, Mr Fielding,' said Jack in a voice intended as a public communication—a score of men were within earshot. 'I am sure you and all hands did their best, but it was a hopeless blaze by the time we reached it: they had certainly spread tar fore and aft. However, here we are alive, and most of us fit for duty. We have many of poor Mr Hadley's tools; there is timber all around us; and I have no doubt we shall find a solution.'

He hoped the words sounded cheerful and that they carried conviction, but he could not be sure. As it usually happened after an engagement, a heavy sadness was coming down over his spirits. To some degree it was the prodigious contrast between two modes of life: in violent hand-to-hand fighting there was no room for time, reflexion, enmity or even pain unless it was disabling; everything moved with extreme speed, cut and parry with a reflex as fast as a sword-thrust, eyes automatically keeping watch on three or four men within reach, arm lunging at the first hint of a lowered guard, a cry to warn a friend, a roar to put an enemy off his stroke; and all this in an extraordinarily vivid state of mind, a kind of fierce exaltation, an intense living in the most immediate present. Whereas now time came back with all its deadening weight—a living in relation to tomorrow, to next year, a flag promotion, children's future—so did responsibility, the innumerable responsibilities belonging to the captain of a man-of-war. And decision: in battle, eye and sword-arm made the decisions with inconceivable rapidity; there was no leisure to brood over them, no leisure at all.

Then again there were all the ugly things to be done after a victory; and the sad ones too. He looked round for a midshipman, for by now most of the people had come up the hill again; but seeing none he called Bonden, the invulnerable Bonden, and told him to ask the Doctor whether a visit would be convenient. 'Aye aye, sir,' said Bonden, and hesitated. 'Which you have a nasty trough up there'—tapping his scalp—'that did ought to be looked to at the same time.'

'So I have,' said Jack, feeling his head, 'but it don't signify. Cut along now.'

Before Bonden could come back Richardson limped up to say that the Dyaks had taken the heads not only of the carpenter and his mate but of all those killed on the lower or middle ground. Some could not be identified: should the bodies be brought up? Were our own dead by the camp to be separated by religion? What was to be done with the dead natives?

'Sir,' said Bonden, with a queer look on his face, 'Doctor's compliments and in five minutes, if you please.'

Every man has his own five minutes: Jack's was shorter than Stephen's and he came into the tent too early. Stephen was carrying a slender arm to a heap of amputated limbs and the bodies of patients who had already died; he put it down on a shattered foot and said 'Show me your scalp, will you now? Sit on this barrel.'

'Whose was that arm?' asked Jack.

'Reade's,' said Stephen. 'I have just taken it off at the shoulder.'

'How is he? May I speak to him? Will he be all right?'

'With the blessing; he may do well,' said Stephen. 'With the blessing. That swivel-gun flung him down with his head against a rock and he is still stunned entirely. Sit on the barrel. Mr Macmillan, hot water and the coarse shears, if you please.' As he mopped and snipped he said 'Of course I have not a full list for you since not all the dead have been counted and there are still some wounded to be brought up the hill; but I am afraid it will be a long one. The midshipmen's berth has suffered very heavily. Your clerk was killed in the charge; so was little Harper; Bennett was virtually disembowelled and though we have sewn him up I doubt he sees tomorrow.'

Butcher, Harper, Bennett, Reade: dead or maimed. As Jack sat there with his head bowed to the swab, the shears and the probe, tears fell steadily on his folded hands.

The first sad, weary days of mass burial—more dead men, both sides taken together, than living—and the visiting of the wounded, seeing faces he had known all this commission, good, decent faces almost all of them, yellow and thin with pain, sometimes with fatal infection, lying there in the heat and the dreadful familiar smell. Then the later funerals as the worst cases dropped off, one, two and even three a day. And all this with extremely little food. Stephen had shot only one small babirussa; the apes were no longer worth his remaining charges; and of the few fishes caught by casting from the rocks or hauling the seine most were scaleless lead-coloured things that even the gulls would not eat.

On the morning after the last patient on the danger-list died—a young Dyak who had borne resection after resection of his gangrenous leg with admirable fortitude—Stephen was late in obeying the pipe of *All hands on deck—all hands aft* that preceded the Captain's address to the ship's company. By the time he slipped into his place Jack was still dealing with naval law, the perennity of commissions, the Articles of War and so on: all hands listened attentively, with grave, judicial expressions as he repeated his main points once again, particularly that which had to do with the continuance of their pay, each according to his rating, and the compensation in lieu of spirits not served out. They stood there close-packed, confined between imaginary rails, exactly as though they were still aboard the *Diane*, and they weighed every word. Stephen, who had heard the essence before, paid little attention; in any case his mind was elsewhere. He had been attached to the Dyak, who showed unlimited trust in his skill and benevolent intent, who would take food only from him, and whom he really thought he had saved as he had in fact saved young Reade, now sitting there wraith-like on a carronade-slide, his empty sleeve pinned across his chest, and as he had saved Edwards, who stood alone, there where the envoy and his suite had always had their place.

'But now, shipmates,' said Jack in his strong deep voice, 'I come to another point. You have all heard of the widow's cruse.' No single officer, seaman or Marine showed the least sign of having heard of the widow's cruse, nor any sign whatsoever of intelligence. 'Well,' continued Captain Aubrey, '*Diane* shipped no widow's cruse. And by that I mean tomorrow is St Famine's Day.' Comprehension, alarm, despondency, extreme displeasure showed in the faces of all the old man-of-war's men present; and the hum of whispered explanation kept Jack silent for a long moment. 'But it is not the worst St Famine I have ever known,' he went on. 'Although it is true that today's is the last issue of grog and the last cheese-paring scrap of tobacco, we still have a little biscuit and a cask of Dublin horse not very badly spoilt and there is always the chance the Doctor may knock down another of the island gazelles. And there is this point too. The officers and I are not going to sit on silk cushions swilling wine and brandy. The gunroom steward and Killick are going to put all our stores into a general pool, under double guard, and as long as it lasts each mess will draw its share by lot. That is what the gunroom steward and Killick are going to do, whether they like it or not.' This was very well received. Killick's extreme jealousy of the Captain's stores, even the oldest heel-taps of his wine, had always been notorious, and the gunroom steward's hardly less so. Both looked pinched and intensely disapproving, but the ship's company in general laughed as they had not laughed since before the battle. 'Then again,' said Jack, 'God helps those that help themselves. We still have Ned Walker and two others who were rated carpenter's crew. We still have plenty of sailcloth and a fair amount of cordage. We can save many of the nails and spikes from the schooner's ashes, and my plan is to run up a six-oared cutter to replace the one they burnt, pick a crew of our best seamen with an officer to navigate and send them off to Batavia for help. I shall stay here, of course.'

All these things coming at once confused his audience. Upon the whole there was a hum of agreement, even of very strong approval, but one man called out 'Two hundred mile in an open boat, with the monsoon like to change?'

'Bligh sailed four thousand in a twenty-three foot launch crammed with people. Besides, the monsoon does not change for close on a fortnight, and even a parcel of grass-combing lubbers can put a seaworthy cutter together in that length of time. In any case, what is the alternative? Sit here and watch the sun go down on the last of the ring-tailed apes? No, no. Better a dead dog than a lead lion. That is to say . . .'

'Three cheers for Captain Aubrey's plan,' cried a perfectly unexpected voice, a taciturn, highly-respected, middle-aged forecastleman named Nicholl. 'Hip, hip, hip . . .'

The cheering was still going on when Stephen, with his rifle in the crook of his arm, walked down past the blackened wreckage in the slip; the skeleton with its elegant curves was still recognizable, and as heavy rain had fallen in the night the whole gave off something of the desolate acrid smell he had caught the first day.

He walked out along the strand westwards, meaning to climb by his usual path behind the cricket-pitch, but after he had been going for some time he saw a moving object in the sea. At this point he was well above the ordinary high-tide mark, in a region where the most uncommon storms, like that which had destroyed the *Diane*, cast up massive debris, among which there grew interesting plants, sometimes with surprising speed. He sat, pleasantly shaded by ferns, on the trunk of a medang and drew out his pocket-glass. As soon as it was focused his first opinion was confirmed: he was gazing into the large insipid kindly square-nosed face of a dugong. It was not the first he had seen, but it was the first in these waters, and certainly he had never had a finer view at any time. A young female dugong, about eight feet long, with her child. Sometimes she held it to her bosom with her flipper, both of them poised upright in the sea, staring straight before them in a very vacant manner; and sometimes she browsed on the seaweed that grew on the rocks out there; but at all times she showed the utmost solicitude for her child, occasionally going so far as to wash its face, which seemed a pointless task in so limpid a sea. Was her presence, and that of some fellow-mermaidens much farther out, a sign of the coming change of season? 'How glad I am that the boat is still only a hypothesis,' he said, having pondered on the question. 'Otherwise it would have been my duty to pursue the innocent dugong. They are said to be excellent eating, like poor Steller's sea-cow: or rather Steller's poor sea-cow, the creature.'

Presently the dugong dived and swam away to join her friends browsing on the far side of the reef and Stephen was thinking of getting up when a strangely familiar sound caught his ear. 'You would swear it was a pig rooting,' he said, moving his head slowly to the right. It was in fact a pig rooting, as fine a babirussa as he had ever seen: the animal was snorting and grunting at a great rate, wholly intent upon a wealth of tubers. It presented a perfect target and Stephen very gently brought up his gun. The babirussa was as innocent as the dugong; he shot it dead without the least compunction.

When at last he had hoisted the boar into a tree with his tackle he said 'Twenty-two score if he weighs an ounce. Mother of God, how happy they will be. I shall follow the back-track as far as I can—never was such a day for tracks—to see where he came from, and then I believe I shall indulge myself with a view of the swifts. I feel no resentment against them now, I find, none at all, and I wish to see the state of the vacated nests. Poor little Reade, alas, will never climb down to take them for me. But Heavens, what youth and stamina and a cheerful mind will do in the face of a shocking injury! He will be running about in a fortnight, whereas the bosun, middle-aged and sunk in gloom, will take a great while to recover from a far less serious wound.' His mind ran on in this way as he followed the clear track as far as a much-favoured wallow in the upper part of the island. In earlier days he would have seen a dozen tracks or more, new or old, converging upon this shallow pool of mud; now there was but this single line, coming from the north-east.

'I shall branch off here,' he said by the tree from which he had shot an earlier boar, and he walked uphill to the edge of the northern cliffs. But he was still quite far from the precipice when he skirted what had been a puddle in the night and was now a broad patch of mud, soft mud. On its farther edge, as clear as well could be, he saw a child's footprint: nothing leading to it, nothing leading from it. 'Either that child is preternaturally agile and leapt a clear eight feet, or it was an angel setting one foot on earth,' he said, his search in the low scrub on either side having revealed nothing. 'We have no ship's boy anything like so small.'

Another hundred yards resolved the puzzle. Near the edge of the precipice, where he had lain with his head down the narrow cleft, the same cleft down which Reade was to have been lowered, stood seven baskets, filled with the finest nests and carefully wedged with stones. And if that was not clear enough there was a junk lying off shore, with boats going to and from the little sandy cove.

When he had sat there for some minutes, his mind turning over the various possibilities he heard children's voices down among the trees. They were raised in anger, mockery, challenge and defiance, in Malay or Chinese indifferently; they rose in a shrill crescendo that ended with a distinct thump, a scream of pain, and a concerted wail.

Stephen walked down and found four children under a tall medang, three little girls howling with woe, one little boy groaning with pain and grasping his bloody leg. They were all Chinese, all dressed in much the same way, with pads on their knees and elbows for cave-climbing.

They turned to him and stopped howling. 'Li Po said we could go and play when we had gathered seven baskets,' said one girl in Malay.

'We never meant him to go right up to the top,' said another. 'It is not our fault.'

'Li Po will whip us past all bearing,' said the third. 'We are only girls.' And she began grizzling again.

Stephen's appearance did not astonish or alarm them—he too was dressed in wide short trousers, an open jacket and a broad hat, while his face, so long exposed to the sun, was now a disagreeable yellow— and the little boy, who in any case was partly stunned, let him examine the leg without resistance.

Having more or less staunched the blood with his handkerchief and made his diagnosis Stephen said 'Lie quite still, and I will cut you seven splints.' This he did with his hunting knife, and although time pressed with very great urgency, professional conscience obliged him to trim them before cutting his thin cloth jacket into strips for pads and bandages. He worked as fast as ever he could, but the little girls, calmed by his grown-up, competent presence, talked faster still. The eldest, Mai-mai, was the boy's sister and their father was Li Po, the owner of the junk. They had come from Batavia to fetch a cargo of ore from Ketapan in Borneo, and as they did every season when the wind was favourable and the sea calm, they had deviated from their course for the bird's-nest island. When they were very young they had had ropes lowered from above, but now they did not need them. They came right up from the bottom, using pegs driven in here and there in the bad places; but generally it was quite easy to creep along the ledges and slopes, carrying a small basket in one's teeth and filling the large ones at the top. Only thin people could get through in some places. Li Po's brother, the one who was killed by Dyak pirates, had grown too fat by the time he was fifteen.

'There,' said Stephen; gently tying a final knot, 'I believe that will answer. Now, Mai-mai, my dear, you must go down at once and tell your father what has happened. Tell him I am a medical man, that I have treated the wound, and that I am going to carry your brother to our camp on the south side. He cannot possibly be lowered to the junk in this state. Tell Li Po there are a hundred Englishmen in a fortified camp nearly opposite the reef, and that we shall be happy to see him as soon as he can bring the junk round. Now run along like a good child and tell him all will be well. The others may go with you or come with me, just as they choose.'

They chose coming with him out of a desire for novelty, an unwillingness to see Li Po just at present, and the glory of carrying the rifle. The path was narrow, their legs short, and they had either to run in front of him and talk over their shoulders or else behind and call out to the back of his head as he carried the boy; for there was no question of their not talking, with so much to communicate and so many important things to learn. The slimmer of the two, whose eyes had that extraordinary purity of curve only to be seen in Chinese children, wished Stephen to know that her best friend in Batavia, whose name could be interpreted Golden Flower of Day, possessed a striped Dutch cat. No doubt the old gentleman had already seen a striped Dutch cat? Would the old gentleman like to hear an account of the plants in their garden, and of the betrothal ceremonies of their aunt Wang? This and a catalogue of the varieties of edible birds' nests, with their prices, lasted almost to the edge of the forest, and they could be heard from the camp well before their forms could be seen.

'Lord, Jack,' said Stephen when the boy had been put into a cot with a basket over his leg and Ahmed at hand to comfort him, and when the little girls had been turned loose to admire the wonders of the camp, 'there is a great deal to be said for the Confucian tradition.'

'So my old nurse always used to tell me,' said Jack. 'Just let me send for your blessed gazelle, and then tell me where you found them and why you are looking so pleased.'

'The tradition or shall I say doctrine of infinite respect for age. As soon as I told that worthy child to run along like a good girl now, she stood up, bowed with her hands clasped before her, and ran off. It was the turning-point, the crisis: either all was wrecked or all succeeded. Had she proved forward, or stubborn, or disobedient I was lost . . . The animal is behind and rather beyond the cricket-field, in a tree one half blackened by lightning, one half green. That is how I shall bring up my daughter.'

'Don't you wish you may succeed? Ha, ha, ha! Bonden, there. Bonden, the Doctor has saved our bacon again—has *saved our bacon*—so take three more hands and a stout spar to the lightning-struck tree by the cricket-pitch as quick as ever you like. Now, sir?'—turning to Stephen.

'Now, sir, prepare to be amazed. There is a vast junk with empty holds lying off the north side of the island: the children had come ashore to collect edible birds' nests. I believe the vessel will come round as soon as the wind serves, and I think it likely that its owner and captain will carry us back to Batavia. That boy in splints is his son. And I have draughts on Shao Yen, a Batavia banker he must necessarily know, draughts that will certainly pay our passage; and if his demands are not exorbitant they will leave enough over for some modest vessel that may still enable us to keep our rendezvous in New South Wales or even before.'

'Oh Stephen,' cried Jack, 'what a glorious thought!' He beat his hands together, as he did when he was very deeply moved, and then said 'He had better not be exorbitant . . . By God, to keep our rendezvous . . . With this wind we should be in Batavia in three days at the most; and if Raffles can help us to something that will swim at something better than five knots we have time in hand for a much earlier rendezvous. Time and to spare. Lord, how providential that you happened to be by when the poor boy broke his leg.'

'Perhaps hurt it would be more exact. I will not absolutely certify the fracture.'

'But he has splints on.'

'In such cases one cannot be too careful. How pleasantly the breeze is freshening.'

'If your junk is at all weatherly—and I am sure she is a wonderfully weatherly craft—it should bring her round by the afternoon. Just how big is she? I mean,' he added, seeing the look of deep stupidity in Stephen's face, 'what does she displace? What is her tonnage? What does she weigh?'

'Oh, I cannot tell. Shall we say ten thousand tons?'

'What a fellow you are, Stephen,' cried Jack. 'The *Surprise* don't gauge six hundred. How does your blessed junk compare with her?'

'Dear *Surprise,*' said Stephen, and then recollecting himself, 'I do not let on to be an expert in nautical affairs, you know; but I think the junk, though not so long as the *Surprise,* is distinctly fatter, and swims higher in the sea. I am fully persuaded that there is room for everybody, sitting close, and for what possessions we may have left.'

'If you please, sir,' said Killick, 'dinner is on table.'

'Killick,' said Jack, smiling on him in a way that Killick would have found incomprehensible if he had not been listening attentively, 'we have not put all our wine into the common pool yet, have we?'

'Oh no, sir. Which there is grog for all hands today.'

'Then rouse out a couple of bottles of the Haut Brion with the long cork, the eighty-nine: and tell my cook to knock up something to stay the little girls' hunger till the gazelle comes in.' To Stephen he said 'The *Haut Brion* should go well with the *Dublin* horse, ha, ha, ha! Ain't I a rattle? You smoked it, Stephen, did you not? No reflexion upon your country of course, God bless it—mere lightness of heart.' Chuckling he drew the cork, passed Stephen a glass, raised his own and said 'Here is to your glorious, glorious junk, the timeliest junk that ever yet was seen.'

The glorious junk appeared round the point before the end of the second bottle and began beating up for the anchorage. 'Before we drink our coffee I shall just look at that dressing,' said Stephen. 'Mr Macmillan,' he called in the hospital-tent, 'be so good as to give me two elegant splints and white bandage galore.'

They unwound the strips of jacket and swabbed the scratch quite clean. 'Something of a sprain do I see, sir,' said Macmillan, 'and a considerable tumescence about the external malleolus; but where is the break? Why the splint?'

'It may exist only in the form of an imperceptible crack,' said Stephen, 'but we must bind it up with as much care and attention as if it were a compound fracture of the most untoward kind; and we shall anoint it with hog's lard mixed with Cambodian bole.'

Returning to his coffee he observed that Jack Aubrey, lighthearted though he was, had not overlooked the necessity for a show of strength: the earthwork was bristling with armed men, all clearly visible from the junk.

Li Po came up the hill therefore with a submissive, deprecating air, accompanied only by a youth carrying a contemptible box of dried litchis and a canister of discreditable green tea: Li Po begged the learned physician's acceptance of these worthless articles—mere shadowy tokens of his respectful gratitude—and might he see his son?

The little boy could not have played his part better. He moaned, groaned, rolled his eyes with anguish, spoke in a faint and dying voice, and shrunk petulantly from his father's caressing hand.

'Never mind,' said Stephen. 'His suffering will be less once we are afloat; I shall attend him every day and when I remove these bandages in Batavia you will find his leg perfectly whole.'

Everest at the Bottom of the Sea
by Bucky McMahon

Veteran journalist Bucky McMahon (born 1955) has made a career of writing about dangerous scuba dives. Here he turns his attention to the Andrea Doria, one of wreck diving's most prestigious—and deadly—sites.

RRIVAL. You toss in your seaman's bunk and dream the oldest, oddest beachcomber's dream: Something has siphoned away all the waters of the seas, and you're taking a cold, damp hike down into the world's empty pool. Beer cans, busted pipes, concrete blocks, grocery carts, a Cadillac on its back, all four tires missing—every object casts a long, stark shadow on the puddled sand. With the Manhattan skyline and the Statue of Liberty behind you, you trek due east into the sunrise, following the toxic trough of the Hudson River's outflow—known to divers in these parts as the Mudhole—until you arrive, some miles out, at Wreck Valley.

You see whole fishing fleets asleep on their sides and about a million lobsters crawling around like giant cockroaches, waving confounded antennae in the thin air. Yeah, what a dump of history you see, a real Coney Island of catastrophes. The greatest human migration in the history of the world passed through here, first in a trickle of dauntless hard-asses, and then in that famous flood of huddled masses, Western man's main manifest destiny arcing across the northern ocean. The whole story is written in the ruins: in worm-ridden middens, mere stinking piles of mud; in tall ships chewed to fish-bone skeletons; five-hundred-foot steel-plated cruisers plunked down onto their guns; the battered cigar tubes of German U-boats; and sleek yachts scuttled alongside sunken tubs as humble as old boots.

You can't stop to poke around or fill your pockets with souvenirs. You're on a journey to the continent's edge, where perhaps the missing water still pours into the Atlantic abyss with the tremendous roar of a thousand Niagaras. Something waits there that might explain, and that must justify, your presence in this absence, this scooped-out plain where no living soul belongs. And you know, with a sudden chill, that only your belief in the dream, the focus of your mind and your will on the possibility of the impossible, holds back the annihilating weight of the water.

You wake up in the dark and for a moment don't know where you are, until you hear the thrum of the diesel and feel the beam roll. Then you realize that what awakened you was the abrupt decrease of noise, the engine throttling down, and the boat and the bunk you lie in subsiding into the swell, and you remember that you are on the open sea, drawing near to the wreck of the *Andrea Doria*. You feel the boat lean into a turn, cruise a little ways, and then turn again, and you surmise that up in the pilothouse, Captain Dan Crowell has begun to "mow the lawn," steering the sixty-foot exploration vessel the *Seeker* back and forth, taking her through a series of slow passes, sniffing for the *Doria*.

Crowell, whom you met last night when you hauled your gear aboard, is a big, rugged-looking guy, about six feet two inches in boat shoes, with sandy brown hair and a brush mustache. Only his large, slightly hooded eyes put a different spin on his otherwise gruff appearance; when he blinks into the green light of the sonar screen, he resembles a thoughtful sentinel owl. Another light glows in the wheelhouse: a personal computer, integral to the kind of technical diving Crowell loves.

The *Seeker*'s crew of five divvies up hour-and-a-half watches for the ten-hour trip from Montauk, Long Island, but Crowell will have been up all night in a state of tense vigilance. A veteran of fifty *Doria* trips, Crowell considers the hundred-mile cruise—both coming and going— to be the most dangerous part of the charter, beset by imminent peril of fog and storm and heavy shipping traffic. It's not for nothing that mariners call this patch of ocean where the *Andrea Doria* collided with another ocean liner the "Times Square of the Atlantic."

You feel the *Seeker*'s engine back down with a growl and can guess what Crowell is seeing now on the forward-looking sonar screen: a spattering of pixels, like the magnetic shavings on one of those draw-the-beard slates, coalescing into partial snapshots of the seven-hundred-foot liner. What the sonar renders is but a pallid gray portrait of the outsized hulk, which, if it stood up on its stern on the bottom, 250 feet below, would tower nearly fifty stories above the *Seeker*, dripping and roaring like Godzilla. Most likely you're directly above her now, a proximity you feel in the pit of your stomach. As much as the physical wreck itself, it's the *Doria* legend you feel leaking upward through the *Seeker*'s hull like some kind of radiation.

"The Mount Everest of scuba diving," people call the wreck, in another useful catchphrase. Its badass rep is unique in the sport. Tell a fellow diver you've done the Great Barrier Reef or the Red Sea, they think you've got money. Tell 'em you've done the *Doria*, they know you've got balls. Remote enough to expose you to maritime horrors— the *Seeker* took a twenty-five-foot wave over its bow on a return trip last summer—the *Doria*'s proximity to the New York and New Jersey coasts has been a constant provocation for two generations. The epitome, in its day, of transatlantic style and a luxurious symbol of Italy's post-World War II recovery, the *Andrea Doria* has remained mostly intact and is still full of treasure: jewelry, art, an experimental automobile, bottles of wine—plus mementos of a bygone age, like brass shuffleboard numbers and silver and china place settings, not so much priceless in themselves but much coveted for the challenge of retrieving them.

But tempting as it is to the average wreck diver, nobody approaches the *Doria* casually. The minimum depth of a *Doria* dive is 180 feet, to the port-side hull, well below the 130-foot limit of recreational diving. Several years of dedicated deep diving is considered a sane apprenticeship for those who make the attempt—that, plus a single-minded focus that subsumes social lives and drains bank accounts. Ten thousand dollars is about the minimum ante for the gear and the training and the dives you need to get under your belt. And that just gets you to the hull and hopefully back. For those who wish to penetrate the crumbling, mazelike interior, the most important quality is confidence bordering on hubris: trust in a lucid assessment of your own limitations and belief in your decision-making abilities, despite the knowledge that divers of equal if not superior skill have possessed those same beliefs and still perished.

Propped up on your elbows, you look out the salon windows and see the running lights of another boat maneuvering above the *Doria*. It's the *Wahoo*, owned by Steve Bielenda and a legend in its own right for its 1992 salvage of the seven-hundred-pound ceramic Gambone Panels, one of the *Doria*'s lost art masterpieces. Between Bielenda, a sixty-four-year-old native of Brooklyn, and Crowell, a transplanted southern Californian who's twenty years younger and has gradually assumed the lion's share of the *Doria* charter business, you have the old King of the Deep and the heir apparent. And there's no love lost between the generations.

"If these guys spent as much time getting proficient as they do avoiding things, they'd actually be pretty good" is Crowell's backhanded compliment to the whole "Yo, Vinny!" attitude of the New York–New Jersey old school of gorilla divers. Bielenda, for his part, has been more pointed in his comments on the tragedies of the 1998 and 1999 summer charter seasons, in which five divers died on the *Doria*, all from aboard the *Seeker*. "If it takes five deaths to make you the number-one *Doria* boat," Bielenda says, "then I'm happy being number two." He also takes exception to the *Seeker*'s volume of business—ten charters in one eight-week season. "There aren't enough truly qualified divers in the world to fill that many trips," Bielenda says.

To which Crowell's best response might be his piratical growl, "*Arrgh!*" which sums up his exasperation with the fractious politics of diving in the Northeast. He says he's rejected divers who've turned right around and booked a charter on the *Wahoo*. But, hell, that's none of his business. His business is making the *Seeker*'s criteria for screening divers the most coherent in the business, which Crowell believes he has. Everyone diving the *Doria* from the *Seeker* has to be Tri-mix certified, a kind of doctoral degree of dive training that implies you know a good deal about physiology, decompression, and the effects of helium and oxygen and nitrogen on those first two. That, or be enrolled in a Tri-mix course and be accompanied by an instructor, since, logically, where else are you gonna learn to dive a deep wreck except on a deep wreck?

As for the fatalities of the last two summer seasons—"five deaths in thirteen months" is the phrase that has been hammered into his mind—Crowell has been forthcoming with reporters looking for a smoking gun onboard the *Seeker* and with fellow divers concerned about mistakes they might avoid. "If you look at the fatalities individually, you'll see that they were coincidental more than anything else," Crowell has concluded. In a good season, during the fair-weather months from June to late August, the *Seeker* will put about two hundred divers on the *Doria*.

Nobody is more familiar with the cruel Darwinian exercise of hauling a body home from the *Doria* than Crowell himself, who has wept and cursed and finally moved on to the kind of gallows humor you need to cope. He'll tell you about his dismay at finding himself on a first-name basis with the paramedics that met the *Seeker* in Montauk after each of the five fatalities—how they tried to heft one body still in full gear, until Crowell reached down and unhooked the chest harness, lightening the load by a couple hundred pounds. Another they tried to fit into a body bag with the fins still on his feet.

But beyond their sobering effect on those who've made the awful

ten-hour trip home with the dead, the accidents have not been spectacularly instructive. Christopher Murley, forty-four, from Cincinnati,
had an outright medical accident, a heart attack on the surface. Vince
Napoliello, a thirty-one-year-old bond salesman from Baltimore and a
friend of Crowell's, "just a good, solid diver," was a physiological
tragedy waiting to happen; his autopsy revealed a 90 percent
obstructed coronary artery. Charlie McGurr? Another heart attack. And
Richard Roost? A mature, skilled diver plain shit-out-of-luck, whose
only mistake seems to have been a failure to remain conscious at
depth, which is never guaranteed. Only the death of Craig Sicola, a
New Jersey house builder, might fit the criticism leveled at the *Seeker* in
Internet chat rooms and God knows where else—that a supercompeti-
tive atmosphere, and a sort of taunting elitism projected by the *Seeker*'s
captain and his regular crew, fueled the fatalities of the last two
seasons.

Did Sicola, soloing on his second trip, overreach his abilities?
Maybe so, but exploring the wreck, and yourself in the process, is the
point of the trip.

"You might be paying your money and buying your ticket just like
at Disney World, but everybody also knows this is a real expedition,"
says Crowell. "You've got roaring currents, low visibility, often horrible weather, and you're ten hours from help. We're pushing the
limits out here."

All this you know because, like most of the guys on the charter, you're
sort of a *Doria* buff. . . . Well, maybe a bit of a nut. You wouldn't be out
here if you weren't. A lot of the back story you know by heart. How on
the night of July 25, 1956, the *Andrea Doria* (after the sixteenth-century
Genoese admiral), 29,083 tons of *la dolce vita*, festively inbound for
New York Harbor, steamed out of an opaque fogbank at a near top
speed of twenty-three knots and beheld the smaller, outbound Swedish
liner *Stockholm* making straight for her. The ships had tracked each other
on radar but lined up head-on at the last minute. The *Stockholm*'s bow,
reinforced for ice-breaking in the North Sea, plunged thirty feet into the

Doria's starboard side, ripping open a six-story gash. One *Doria* passenger, Linda Morgan, who became known as the miracle girl, flew from her bed in her nightgown and landed on the forward deck of the *Stockholm*, where she survived. Her sister, asleep in the bunk below, was crushed instantly. In all, fifty-one people died.

Eleven hours after the collision, the *Andrea Doria* went down under a froth of debris, settling onto the bottom on her wounded starboard side in 250 feet of cold, absinthe-green seawater. The very next day, Peter Gimbel, the department-store heir (he hated like hell to be called that) and underwater filmmaker, and his partner, Joseph Fox, made the first scuba dive to the wreck, using primitive doublehosed regulators. The wreck they visited was then considerably shallower (the boat has since collapsed somewhat internally and hunkered down into the pit the current is gouging) and uncannily pristine; curtains billowed through portholes, packed suitcases knocked around in tipped-over staterooms, and shoes floated in ether. That haunted-house view obsessed Gimbel, who returned, most famously, for a month-long siege in 1981. Employing a diving bell and saturation-diving techniques, Gimbel and crew blowtorched through the first-class loading-area doors, creating "Gimbel's Hole," a garage-door-sized aperture amidships, still the preferred entry into the wreck, and eventually raised the Bank of Rome safe. When Gimbel finished editing his film, *The Mystery of the Andrea Doria*, in an event worthy of Geraldo, the safe was opened on live TV. Stacks of waterlogged cash were revealed, though much less than the hoped-for millions.

In retrospect, the "mystery" and the safe seem to have been invented after the fact to justify the diving. Gimbel was seeking something else. He had lost his twin brother to illness some years before, an experience that completely changed his life and made of him an explorer. He got lost in jungles, filmed great white sharks from the water. And it was while tethered by an umbilicus to a decosphere the divers called Mother, hacking through shattered walls and hauling out slimed stanchions in wretchedly constrained space and inches of visibility, always cold, that Gimbel believed he encountered and narrowly escaped a "malevolent spirit," a spirit he came to believe inhabited the *Doria*.

But while Gimbel sought absolute mysteries in a strongbox, salvagers picked up other prizes—the *Andrea Doria*'s complement of fine art, such as the Renaissance-style life-sized bronze statue of Admiral Doria, which divers hacksawed off at the ankles. The wreckage of the first-class gift shop has yielded trinkets of a craftsmanship that no longer exists today—like Steve Bielenda's favorite *Doria* artifact, a silver tea fob in the form of a locomotive with its leather thong still intact. A handful of Northeastern deep divers who knew one another on a first-name basis (when they were on speaking terms, that is) spread the word that it was actually fun to go down in the dark. And by degrees, diving the *Doria* and its two-hundred-foot-plus interior depths segued from a business risk to a risky adventure sport. In the late eighties and early nineties, there was a technical-diving boom, marked by a proliferation of training agencies and a steady refinement of gear. Tanks got bigger, and mixed gases replaced regular compressed air as a "safer" means of diving at extreme depths.

Every winter, the North Atlantic storms give the wreck a rough shake, and new prizes tumble out, just waiting for the summer charters. The *Seeker* has been booked for up to three years in advance, its popularity founded on its reputation for bringing back artifacts. The most sought-after treasure is the seemingly inexhaustible china from the elaborate table settings for 1,706 passengers and crew. First-class china, with its distinctive maroon-and-gold bands, has the most juju, in the thoroughly codified scheme of things. It's a strange fetish, certainly, for guys who wouldn't ordinarily give a shit about the quality of a teacup and saucer. Bielenda and Crowell and their cronies have so much of the stuff that their homes look as if they were decorated by maiden aunts.

Yet you wouldn't mind a plate of your own and all that it would stand for. You can see it in your mind's eye—your plate and the getting of it—just as you saw it last night on the cruise out, when someone popped one of Crowell's underwater videos into the VCR. The thirty-minute film, professionally done from opening theme to credits, ended beautifully with the *Seeker*'s divers fresh from their triumphs, still blushing in their dry suits like lobsters parboiled in adrenaline, holding up *Doria* china while Vivaldi plays. A vicarious victory whose emotions were overshadowed, you're sorry to say, by the scenes inside the *Doria*, and specifically by the shots of *Doria* china, gleaming bone-white in the black mud on the bottom of some busted metal closet who knew how far in or down how many blind passageways. Crowell had tracked it down with his camera and put a beam on it: fine Genoa china, stamped ITALIA, with a little blue crown. The merit badge of big-boy diving, the artifact that says it best: I fuckin' did it—I dove da *Doria*! Your hand reaches out . . .

The cabin door opens and someone comes into the salon, just in time to cool your china fever. It's Crowell's partner Jenn Samulski, who keeps the divers' records and cooks three squares a day. Samulski, an attractive blond from Staten Island who has been down to the *Doria* herself, starts the coffee brewing, and eyes pop open, legs swing out over the sides of the bunks, and the boat wakes up to sunrise on the open sea, light glinting off the steely surface and the metal rows of about sixty scuba tanks weighing down the stern.

On a twelve-diver charter, personalities range from obnoxiously extroverted to fanatically secretive—every type of type A, each man a monster of his own methodology. But talk is easy when you have something humongous in common, and stories are the coin of the lifestyle. You know so-and-so? someone says around a mouthful of muffin. Wasn't he on that dive back in '95? And at once, you're swept away by a narrative, this one taking you to the wreck of the *Lusitania*, where an American, or a Brit maybe—somebody's acquaintance, somebody's friend—is diving with an Irish team. He gets entangled, this diver does, in his own exploration line, on the hull down at 280 feet. His line is just pooling all around him and he's thrashing, panicking, thinking—as everybody always does in a panic—that he has to get to the surface, like *right now*. So he inflates his buoyancy compensator to the max, and now he's like a balloon tied to all that tangled line, which the lift of the b.c. is pulling taut. He's got his knife out, and he's hacking away at the line. One of the Irish divers sees what's happening and swims over and grabs the guy around the legs just as the last line is cut. They both go rocketing for the surface, this diver and his pumped-up b.c. and the Irishman holding on to him by the knees. At 160 feet, the Irishman figures, Sorry, mate, I ain't dying with you, and has to let him go. So the diver flies up to the top and bursts internally from the violent change of depth and the pressurized gas, which makes a ruin of him.

Yeah, he should never have been diving with a line, someone points out, and a Florida cave diver and a guy from Jersey rehash the old debate—using a line for exploration, the cave diver's practice, versus progressive penetration, visual memorization of the wreck and the ways out.

Meanwhile, a couple of the *Seeker*'s crew members have already been down to the wreck to set the hook. The rubber chase boat goes over the bow, emergency oxygen hoses are lowered off the port-side rail, and Crowell tosses out a leftover pancake to check the current. It slaps the dead-calm surface, spreading ripples, portals widening as it drifts aft. Because the *Doria* lies close to the downfall zone, where dense cold water pours over the continental shelf and down into the Atlantic Trench, the tidal currents can be horrendously strong. Sometimes a boat anchored to the *Doria* will carve a wake as if it were underway, making five knots and getting nowhere. An Olympic swimmer in a Speedo couldn't keep up with that treadmill, much less a diver in heavy gear. And sometimes the current is so strong, it'll snap a three-quarter-inch anchor line like rotten twine. But on this sunny July morning, already bright and heating up fast, Crowell blinks beneath the bill of his cap at the bobbing pancake and calculates the current at just a couple of knots—not too bad at all, if you're ready for it.

Crowell grins at the divers now crowded around him at the stern. "Pool's open," he says.

You can never get used to the weight. When you wrestle your arms into the harness of a set of doubles, two 120-cubic-foot-capacity steel tanks yoked together on metal plates, you feel like an ant, one of those leaf-cutter types compelled to heft a preposterous load. What you've put on is essentially a wearable submarine with its crushed neoprene dry-suit shell and its steel external lungs and glass-enclosed command center. Including a pony-sized emergency bottle bungee-strapped between the steel doubles and two decompression tanks clipped to your waist, you carry five tanks of gas and five regulators. You can barely touch your mittened hands together in front of you around all the survival gear, the lift bags, lights, reels, hoses, and instrument consoles. And yet, for all its awkwardness on deck, a deep-diving rig is an amazing piece of technology, and if you don't love it at least a little you had better never put it on. It's one thing you suppose you all have in common on this charter—stockbrokers, construction workers, high school teachers, cops—you're all Buck Rogers flying a personal ship through inner space.

The immediate downside is that you're slightly nauseated from reading your gauges in a four-foot swell, and inside your dry suit, in expedition-weight socks and polypropylene long johns, you're sweating bullets. The way the mind works, you're thinking, To hell with this bobbing world of sunshine and gravity—you can't wait to get wet and weightless. You strain up from the gearing platform hefting nearly two hundred pounds and duckwalk a couple of steps to the rail, your fins smacking the deck and treading on the fins of your buddies who are still gearing up.

Some of the experienced *Doria* divers from Crowell's crew grasp sawed-off garden rakes with duct-taped handles, tools they'll use to reach through rubble and haul in china from a known cache. Crowell gestures among them, offering directions through the *Doria*'s interior maze. Your goal is just to touch the hull, peer into Gimbel's Hole. An orientation dive. You balance on the rail like old Humpty-Dumpty and crane your neck to see if all's clear on the indigo surface. Scuba lesson number one: Most accidents occur on the surface. There was a diver last summer, a seasoned tech diver, painstaking by reputation, on his way to a wreck off the North Carolina coast. Checked out his gear en route—gas on, take a breath, good, gas off—strapped it on at the site, went over the side, and sank like a dirt dart. His buddies spent all morning looking for him everywhere except right under their boat, where he lay, drowned. He had never turned back on his breathing gas.

And there was a diver on the *Seeker* who went over the side and then lay sprawled on his back in the water, screaming, "Help! Help!" The fuck was the matter with the guy? Turns out he'd never been in a dry suit before and couldn't turn himself over. Crowell wheeled on the guy's instructor. "You brought him out here to make his first dry-suit dive on the *Doria*? Are ya *crazy*?" Then the instructor took an underwater scooter down with him, and he had to be rescued with the chase boat. *Arrgh!* Crowell laments that there are divers going from Open Water, the basic scuba course, to Tri-mix in just fifty dives; they're booksmart and experience-starved. And there are bad instructors and mad instructors, egomaniacal, gurulike instructors.

"You will dive only with me," Crowell says, parodying the Svengalis. "Or else it's a thousand bucks for the cape with the clouds and the stars on it. Five hundred more and I'll throw in the wand."

"Just because you're certified don't make you qualified" is Steve Bielenda's motto, and it's the one thing the two captains can agree on.

You take a couple of breaths from each of your regs. Click your lights on and off. You press the inflator button and puff a little more gas into your buoyancy compensator, the flotation wings that surround your double 120's, and experience a tightening and a swelling up such as the Incredible Hulk must feel just before his buttons burst. Ready as you'll ever be, you plug your primary reg into your mouth and tip the world over . . . and hit the water with a concussive smack. At once, as you pop back up to the surface, before the bubbles cease seething between you and the image of the *Seeker*'s white wooden hull, rocking half in and half out of the water, you're in conflict with the current. You grab the floating granny line and it goes taut and the current dumps buckets of water between your arms and starts to rooster-tail around your tanks. This is two knots? You're breathing hard by the time you haul yourself hand over hand to the anchor line, and that's not good. Breath control is as important to deep divers as it is to yogis. At two hundred feet, just getting really excited could knock you out like a blow from a ball-peen hammer. As in kill you dead. So you float a moment at the surface, sighting down the parabola of the anchor line to the point where it vanishes into a brownish-blue gloom. Then you reach up to your inflator hose and press the other button, the one that splutters out gas from the b.c., and feel the big steel 120's reassert their mass, and calmly, feetfirst, letting the anchor line slide through your mitts, you start to sink.

For the thin air of Everest, which causes exhaustion universally and pulmonary and cerebral events (mountain sickness) seemingly randomly, consider the "thick" air you must breathe at 180 feet, the minimum depth of a dive to the *Doria*. Since water weighs sixty-four pounds per cubic foot (and is eight hundred times as dense as air), every foot of depth adds significantly to the weight of the water column above you. You feel this weight as pressure in your ears and sinuses almost as soon as you submerge. Water pressure doesn't affect the gas locked in your noncompressible tanks, of course, until you breathe it. Then, breath by breath, thanks to the genius of the scuba regulator—Jacques Cousteau's great invention—the gas becomes ambient to the weight of the water pressing on your lungs. That's why breathing out of steel 120's pumped to a pressure of 7,000 psi isn't like drinking out of a fire hose, and also why you can kick around a shallow reef at twenty feet for an hour and a half, while at a hundred feet you'd suck the same tank dry in twenty minutes; you're inhaling many times more molecules per breath.

Unfortunately, it's not all the same to your body how many molecules of this gas or the other you suck into it. On the summit of Everest, too few molecules of oxygen makes you light-headed, stupid, and eventually dead. On the decks of the *Doria*, too many molecules of oxygen can cause a kind of electrical fire in your central nervous system. You lose consciousness, thrash about galvanically, and inevitably spit out your regulator and drown. A depth of 216 feet is generally accepted as the point at which the oxygen in compressed air (which is 21 percent oxygen, 79 percent nitrogen) becomes toxic and will sooner or later (according to factors as infinitely variable as individual bodies) kill you. As for nitrogen, it has two dirty tricks it can play at high doses. It gets you high—just like the nitrous oxide that idiot adolescents huff and the dentist dispenses to distract you from a root canal—starting at about 130 feet for most people. "I am personally quite receptive to nitrogen rapture," Cousteau writes in *The Silent World*. "I like it and fear it like doom."

The fearsome thing is that, like any drunk, you're subject to mood swings, from happy to sad to hysterical and panicky when you confront the dumb thing you've just done, like getting lost inside a sunken ocean liner. The other bad thing nitrogen does is deny you permission to return immediately to the surface, every panicking person's solution to the trouble he's in. It's the excess molecules of nitrogen lurking in your body in the form of tiny bubbles that force you to creep back up to the surface at precise intervals determined by time and depth. On a typical *Doria* dive, you'll spend twenty-five minutes at around two hundred feet and decompress for sixty-five minutes at several stopping points, beginning at 110 feet. While you are hanging on to the anchor line, you're off-gassing nitrogen at a rate the body can tolerate. Violate deco and you are subject to symptoms ranging from a slight rash to severe pain to quadriplegia and death. The body copes poorly with big bubbles of nitrogen trying to fizz out through your capillaries and bulling through your spinal column, traumatizing nerves.

Enter Tri-mix, which simply replaces some of the oxygen and nitrogen in the air with helium, giving you a life-sustaining gas with fewer molecules of those troublesome components of air. With Tri-mix, you can go deeper and stay longer and feel less narced. Still, even breathing Tri-mix at depth can be a high-wire act, owing to a third and final bad agent: carbon dioxide. The natural by-product of respiration also triggers the body's automatic desire to replenish oxygen. When you hyperventilate—take rapid, shallow breaths—you deprive yourself of CO_2 and fool the body into believing it doesn't need new oxygen.

Breath-hold divers will hyperventilate before going down as a way to gain an extra minute or two of painless O_2 deprivation. But at depth (for reasons poorly understood), hypercapnia, the retention of CO_2 molecules, has the same "fool the brain" effect. It's a tasteless, odorless, warningless fast track to unconsciousness. One moment you are huffing and puffing against the current, and the next you are swimming in the stream of eternity.

Richard Roost, a forty-six-year-old scuba instructor from Ann Arbor, Michigan, one of the five *Doria* fatalities of the last two seasons, was highly skilled and physically fit. His body was recovered from the *Doria*'s first-class lounge, a large room full of shattered furniture deep in the wreck. It's a scary place, by all accounts, but Roost seemed to be floating in a state of perfect repose. Though he had sucked all the gas from his tanks, there was no sign that he had panicked. Crowell suspects that he simply "took a nap," a likely victim of hypercapnia.

So it is that you strive to sink with utter calm, dumping a bit of gas into your dry suit as you feel it begin to vacuum-seal itself to you, bumping a little gas into the b.c. to slow your rate of descent, seeking neutrality, not just in buoyancy but in spirit as well. Soon you've sunk to that zone where you can see neither surface nor bottom. It's an entrancing, mystical place—pure inner space. Things appear out of nowhere—huge, quick things that aren't there, blocks of blankness, hallucinations of blindness. Drifting, drifting . . . reminds you of something Steve Bielenda told you: "The hard part is making your brain believe this is happening. But, hey, you know what: It really is happening!" You focus on the current-borne minutiae—sea snow, whale food, egg-drop soup—which whizzes by outside the glass of your mask like a sepia-colored silent movie of some poor sod sinking through a blizzard.

Your depth gauge reads 160 feet, and you hit the thermocline, the ocean's deep icebox layer. The water temp plunges to 45 degrees and immediately numbs your cheeks and lips. Your dry suit is compressed paper-thin; you don't know how long you can take the cold, and then something makes you forget about it completely: the *Doria*, the great

dome of her hull falling away into obscurity, and the desolate rails van-
ishing in both directions, and a lifeboat davit waving a shred of trawler
net like a hankie, and the toppled towers of her superstructure. And it's
all true what they've said: You feel humbled and awed. You feel how
thin your own audacity is before the gargantuan works of man. You
land fins-first onto the steel plates, kicking up two little clouds of silt.
Man on the moon.

You've studied the deck plans of the Grande Dame of the Sea—her
intricacy and complexity and order rendered in fine architectural lines.
But the *Doria* looks nothing like that now. Her great smokestack has
tumbled down into the dark debris field on the seafloor. Her raked-
back aluminum forecastle decks have melted like a Dali clock in the
corrosive seawater. Her steel hull has begun to buckle under its own
weight and the immense weight of water, pinching in and splintering
the teak decking of the promenade, where you kick along, weaving in
and out of shattered windows. Everything is moving: bands of water,
now cloudy, now clear, through which a blue shark twists in and out of
view; sea bass darting out to snatch at globs of matter stirred up by
your fins. They swallow and spit and glower. Everywhere you shine
your light inside, you see black dead ends and washed-out walls and
waving white anemones like giant dandelions bowing in a breeze.

You rise up a few feet to take stock of your location and see that on
her outer edges she is Queen of Snags, a harlot tarted up with torn nets,
bristling with fishermen's monofilament and the anchor lines of dive
boats that have had to cut and run from sudden storms. She's been grap-
pled more times than Moby Dick, two generations of obsessed Ahabs
finding in her sheer outrageous bulk the sinews of an inscrutable
malice, a dragon to tilt against. In your solitude you sense the bleak
bitch of something unspeakably larger still, something that shrinks the
Doria down to the size of Steve Bielenda's toy-train tea fob: a hurricane
of time blowing through the universe, devouring all things whole.

On the aft deck of the *Wahoo*, Steve Bielenda, a fireplug of a man, still
sinewy in his early sixties, is kicked back in his metal folding-chair

throne. He wears his white hair in a mullet cut and sports a gold ear-ring. He was wild as a kid, by his own account, a wiseguy, wouldn't listen to nobody. The product of vocational schools, he learned auto mechanics and made a success of his own repair shop before he caught the scuba bug. Then he would go out with fishermen for a chance to dive—there weren't any dive boats then—and offered his services as a salvage diver, no job too small or too big. When he sold his shop and bought the *Wahoo*, it was the best and the biggest boat in the business. Now, as the morning heats up, he's watching the bubbles rise and growling out *Doria* stories in his Brooklyn accent.

"When you say Mount Everest to somebody," he says, "you're sayin' something. Same with da *Doria*. It was the pinnacle wreck. It was some-thing just to go there."

And go there he did—more than a hundred times. The first time in '81, with a serious *Doria* fanatic, Bill Campbell, who had commissioned a bronze plaque to commemorate the twenty-fifth anniversary of the sinking; and often with maritime scholar and salvager John Moyer, who won salvage rights to the *Doria* in federal court and hired the *Wahoo* in '92 to put a "tag" on the wreck—a tube of PVC pipe, sealed watertight, holding the legal papers. Tanks were much smaller then, dinky steel 72's and aluminum 80's, compared with the now-state-of-the-art 120-cubic-foot-capacity tanks. "You got air, you got time," is how Bielenda puts it. And time was what they didn't have down at 180 feet on the hull. It was loot and scoot. Guys were just guessing at their decompression times, since the U.S. Navy Dive Tables expected that nobody would be stupid or desperate enough to make repetitive dives below 190 feet with scuba gear. "Extrapolating the tables" was what they called it; it was more like pick a lucky number and hope for the best. But Bielenda's quick to point out that in the first twenty-five years of diving the *Doria*, nobody died. Back then the players were all local amphibians, born and bred to cold-water diving and watermen to the *n*th degree. Swimming, water polo, skin diving, then scuba, then deep scuba—you learned to crawl before you walked in those days.

A thousand things you had to learn first. "You drive through a tollbooth at five miles an hour—no problem, right? Try it at fifty miles an hour. That hole gets real small! That's divin' da *Doria*. To dive da *Doria* it's gotta be like writin' a song," the captain says, and he hops up from his chair and breaks into an odd little dance, shimmying his 212 pounds in a surprisingly nimble groove, tapping himself here, here, here—places a diver in trouble might find succor in his gear.

"And you oughta wear yer mask strap under yer hood," he tells a diver who's gearing up. "There was this gal one time . . ." and Bielenda launches into the story about how he saved Sally Wahrmann's life with that lesson.

She was down in Gimbel's Hole, just inside it and heading for the gift shop, when this great big guy—John Ornsby was his name, one of the early *Doria* fatalities—comes flying down into the hole after her and just clobbers her. "He rips her mask off and goes roaring away in a panic," Bielenda says. "But see, she has her mask under her hood like I taught her, so she doesn't lose it. It's still right there around her neck."

The blow knocked Wahrmann nearly to the bottom of the wreck, where an obstruction finally stopped her fall seven sideways stories down. But she never panicked, and with her mask back on and cleared, she could find her way out toward the tiny speck of green light that was Gimbel's Hole, the way back to the world. "She climbs up onto the boat and gives me a big kiss. 'Steve,' she says, 'you just saved my life.'"

As for Ornsby, a Florida breath-hold diver of some renown, his banzai descent into Gimbel's Hole was never explained, but he was found dead not far from the entrance, all tangled up in cables as if a giant spider had been at him. It took four divers with cable cutters two dives each to cut the body free. Bielenda has been lost inside of wrecks and has found his way out by a hairbreadth. He and the *Wahoo* have been chased by hurricanes. One time he had divers down on the *Doria* when a blow came up. He was letting out anchor line as fast as he could, and the divers, who were into decompression, they were scrambling up the line hand over hand to hold their depth. The swells rose up to fifteen feet, and Bielenda could see the divers in the swells hanging on to the anchor line, ten feet underwater but looking down into the *Wahoo!* A *Doria* sleigh ride—that's the kind of memories the *Doria*'s given him. Strange sights indeed. He knows he's getting too old for the rigors of depth, but he's not ready to let go of the *Doria* yet, not while they still have their hooks in each other.

Up in the pilothouse of the *Seeker*, Dan Crowell is fitting his video camera into its watertight case, getting ready to go down and shoot some footage inside the wreck. He tries to make at least one dive every charter trip, and he never dives without his camera anymore if he can help it.

The more you learn about Crowell, the more impressed you are. He's a voracious autodidact who sucks up expertise like a sponge. He has worked as a commercial artist, a professional builder, a commercial diver, and a technical scuba instructor, as well as a charter captain. His passion now is shooting underwater video, making images of shipwrecks at extreme depths. His footage of the *Britannic* was shot at a whopping depth of 400 feet. When Crowell made his first *Doria* dive in 1990, a depth of 200 feet was still Mach I, a real psychological and physical barrier. He remembers kneeling in the silt inside Gimbel's Hole at 210 feet and scooping up china plates while he hummed the theme from *Indiana Jones*, "and time was that great big boulder coming at you."

In '91, Crowell didn't even own a computer, but that all changed with the advent of affordable software that allowed divers to enter any combination of gases and get back a theoretically safe deco schedule for any depth. "In a matter of months, we went from rubbing sticks together to flicking a Bic," Crowell says. It was the aggressive use of computers—and the willingness to push the limits—that separated the *Seeker* from the competition. When Bill Nagle, the boat's previous captain, died of his excesses in '93, Crowell came up with the cash to buy the *Seeker*. He'd made the money in the harsh world of hard-hat diving.

Picture Crowell in his impermeable commercial diver's suit, with its hose-fed air supply and screw-down lid, slowly submerging in black, freezing water at some hellish industrial waterfront wasteland. The metaphorical ball cock is stuck and somebody's gotta go down and unstick it. Hacksaw it, blast it, use a lift bag and chains—the fuck cares how he does it? Imagine him slogging through thigh-deep toxic sludge hefting a wrench the size of a dinosaur bone. His eyes are closed—can't see a damned thing down there anyway—and he's humming a tune to himself, working purely by touch, in three-fingered neoprene mitts. Think of him blind as a mole and you'll see why he loves the camera's eye so much, and you'll believe him when he says he's never been scared on the *Andrea Doria*.

"Well, maybe once," Crowell admits. "I was diving on air and I was pretty narced, and I knew it. I started looking around and realized I had no idea where I was." He was deep inside the blacked-out maze of the wreck's interior, where every breath dislodges blinding swirls of glittering rust and silt. "But it just lasted a few seconds. When you're in those places, you're seeing things in postage-stamp-sized pieces. You need to pull back and look at the bigger picture—which is about eight and a half by eleven inches." Crowell found his way out, reconstructing his dive, as it were, page by page.

You've always thought that the way water blurs vision is an apt symbol of a greater blurring, that of the mind in the world. Being matter, we are buried in matter—we are buried alive. This is an idea you first encountered intuitively in the stories of Edgar Allan Poe. Madman! Don't you see? cries Usher, before his eponymous house crashes down on top of him. And the nameless penitent in "The Pit and the Pendulum" first creeps blindly around the abyss, and then confronts the razor's edge of time. He might well be looking into Gimbel's Hole and at the digital readout on his console; he is literature's first extreme deep diver immersed in existential fear of the impossible present moment. But the diver's mask is also a miraculous extra inch of perspective; it puts you at a certain remove from reality, even as you strike a Mephistophelian bargain with physics and the physical world.

You're twelve minutes into your planned twenty-five-minute bottom time when the current suddenly kicks up. It's as if God has thrown the switch—*ka-chung!*—on a conveyor belt miles wide and fathoms thick. You see loose sheets of metal on the hull sucking in and blowing out, just fluttering, as if the whole wreck were breathing. If you let go, you would be whisked away into open sea, a mote in a maelstrom. The current carries with it a brown band of bad visibility, extra cold, direly menacing. Something has begun to clang against the hull, tolling like a bell. Perhaps, topside, it has begun to blow. Keep your shit together. Control your breath. Don't fuck up. And don't dream that things might be otherwise, or it'll be the last dream you know. Otherwise? Shit . . . this is it. Do something. Act. Now! You're going to have to fight your way back to the anchor line, fight to hold on for the whole sixty-five minutes of your deco. And then fight to get back into the boat, with the steel ladder rising and plunging like a cudgel. What was moments ago a piece of cake has changed in a heartbeat to a life-or-death situation.

Then you see Dan Crowell, arrowing down into Gimbel's Hole with his video camera glued to his eyes. You watch the camera light dwindle down to 200 feet, 210, then he turns right and disappears inside the wreck. Do you follow him, knowing that it is precisely that—foolish emulation—that kills divers here? Consider the case of Craig Sicola, a talented, aggressive diver. On his charter in the summer of '98, he saw the crew of the *Seeker* bring up china, lots of it. He wanted china himself, and if he'd waited, he would've gotten it the easy way. Crowell offered to run a line to a known cache—no problem, china for everybody. But it wouldn't have been the same. Maybe what he wanted had less to do with plates than with status, status within an elite. He must've felt he'd worked his way up to the top of his sport only to see the pinnacle recede again. So he studied the *Doria* plans posted in the *Seeker*'s cabin and deduced where china ought to be—his china—and jumped in alone to get it. He came so close to pulling it off, too.

Dropping down into Gimbel's Hole, he found himself in the first-class foyer, where well-dressed passengers once made small talk and smoked as they waited to be called to dinner. He finessed the narrow passageway that led to the first-class dining room, a huge, curving space that spans the width of the *Doria*. He kicked his way across that room, playing his light off lumber piles of shattered tables. Down another corridor leading farther back toward the stern, he encountered a jumble of busted walls, which may have been a kitchen—and he found his china. He loaded up his goody bag, stirring up storms of silt as the plates came loose from the muck. He checked his time and gas supply—hurry now, hurry—and began his journey back. Only he must have missed the passage as he recrossed the dining room. Easy to do: Gain or lose a few feet in depth and you hit blank wall. He would've sucked in a great gulp of gas then—you do that when you're lost; your heart goes wild. Maybe the exit is inches away at the edge of vision, or maybe you've got yourself all turned around and have killed yourself, with ten minutes to think about it.

Sicola managed to find his way out, but by then he must've been running late on his deco schedule. With no time to return to the anchor line, he unclipped his emergency ascent reel and tied a line off to the wreck. Which was when he made mistake number two. He either became entangled in the line, still too deep to stop, and had to cut himself free, or else the line broke as he ascended. Either way, he rocketed to the surface too fast and died of an embolism. Mercifully, though, right up to the last second, Sicola must have believed he was taking correct and decisive action to save himself. Which, in fact, is exactly what he was doing.

But with a margin of error so slender, you have to wonder: Where the hell does someone like Crowell get the sack to make fifty turns inside that maze? How can he swim through curtains of dangling cables, twisting through blown-out walls, choosing stairways that are now passages, and taking passages that are now like elevator shafts, one after another, as relentlessly as one of the blue sharks that school about the wreck? By progressive penetration, he has gone only as far at a time as his memory has permitted. Only now he holds in his mind a model of the ship—and he can rotate that model in his mind and orient himself toward up, down, out. He's been all the way through the *Doria* and out the other side, through the gash that sank her, and brought back the images. This is what it looks like; this is what you see.

But how does it feel? What's it like to know you are in a story that you will either retell a hundred times or never tell? You decide to drop down into the black hole. No, you don't decide; you just do it. Why? You just do. A little ways, to explore the wreck and your courage, what you came down here to do. What is it like? Nothing under your fins now for eighty feet but the mass and complexity of the machine on all sides—what was once luminous and magical changed to dreary chaos. Drifting down past the cables that killed John Ornsby, rusty steel lianas where a wall has collapsed. Dropping too fast now, you pump air into your b.c., kick up and bash your tanks into a pipe, swing one arm and hit a cable, rust particles raining down. You've never felt your attention so assaulted: It is everything at once, from all directions, and from inside, too. You grab the cable and hang, catching your breath— bubble and hiss, bubble and hiss. Your light, a beam of dancing motes, plays down a battered passageway, where metal steps on the left-hand wall lead to a vertical landing, then disappear behind a low, sponge-encrusted wall that was once a ceiling. That's the way inside the *Doria.*

There is something familiar about that tunnel, something the body knows. All your travels, your daily commutes, the Brownian motion of your comings and goings in the world, straining after desires, reaching for your beloved—they've all just been an approach to this one hard turn. You can feel it, the spine arching to make the corner, a bow that shoots the arrow of time. In the final terror, with your gauges ticking and your gas running low, as dead end leads to dead end and the last corridor stretches out beyond time, does the mind impose its own order, seizing the confusion of busted pipes and jagged edges and forcing them into a logical grid, which you can then follow down to the bottom of the wreck and out—in a gust of light and love—through the wound in her side? Where you find yourself standing up to your waist in water, in the pit the current has gouged to be the grave of the *Andrea Doria.* Seagulls screech in the air as you take off your gear piece by piece and, much lightened, begin to walk back to New York across the sandy plane. And it comes as no surprise at all to look up and behold the *Seeker* flying above you, sailing on clouds. On the stern deck, the divers are celebrating, like rubber-suited angels, breaking out beers and cigars and holding up plates to be redeemed by the sun.

from North to the Night
by Alvah Simon

Alvah Simon and his wife Diana in 1994 sailed their 36-foot sloop Roger Henry *into Canada's arctic Tay Bay. Their plan: drop anchor and let the ice lock them in for the winter. Diana had to be evacuated to be with her sick father in New Zealand, leaving Alvah with only a cat named Halifax for company. Simon found that coping with polar bears and arctic cold was easier than coming to grips with his solitude.*

P aralyzed, petrified, I felt around my thighs. *What is this, is it ice? Am I sleeping in a pool of freezing water? Is the boat sinking? No, how could the boat sink? It's in solid ice. Calm, stay calm . . . think.*

Slowly, I realized what must have happened. The cabin walls had been glazed with a half-foot of ice. I had fallen asleep with the lantern burning. In this confined space, the heat would have melted the ice. Water had run down the cabin walls onto the berth, which had a waterproof sheet on the mattress. The water had flowed to the low spot beneath me, and when the lantern went out, the cabin had cooled and the water had frozen.

My frozen clothing and bedding had me pinned down like Gulliver in Lilliput. My normally mild claustrophobia gave way to panic, which gave me the strength to rip myself free. I stumbled into the main cabin, dragging a train of frozen fabric stuck to me. My body was numb. My mind was the dangerous kind of sluggish that comes when the body's core temperature drops precipitously. Exposed to the frigid cabin air, my wet clothing quickly started to freeze. I stripped naked while I could and stood there mumbling stupidly in the dark. In a daze, I crawled into my insulated overalls. The nylon surface of that clothing was searing cold and sucked heat right from my center. Spots on my skin instantly frostbit. I rubbed them back into softness. I shivered hard, rubbed myself, and rocked from foot to foot, but I could not get warm. My teeth chattered uncontrollably. My hands shook so hard I could barely get into my boots, facemask, gloves, and parka. The coat was large enough to serve as a day pack, and in its pockets, fortunately, I had stashed food, hand warmers, extra gloves, and shotgun shells. I shoved a piece of fatty sausage into my mouth and put my clacking teeth to use.

I knew walking was the only way to warm my body and blood slowly. Sitting doesn't burn enough fuel to restart the inner furnace, while the exertion of running forces you to suck in huge amounts of cold air before your muscles are truly warmed. I climbed out of the boat, somehow remembering my shotgun but barely noticing that the night was clear and showed no threat of a blizzard. Because the snow is so dry in the desert air of the Arctic, the slightest wind whips up a blinding ground squall, and navigation is hopeless. I stumbled out across the broken sea-ice at a slow but steady pace. I pushed hard for an hour, walking until I could think, then until I could feel a severe but comforting pain in my feet.

Each footfall sounded like a cannon shot in the absolute silence surrounding me. Each rumble or shift in the snow might have been a precursor to a charging bear, but I could not concern myself with bears just now. I had to deal with my problems one at a time, starting with the most pressing: regaining warmth.

Disoriented, I had to pay close attention to the lay of the land to establish where I was and where I was going. The tundra sloped left and was blown nearly clear of snow. That meant I was on the windward side facing southeast. If I followed it downhill it would lead me to the cliffs off the vessel's starboard beam. I was relieved to find my mind now working clearly.

But when I came to what I thought was the spot in which we had first tried to anchor, I was confused, for a huge uplifting of ice boulders rose above me in the shape of Stonehenge. *Wait, this should be sea-ice outside the tidal fracture zone, only moderately rough, not cliffs or boulders!* It took discipline to calm myself and think it through. If I was where I thought, then some disturbance, a ledge or boulder, must be hidden beneath the water's surface. As the ice thickened, this caused uplifting right at our anchoring location. Assuming that to be my position, I cut off at the angle that should lead to the cliffs beneath Raven's Rock. When those cliffs appeared, a flush of relief flowed through me. But still I felt unsettled when I realized that, had we remained where we originally anchored, the *Roger Henry* would have been severely damaged.

I came up to the cliffs, which cut a high swath even darker than the night behind them. I climbed up the rocky slope of a gully to the cliff top and followed the rim around toward Raven's Rock. The air was perversely cold, near forty-five below zero and compounded in its deadliness by a rising wind, yet there the old black sorcerer sat on top of his rock, fully exposed against the starlight that the ancient Inuit believed the bird had a hand in forming.

Ravens, unlike ptarmigan, snowy owl, musk ox, or bear, have no outer protection from these extremes. But they, like other Arctic birds, do have the special adaptation of a countercurrent circulatory system in their legs that maintains their body heat at 104 degrees while their legs and feet fall to close to freezing.

I did not think of the Raven as my enemy, nor did I find his black countenance forbidding. He was more like a fellow gambler sitting across the table from me—an opponent, but not an enemy. Make no mistake, this was a game with high stakes, and there had to be a winner and a loser, but it was a game we both enjoyed and to which we were inexorably tied.

The Raven sat there unsuspecting, deep in his own thoughts—perhaps profound thoughts, for again we underestimate our fellow earthly species. We have maligned their intelligence by calling anything apparently stupid a "bird brain," based on our simple logic that a small cerebral cortex equals a smallness of smarts. But recent studies discovered that bird brains do not function at all like ours. Their cognizance is centered in the hyperstriatum, which mammals lack. Researchers were startled to find that the *Corvidae*, the family including crows and ravens, possess brain-size-to-body-weight ratios equaling that of dolphins and nearly matching ours. In addition, Corvid brains were found to be packed with an enormous number of brain cells. In the mid-1800s, the Reverend Henry Ward Beecher said all this sooner and simpler: "If men had wings and black feathers, few of them would be clever enough to be ravens." Of course, native people have always credited this bird with a cunning intelligence, as their many legends about the great trickster attest.

I slipped up out of the darkness. It was important to the game that I put on a good face, so I shouted, "I'm fit as a fiddle, old buddy." Startled, the Raven leapt up and cawed a holy hell of protest. It was wonderful to hear a voice other than my own echo across Tay Bay. I cut off from the cliffs at the angle I knew would lead to the boat. The tidal fracture zone extending one hundred feet out from the land had become a chaotic field of splintered ice sheets and ice boulders, one tossed upon the other. The bears never walked directly across the bay but stuck to the fringes of this tumble, looking for seal lairs. Without incident, I wound through the boulders onto the smoother sea-ice, found my way to the boat, and slid below.

I lit the heater and hung the frozen bedding in front of it on a long cord. Our salon table is offset from the centerline to port and is surrounded by a U-shaped settee of cushioned benches. The table is on a collapsible pedestal, which I dropped to seat level, creating a wide bed when I laid the back cushions on the table. I rummaged through the dirty clothes bag and layered myself with some disgustingly dirty long underwear. As each piece of bedding dried, I peeled off a layer of clothing. It took two days to regain complete control.

I surrendered the aft cabins to the cancerous ice by shutting the foil-backed doors. This shrank my already small world, but it reduced the space I had to heat. In my Western orderliness, I had not wanted to eat where I slept—here for cooking, there for sleeping—but that was an extravagance the Arctic would not allow. Within one day of living in my new arrangement, it struck me yet again how highly attuned the Inuit are to their environment. I had accidentally come to the same conclusions they had made millennia earlier. My sleeping platform, which they call an *ikliq*, was now well above the flooring, and being just those few inches higher than the aft-cabin berth made it noticeably warmer. Also, by creating one living space I concentrated the effects of my body heat, kept all the equipment of daily life easily at hand, and found a psychological lift in the relative expansiveness of the main cabin.

The day or date became less relevant in tracking the passage of time. Nature provided more meaningful milestones. Dreadful temperatures, howling blizzards, and total blackness pinned me below. Besides the drudgery of daily chores, there was little to do. Thinking became my sole entertainment, and I grew playful. In the darkness, with no external distractions, it was easy to focus my mediocre mental amperage on a single subject. What I could not cut through with brilliance, I bludgeoned with persistence. I decided to mop up some of the world's most often asked yet lingering questions. I started with:

> Q. Which came first, the chicken or the egg?
> A. Our Western insistence on the strict delineation of species means that, in evolutionary terms, there was a precise moment when a very-nearly-chicken animal laid an egg, within which developed the first true chicken. Thus, the egg came first. Why the chicken crossed the road remains a mystery.
> Q. If God is omnipotent, can He create a rock so big that even He can't lift it?
> A. As we define God as Spirit, and acknowledge Him to be the creator of the material universe, we have established a cause-and-effect order and, clearly, a case for the superiority

of Mind over Matter. Therefore, God can lift any rock he can create, but He should remember to bend at the knees and always wear His support belt.

Q. How many angels can dance on the head of a pin?

A. None. There are serious religious duties to attend to in Heaven, and pinhead dancing is strictly forbidden.

When one blizzard blew itself out, I boiled up a thick beef stew, poured it over a cookie sheet, and laid it up on deck. A half hour later I pulled on my overalls, big pack boots, and stuffed parka and crawled out into the black cockpit with a lantern in one hand and a hammer in the other. I smashed the frozen stew once with the hammer, and it shattered into small pieces that fit nicely into meal-sized plastic bags. I laid these up next to the stack of soup bricks. If I fell sick or injured, or if the diesel gelled into wax in the stove's fuel line, I could start up the camp stove, hacksaw off a nice thick slice of soup, and be warm and fed in minutes.

Staying ahead on my water supply was even more critical, and that meant venturing out to find and chip freshwater ice. The tunneled hood of my parka kept my face warm but severely restricted both my field of vision and hearing. With hobbled senses, I became apprehensive about my surroundings. As I sat in the cockpit, waiting to make my move into the unknown, the thin fabric of the tent constituted my last line of defense. I sat absolutely still for ten minutes, trying to pierce the darkness with my ears, probing for the faintest sound of a bear lying in ambush outside. On some days I burst out the back of the tent. On others I threw something out first as a feint. On still others I slipped my head out as quietly as a church mouse. I did not want to establish any pattern of behavior. Initially, I wanted to throw Halifax out there first, armed only with her keener senses. But as our friendship and partnership grew, I could not bring myself to do that. My life had no more inherent value than hers.

There were times—especially the ones when I dramatically crashed out onto the ice, whirled, and prepared for mortal combat with empty air—that this all seemed silly, tempting me to just get up, go out, and get my damn ice. That would be okay ninety-nine out of a hundred times. Then one day, a crushing blow would smash my head like an overripe papaya. The big beast would then hold my corpse down with one ponderous paw and with his massive jaws snap my head from my body like a berry from a bush.

Fortunately, this night was one of the ninety-nine. After gathering ice and returning to the cockpit tent, I sat there for hours chipping ice boulders into fine flakes. I had experimented with melting times of different-sized ice bits and concluded that minimizing them was well worth the extra effort, considering that I had lots of time and little fuel. I stopped, pulled back my hood for as long as my ears could take the cold, and listened for bears. I pumped up the pressure lantern. Its dim light filled my tent, and its comforting hiss broke the silence. My hands chipped, chipped, chipped, as my mind wandered the world. Occasionally, I slipped below to add a bucket of chips to the melting water on the stove.

Back in the cockpit, my mind wandered to some balmy beach. Condensation formed on the outside of the pot, then ran down to the burner and doused the flame. Soot and toxic smoke filled the cabin, forcing me to open up the boat and release my precious heat into the night air. I regrouped, vowed I would concentrate on my task, and began again. When the pot filled, I carefully poured it into the insulated water barrel. I laid up a full six gallons of water, which would cover my every need for four days and should span any blizzard.

To reward myself, I fried several slices of smoked bacon and dehydrated eggs, then poured maple syrup over the lot. For dessert I crawled between the covers of a good book. Exactly a century before my Arctic vigil, Norwegian explorers Fridtjof Nansen and Hjalmar Johansen left their icebound ship *Fram* drifting in the Arctic Ocean pack ice and made a bold dash for the North Pole. Turned back short of their goal, they were forced to winter on a wilderness island. With a walrus-hide tent, skins to sleep under, blubber to burn, bear meat to eat, and some luck, they had everything they needed to survive. But when asked what

they missed most, Nansen replied, "Oh, how we longed for a book."
Forewarned is forearmed. Cocooned in my sleeping bag, I began
devouring *Endurance, Tundra, Kabloona, Arctic Dreams, Arctic Grail,* and
three more feet of bookshelf.

First I tried to read the "Gee, what a guy" novels, to save my good
biographies, histories, and travel books, resources that were no less
vital than food or fuel. I invested two hundred pages into one mad
genius's plot to destroy the world. The President reluctantly told his
cabinet, "There is only one man who can save us now." They called in
the chiseled-jaw rogue agent, Lance Sterling, who, through episodes of
cool gun play, gratuitous sex, and unbelievable coincidence, crushed
the forces of darkness. I lost it completely and shouted, "Fuck you,
Lance Sterling, and the man who wrote you! Life is too short, even if I
do have time to burn. I need intellectual meat, not cream donuts!" I
angrily threw the book into the black void. I heard smashing glass.
Lance had just crushed the forces of light—my spare lantern. My raw
nerves and intense emotions always cost me something. The next day,
to be sure my opinion was perfectly understood, I wiped my butt with
the pages of that book. Take that, Lance.

I raided the spot on the shelf earmarked for February. I tried to read
slowly, stop early, but the books were just too damned good. My
gloved hands clumsily plowed through thousands of pages. William
Manchester's *The Last Lion,* covering Winston Churchill's early years,
filled me with wonder about this giant of an era. I sank into the plush
leather chairs of mahogany men's clubs, tasted the claret and Highlands whiskey, smelled the cigar smoke. I rose in jubilation and fell
into despair with Winston through his changing fortunes. And when I
laughed, which was often, or cried, which also was often, I thanked
gifted authors Pierre Berton, Steven Ambrose, Arthur M. Schlesinger, Jr.,
and Michael Caro for touching my day.

I read until my nose froze, and then I slipped under the bag and
thought about what lay between those lines. If I were Winnie, what
would I have done? Could I have stooped so low to rise so high, as
L.B.J. had? Is it goodness of heart that makes men seem simple of

mind? As a senior at West Point, Dwight Eisenhower stopped a plebe to haze him, as tradition demanded. He said in a sneering tone, "You don't look like a soldier. You look more like a barber." The plebe, standing at terrified attention, flushed red and said, "Yes sir, I was a barber before I came here." Eisenhower went to his room and told his roommate, "I have just mocked a man for the way he makes an honest living. It is the worst thing that I have ever done, and it will never happen again."

Breaking a lantern did not break the tension. A good laugh was better for that. I do not mean a little chuckle, I mean a belly-aching, knee-slapping, tension-snapping laugh, set off by something that might otherwise have been only mildly amusing but in my solitary confinement became hilarious. Example: While Winston was in his rabidly conservative days, he walked into the Parliamentary urinals only to find his very liberal archrival, Attlee, standing at the trough. Churchill walked down to the far end to relieve himself. Attlee teased, "Feeling a little stand-offish today, are we, Winston?" Churchill replied, "Naturally, sir, every time that you see something big, you try to nationalize it." I spit out my tea, and it took me five minutes to catch my breath.

Without light and darkness to define time, I cannot say how long I sat and read, wrote, thought, or did absolutely nothing. Once, I drifted off to sleep with the ship's clock saying six o'clock. (a.m. or p.m.? It mattered little, anyway.) When I woke, it still said six. Had I really slept twelve hours? I couldn't believe that, so I warmed up the cabin and turned on the satellite navigator for a time update. It was worse than I thought; I had lapped the clock and slept through a full twenty-four hours. That depressed me so much, I went back to sleep. When I woke to that same six o'clock, I panicked. Was my life flashing by in nanosecond days? I vowed to quit looking at the clock, but two days later I weakened and turned my headlamp on it. Sure enough, six o'clock. A vague fear gripped me. I lay still in the darkness, listening to a silence too absolute. Then it hit me: *The damn clock has stopped. I am being toyed with like a mouse.*

Allies and strategies helped control my waking moments, but when I fell asleep, those excruciating nightmares still racked me. I dreamed Diana was cruel to me. *It had started almost the day after the wedding. I had grown used to her infidelities, but never her indifference. I begged her to tell me why she had shut me out physically and emotionally for years. What had I done? Why had she married me if that was how she felt? She just sneered, knowing that my not knowing was killing me. She walked away.* I woke up sweating and breathless. I was convinced it was not a dream; it was a psychic premonition. My mind raced. After all, she had not contacted Peter last Sunday. Where was she? She would be distraught and lonely and would need someone to talk to. She is an attractive woman. Men would want to help her, men who would not ask her to camp out as a permanent lifestyle, men who would not drag her into war zones or the dens of wild animals, men who had professions, prestige, income, and fine things, who offered security, who would give her that garden behind a nice house. She would be home and happy. Who could blame her?

I felt nauseous with a chilling certainty that all this was occurring as I sat there, helpless. A hiss of murderous jealousy swept up my spine. I screamed, "You bastards! I could hike out of here, fly to New Zealand, and get my hands on you. You excite Diana only because you're new. In six months she'll discover that you fart in bed and tell the same jokes over and over." My mind covered every mile, my taxi pulling up unexpectedly, me barging in, fists clenched, and there . . . there . . . would lie my dying father-in-law beside my grieving wife. *My God, am I going insane? This poor woman is* not *on vacation. You have to stop this, Alvah. You have to stop.* I was afraid to fall back asleep for fear the dream would repeat itself.

I got up and went through the cumbersome exercise of dressing for the minus-forty-degree cold outside. With a kerosene lantern in hand, I crawled out onto the buried deck. Fox prints covered the snow. Halifax followed me, her tail puffed up like a raccoon's. She was mad at me; after all, a deal is a deal. It was my job to fend off the foxes and bears so she could take her daily constitution. She dug a hole in the cockpit snow, squatted over it, very smartly did her thing, and dove below.

I stayed on deck—or, more precisely, on the hummock of snow that hid the deck. The wind was still, the air crystal clear, and the sky could not have held a single star more. Above me sparkled an entirely new cosmos; new because it has been viewed and named differently by the native people of this land. Our Big Dipper is to them *Tuktu*, "the caribou." Our Pleiades scampers across their mind and sky as "the Little Foxes." And of course, everybody knows that our Milky Way is really the tracks of Raven, made when the universe was fresh and everything was possible. I walked away from the boat, my footsteps unnaturally loud in the stillness. I lay down on a snowbank. Just those few yards flushed me with the joy of freedom. A Muslim moon bounced a shimmering light off the glacier. The night was many shades of beautiful black. Its beauty calmed me, and the fresh air woke me.

I wrote my diary entry right there in my head, knowing that I would not forget a single word, comma, or period.

> December 10: Two months alone. Look, I can handle the cold, the threat of ending up bear shit, the idea that, if I get sick, I die up here alone. I can take this, but these dreams are tearing me up. It is like fighting water, like falling. If it's not Diana, it's Jon's death. If I could have just found his body, if I could have put my fingers in the wounds made by his speedboat propeller, like Doubting Thomas placing his in Jesus' side, if I could have thrown the first clod of dirt on his casket . . . But he is out there, part of the Atlantic Ocean.
>
> In my dreams, I find Jon alive. A tall, athletic man catches a Frisbee in a park, and I know it is him because I know how he moves and I recognize his unique handsomeness. I dreamed he faked his death to avoid the draft or because he was gay or HIV-positive and could not tell his wife and family. In each dream I create another reason. In each, when I call to him, he tries to run. I catch him and we wrestle. Jon

was always bigger, stronger, and faster than me, but he could never beat me in a fight because he was the nicer man. In the dream, I always punch him hard, just once, for the pain he caused me, then I hug him with all my soul. Then I wake up and can't tell where I am or if the dream is true or not. Then I feel the cold, and I know, and I cry.

It is not just me going crazy; Halifax's behavior is altering noticeably. The snow leopard is well suited to the cold but lives near the equator, so it never has to face extended darkness. Felines are not natural Arctic dwellers. Why *wouldn't* Halifax go as crazy as me? She has the classic symptoms of cabin fever. She whines and wails all the time. She is broody and petulant. How can you quarrel with a cat? But I do. She waits for me to watch, then she destroys things with obvious rage. She'd rather risk my wrath than be ignored. It is a dangerous game she is playing, because my temper is terrible, uncontrollable, and I don't know why. She was determined to lure me out of my bag by tearing up the foil on the backside of the forepeak door. I was determined this would be the last time. I had to teach her once and for all. I lit into her with the blind fury of a baby shaker. I could not believe that it was I doing this. I love animals. I have never been a cruel man. For the next two days, every time I tried to pet her, she bit me.

My back is hurting and my eyes are failing. Unless I come out here in the starlight or moonlight, everything I see is no more than two feet in front of me. It doesn't matter, because I cannot write worth a damn. It's all this angry drivel. I heard on the radio that Boris Yeltsin said the Russian troops were in Chechnia to spread peace and harmony, but if the Chechnians resist, they will be annihilated. Words disgust me. They stink of piss or sting like poison. There is no truth in anything we hear. Who asked me anyway? Why do I keep working with words? A mason uses bricks. He builds his wall. It is what it is. It has lasting purpose. But . . . I agonized over a nearly finished short story for fourteen hours. I read once about an author telling a friend that he had a busy day—he took a comma out in the morning, then put it back in the afternoon.

The dreadful cold interrupted my thoughts. I had been lying in the snow for several hours, and I started to shake. There was no avoiding it—I had to return to the boat, and I had to fall asleep eventually and face my dreams, so I got up and shuffled back through the dark. I crawled into my bag and, when I was warm enough, I fell asleep. But the next dream was different. I ran over sparkling snow dunes. I came upon a mystical fox, all fluffy, white, and pure, with soft brown eyes. We recognized each other. We were old friends, the kind that find sheer joy in each other's silent presence. We played and played, he deftly nipping my heels and me chasing him in circles. Then the fox sat on his haunches and stared at me with serious concern. He cocked his sharp little head and yelped little burps and barks, trying to tell me something very important. I could not understand. He tried so hard to make the sounds of human words, and I tried so hard to understand. I grew frustrated, then agitated, then afraid. This could be terribly important. I thought I would burst from turmoil, when suddenly a golden light washed over me, and I was filled with a peace I had never known. The message was somehow clear; I was just not yet ready for what the fox was trying to teach me. Everything unfolds perfectly and in its own time. I patted the fox's head and scratched his chin. I thanked him but told him it was more important that we play in the moment and leave the future to itself.

In mid-December, Peter radioed with the sad news that his ninety-one-year-old mother had fallen very ill and was not expected to pull through. He was going south on extended leave to be with her; he anticipated an absence of eight weeks. I offered sincere condolences, for even though we had never met in person, I now thought of this man as my close friend. He was concerned about me, but I tried to play it down with weak humor.

Peter had been a voice of reason, and having to mask my madness from him had, in fact, helped me keep it in check. Now I was left truly on my own in the darkest and coldest of times.

William James defined religion as "the feelings, acts, and experiences of individuals in their solitude." My need for constant talk, action, and adventure indicated my babe-in-arms spiritual immaturity, an immaturity I would gladly have clung to. But now I was left no option but to turn my whole attention inward.

Above all else, mystics prize silence and solitude. From cloistered cells to mountaintop retreats, in isolation they find inspiration. St. Augustine's search for the mystic began with a meditative state he called "the cloud of unknowing." The setting he created to encourage this differed little from mine, except for its temperatures. Mother Teresa laid out what she called "the Simple Path." It has five steps but is bedrocked on the first: "In silence there is prayer, and in prayer, peace." Yet powerful religious institutions have traditionally been in outspoken, flesh-burning disagreement. Priests, parsons, rabbis, and elders sternly warned us that "an idle mind is the Devil's playground." Did they fear that, left to ourselves, we would each naturally find our own God, a God who did not demand obedience to a manmade structure nor contributions to maintain its earthly edifices? In the Far East one finds keener insight into the relationship of time and self. The Buddhist philosophy inverts the Western phrase, "Don't just sit there, do something!" into "Don't just do something, sit there!"

And so I sat, through moments and months, through elation and despair, through hissing mental clarity and numbed, beast-of-burden stupidity. On my climbs to the emotional peaks and frightening falls to the valley bottoms, I passed a specific midpoint of perfect balance, but I moved so fast I could but glimpse it: ephemeral, simple, comforting. Now if only I could quiet the white noise, still my chatterbox mind, a natural spring of well-being might fill me, and, if left in peace, begin to pour out.

I recalled my treks through the scorched plains of Africa; climbs in the high, thin air of the Andes; paddles down verdant rivers of Borneo.

I had seen third world disease, disorder, and death. But beneath it I had also seen the grace of unhurried human movement, noticed the serenity of acceptance reflected in elderly but unfretted faces, heard a ripple of laughter too light to be called hilarious, for native people do not seem to store the tensions necessary for that. I wondered if the reasons for this might be no more complicated than the pace of life, the quiet time to process the natural signals from without *and* within. These people might not spend time alone, but they do spend time with themselves. I thought about times I had said, "I really enjoyed myself last night." What I really meant was, "I really enjoyed some person or activity outside and other than myself last night." I was beginning now to feel as if my whole life had been outside and other than myself.

At first I was frightened by my solitude. There were moments, difficult to describe, that I would not wish on anyone. But whenever I could slow my train at this midpoint stop, I felt content, fulfilled and, surprisingly, often more alone than lonely.

On a very still day in mid-December, I closed my useless eyes and listened hard. There was only the wispy sound of a zephyr, or *is that my breathing? Being here is like dancing in the dark. It is the Zen sound of one hand clapping. If a tree falls in the woods, and there is no one there to hear it, does it still make a noise? Is our definition of personal self formed from within or by the collected impressions of how others perceive us? There is no one here to perceive me, nor has there been for a long time. I feel as if I am coming apart, becoming transparent, light, unreal. Sometimes, I see my hand move in the dim light and I wonder what it is. But is there really no one to see me? What if there is a God? What if I am in the eyes of God right now? I was taught that not a sparrow falls from the sky that God does not see.*

Think about that, but not too much. I intellectualize everything into mush. Take that phrase, In the eyes of God. It could mean exactly what it says. Not God, standing back, watching. It could mean we are in *his eyes. No, that is still vague. Get it precise. We are his eyes. We are not being watched, we are the process of watching.* I tried to open my eyes but could not. Something was happening. For a fleeting moment, I saw something—no, I knew something. But my mind could not hold it. I held out my hand in the dark trying to grasp it physically, but it swirled away.

Start from the beginning. "In the beginning was the Word." *What word? Maybe not a particular word, but a sound, a vibration. To find the building block of all matter, physicists have probed deeper and deeper into the atom. They end only energy, and when they peel back the onionskin layers of energy, ultimately they find only vibration. The brute paw that might crush my head is made of muscle, blood, and bone, which are made of molecules, which are made of atoms, which are made of electrons, which are made of sparks and quarks, which are made of nothing that can be measured or weighed. Everything is made of nothing! My head will be crushed by illusion. My illusory brain will drip onto the illusory ground. My death itself will be an illusion and therefore so too must be my life. In the beginning was the Word. The Word was God. God is that vibration, that vibration that creates form through visualization alone . . . Well, shake, rattle, and roll, Big Daddy! Is* this *my grand conclusion?* I cringed at its triteness. My mind flickered like the lamplight, and I tried again, and again.

As my days of darkness passed, a duality started to form in my consciousness. I became actor and audience. For my every thought and action, I was both creator and critic. My present play received endurable reviews, but when I drifted back into my past with astonishing power of recall, the critics savaged me. I could remember what shirt I wore on the day I committed a particular unkindness or infidelity. I'd had so many opportunities to do good, but each opportunity was but a brief moment, and I'd missed many. I felt terrible. I found no atonement in sorrow or regret. I tried to shrink my heart to avoid the pain. I sneered, "Yeah, well nobody's perfect."

I turned on my headlamp and grabbed a travel book off the shelf, impatient to rid my mind of all this. A card fell out. I picked it up and was stunned by what it said.

Lord, make me an instrument of your peace
where there is hatred, let me sow love
where there is injury, pardon

where there is doubt, faith
where there is despair, hope
where there is darkness, light
where there is sadness, joy
Oh divine Master, grant that I may not so much seek
To be consoled . . . as to console
To be understood . . . as to understand
To be loved . . . as to love
For it is in giving that we receive
It is in pardoning, that we are pardoned
It is in dying that we are born into eternal life.

—St. Francis of Assisi

I yelled, "Leave me alone, damn it. I'm just an ordinary adventurer, not some fucking saint. Anyway, I don't even believe in you."

I was spitting angry. Increasingly, what I wanted to do with my life was to write one thing of lasting value. Instead, I dabbled and dribbled, and I knew it. Even if I could cast aside its message, this passage was the most perfectly written I had ever read. The cadence and balance were masterfully crafted and lyrical. It mocked my mediocrity. "Stuff it!" I yelled into the dark. "So you devote your life to achieving that perfection and what do you get? Birds shitting on your shoulder!" But an inner voice said loudly, "Wrong. What you get is one bright shining moment, one chance to create something of lasting value. Francis, this simple man in sackcloth, sworn to poverty, was so at peace with every living thing that foxes followed in his footsteps and birds perched on his shoulders. This simple man painted with a few pen strokes the path to peace, to heaven on earth."

Seven hundred years later his words fell out of a book I opened specifically in an attempt to escape the very uncomfortable awakening of my spiritual self. A man too young for such wisdom once told me that anyone who believes in coincidence is not paying attention. Down deep, I knew that events outside my control were aligning themselves. In this journey, rough spots had been inexplicably smoothed, dangerous mistakes had been forgiven by nature. I felt I had been led to this specific place and time. It was eerie, and I was afraid. I didn't think I was ready, but some stubbornly resistant strand in my willful ego snapped.

I could accept the idea of burning bushes on the road to Damascus, but in the Arctic? If the rough terrain of my psyche could be mapped, this moment would mark a watershed. The collection of events that I called my life flowed from this high spot backward, and the man and person I could become through this difficult, black experience trickled forward as a new river seeking outlet in a body of water larger than itself.

Each time I woke after that day, I found myself feeling less alone, more purposeful, and deeply grateful just to be alive. Daily, that gratitude escaped my lips with an audible "Thank you." Then, as now, I had no earthly idea who I was thanking. But I think I know what I was thankful for: the privilege of being a small, frail, faulted, but integral part of the magic and mystery of life on earth.

You can do worse.

from The Boat Who Wouldn't Float
by Farley Mowat

Farley Mowat (born 1921) and Jack McClelland got drunk together decided to buy a boat—for no more than $1,000—and sail it to distant lands. Mowat went to Newfoundland, and—drunk again—purchased a rotting hulk of a schooner. He commissioned the boat's builder, a crotchety local named Enos, to perform repairs, which included installing an ancient motor Mowat called "the bullgine." Mowat and McClelland ironically named the ship Happy Adventure.

Seamen refer to the first tentative voyage of a newly commissioned ship as her trials. *Happy Adventure*'s trials began at 1400 hours the next day, and so did ours.

It was a "civil" day (in Newfoundland this means the wind is not blowing a full hurricane) and a stiff easterly was whitening the waters of the harbor. Because this was our first departure, and because we were being watched by most of the inhabitants of Muddy Hole, we felt compelled to leave the stage under full sail.

We did not do too badly. With main, foresail, jib, and jumbo hoisted, Jack cast off our moorings. We sheeted everything home, the heavy sails began to draw, and *Happy Adventure* slowly picked up way. In a few moments she was standing swiftly across the harbor.

In order to get out of the long, narrow harbor of Muddy Hole against an east wind, a vessel under sail must beat to weather—that is, she must tack back and forth against the wind. We were, of course, aware of this necessity. We were also aware that, as we left the stage, directly ahead of us there lay a covey of two dozen dories and skiffs, moored fifty yards offshore. As we approached them I prepared to come about on the other tack.

"Ready about!" I sang out to Jack. Then, pushing the big tiller over, "Hard a'lee!"

Happy Adventure's head came up into the wind. She shook herself a bit, considered whether she would come about or not—and decided not. Her head fell off again and she resumed her original course.

Jack was later to claim that this was one of the few honest things she ever did. He claimed she knew perfectly well what would happen if we ever took her to sea, and so she decided it would be better for all of us if she committed suicide immediately by skewing herself on the rocky shores of her home port, where her bones could rest in peace forever.

I disagree. I think that, never having been under sail before, the poor little vessel simply did not know what was expected of her. I think she was as terrified as I was as she bore down on the defenseless mess of little boats and the rocks that lay beyond them.

It was Jack who saved us all. He did not even pause to curse, but leapt into the engine room with such alacrity that he caught the bullgine sleeping. Before it knew he was there he had spun the flywheel and, even without a prime, the green beast was so surprised she fired. She had been taken totally off guard, but even as she belched into life she struck back at us, thinking to make us pay for our trickery by starting in reverse.

There were a good many people watching from the fish plant wharf. Since they could not hear the roar of the bullgine above the thunder of the plant machinery they were incredulous of what they saw. Under full sail and snoring bravely along, *Happy Adventure* slowly came to a stop. Then with all sails still set and drawing—she began to back up. The fish plant manager, a worldly man who had several times seen motion picture films, said it was like watching a movie that had been reversed. He said he expected to see the schooner back right up Obie's stage, lower her sails, and go to sleep again.

I would have been happy to have had this happen. To tell the truth I was so unnerved that it was on the tip of my tongue to turn command over to Jack, jump into our little dory which we were towing astern, and abandon the sea forever. However, pride is a terrible taskmaster and I dared not give in to my sounder instincts.

It was now obvious to Jack and to me that we were not going to be able to beat out of the harbor and that we would have to go out under power if we were to get out at all. But neither of us cared to try to make the bullgine change direction and drive the boat ahead. We knew perfectly well she would stop, and refuse to start, and leave us to drift ignominiously ashore. Consequently, *Happy Adventure backed* all the way out of Muddy Hole harbor under full sail. I think it must have been the most reluctant departure in the history of men and ships.

Once we were at sea, and safely clear of the great headlands guarding the harbor mouth, Jack did try to reverse the engine and she reacted as we had known she would. She stopped and would not start. It no longer mattered. *Happy Adventure* lay over on her bilge, took the wind over her port bow and went bowling off down the towering coast as if she were on her way to a racing rendezvous.

During the next few hours all the miseries, doubts, and distresses of the past weeks vanished from our minds. The little ship sailed like a good witch. She still refused to come about, but this was no great problem in open water since we could jibe her around, and her masts and rigging were so stout that this sometimes dangerous practice threatened her not at all. We sailed her on a broad reach; we sailed her hard on the wind; we let her run, wrung-out with foresail to starboard and mainsail to port; and we had no fault to find with her seakeeping qualities.

She had, however, some other frailties. The unaccustomed motion of bucketing through big seas under a press of canvas squeezed out most of the fish gunk with which she had sealed her seams, and she began to leak so excessively that Jack had to spend most of his time at the pump. Also, the massive compass I had brought with me from Ontario demonstrated an incredible disdain for convention and insisted on pointing as much as forty degrees off what should have been the correct course. It was apparent that, until we found someone who could adjust the compass, our navigation would have to be, in the time-honored phrase, "by guess and by God." Neither of us was a very good guesser and we did not know how much we could rely on God.

In our temporarily euphoric mood we dared to sail several miles off shore to reconnoiter a belated iceberg. We were circling it at a discreet distance, for the great bergs become unstable in late summer and sometimes turn turtle, setting up tidal waves that can swamp a small vessel, when the sun began to haze over. The Grand Banks fog was rolling in upon the back of the east wind.

We fled before it and *Happy Adventure* carried us swiftly between the headlands of the harbor just as the fog overtook us, providing a gray escort as we ran down the reach and rounded to in fine style at Obie's stage.

Despite her unorthodox departure, and despite the leaks and the compass, we felt reasonably content with our little vessel and not a little proud of ourselves as well. We were as ready as we would ever be to begin our voyage.

One small difficulty still remained. We had no charts of the east coast of Newfoundland. The lack of charts, combined with a misleading compass and the dead certainty of running into fog, suggested we would do well to ship a pilot until we could make a port where charts could be bought and the compass adjusted.

The obvious choice for a pilot was Enos. Like most Newfoundland seamen he possessed, we presumed, special senses which are lost to modern man. He had sailed these waters all his life, often without a compass and usually without charts. When you asked him how he managed to find his way to some distant place he would look baffled and reply:

"Well, me son, I *knows* where it's at."

We needed somebody like that. However, when we broached the matter to Enos he showed no enthusiasm. For a man who was usually as garrulous as an entire pack of politicians, his response was spectacularly succinct.

"No!" he grunted, and for emphasis spat a gob of tobacco juice on our newly painted cabin top.

There was no swaying him either. Persuasion (and Jack is a persuader par excellence) got us nowhere. He kept on saying "No" and spitting until the cabin top developed a slippery brown sheen over most of its surface and we were prepared to give up. I was, at any rate, but Jack was made of sterner stuff.

"If the old bustard won't come willingly," Jack told me after Enos left, "we'll shanghai him."

"The hell with him, Jack. Forget it. We'll manage on our own."

"Forget it nothing! If this goddamn boat sinks I'm at least going to have the satisfaction of seeing him sink with it!"

There was no arguing with Jack in a mood like that.

He arranged a small farewell party on board that night. It was one of the gloomiest parties I have ever attended. Six or seven of our fishermen friends squeezed into the cabin and ruminated at lugubrious length on the manifold perils of the sea. When they got tired of that, they began recalling the small schooners that had sailed out of Southern Shore ports and never been heard of again. The list went on and on until even Enos began to grow restive.

"Well, byes," he interjected, "them was mostly poorbuilt boats. Not fitten to go to sea. Not proper fer it, ye might say. Now you takes a boat like this 'un. Proper built and found. *She* won't be making any widows on the shore."

This was the opening Jack had been waiting for.

"You're so right, Enos. In a boat as good as this a fellow could sail to hell and back."

Enos eyed Jack with sudden suspicion. "Aye," he replied cautiously. "She be good fer it!"

"*You* certainly wouldn't be afraid to sail in her, now would you Enos?"

The trap was sprung.

"Well, now, me darlin' man, I don't say as I wouldn't, but a 'course . . ."

"Good enough!" Jack shouted. "Farley, hand me the log. Enos, we'll sign you on as sailing master for the maiden voyage of the finest ship you ever built."

Enos struggled mightily but to no avail. He was under the eyes of six of his peers and one of them, without realizing it, became our ally:

"Sign on, sign on, Enos, me son. We knows you'm not afeard!"

So Enos signed his mark.

Happy Adventure sailed an hour after dawn. It was a fine morning, clear and warm, with a good draft of wind out of the nor'west to help us on our way and to keep the fog off shore. We had intended to sail *at* dawn but Enos did not turn up and when we went to look for him his daughters said he had gone off to haul a herring net. We recognized this as a ruse, and so we searched for him in the most likely place. He was savagely disgruntled when we found him, complaining bitterly that a man couldn't even "do his nature" without being followed. Little by little we coaxed him down to the stage, got him aboard and down below, and before he could rally, we cast off the lines.

Happy Adventure made a brave sight as she rolled down the reach toward the waiting sea. With all sails set and drawing she lay over a little and snored sweetly through the water, actually overtaking and passing two or three belated trap skiffs bound out to the fishing grounds. Their crews grinned cheerfully at us, which is as close to a farewell as a Newfoundlander seaman will allow himself. There is bad luck in farewells.

Before we cleared the headlands I celebrated a small ritual that I learned from my father. I poured four stiff glasses of rum. I gave one of these to Enos and one to Jack, and I kept one for myself. The fourth I poured overboard. The Old Man of the Sea is a sailor and he likes his drop of grog. And it is a good thing to be on friendly terms with the Old Man when you venture out upon the gray waters that are his domain.

All that morning we sailed south on a long reach, keeping a two- or three-mile offing from the grim sea cliffs. We came abeam of Cape Ballard and left it behind, then the wind began to fall light and fickle, ghosting for a change. The change came and the wind picked up from sou'east, a dread muzzler right on our bows, bringing the fog in toward us.

Enos began to grow agitated. We were approaching Cape Race, the southeast "corner" of Newfoundland and one of the most feared places in the western ocean. Its peculiar menace lies in the tidal currents that sweep past it. They are totally unpredictable. They can carry an unwary vessel, or one blinded by fog, miles off her true course and so to destruction on the brooding rocks ashore.

In our innocence Jack and I were not much worried, and when Enos insisted that we down sail and start the engine we were inclined to mock him. He did not like this and withdrew into sullen taciturnity, made worse by the fact that I had closed off the rum rations while we were at sea. Finally, to please him, we started the bullgine, or rather Jack did, after a blasphemous half-hour's struggle.

The joys of the day were now all behind us. Somber clouds began closing off the sky; the air grew chill, presaging the coming of the fog; and the thunderous blatting of the unmuffled bullgine deafened us, while the slow strokes of the great pistol shook the little boat as an otter shakes a trout.

By four o'clock we still had reasonably good visibility and were abeam of Cape Race—and there we stuck. The engine thundered and the water boiled under our counter, but we got no farther on our way. Hour after hour the massive highlands behind the cape refused to slip astern. Jack and I finally began to comprehend something of the power of the currents. Although we were making five knots through the water, a leebow tide was running at almost the same speed against us.

The fog was slow in coming but the wall of gray slid inexorably nearer. At six-thirty Jack went below to rustle up some food. An instant later his head appeared in the companionway. The air of casual insouciance, which was as much a part of his seagoing gear as his jaunty yachting cap, had vanished.

"Christ!" he cried, and it was perhaps partly a prayer. "This bloody boat is sinking!"

I jumped to join him and found that he was undeniably right. Water was already sluicing across the floor boards in the main cabin. Spread-eagling the engine for better purchase, Jack began working the handle of the pump as if his life depended on it. It dawned on me his life *did* depend on it, and so did mine.

The next thing I knew Enos had shouldered me aside. Taking one horrified look at the private swimming pool inside *Happy Adventure* he shrieked:

"Lard Jasus, byes, she's gone!"

It was hardly the remark we needed to restore our faith in him or in his boat. Still yelling, he went on to diagnose the trouble.

He told us the stuffing box had fallen off. This meant that the ocean was free to enter the boat through the large hole in the sternpost that housed the vessel's shaft. And since we could not reach it there was nothing we could do about it.

Enos now retreated into a mental room of his own, a dark hole filled with fatalistic thoughts. However, by giving him a bottle of rum to cherish, I managed to persuade him to take the tiller (the little boat had meanwhile been going in circles) and steer a course for Trepassey Bay, fifteen miles to the eastward, where I thought we might just manage to beach the vessel before she sank.

There was never any question of abandoning her. Our dory, so called, was a little plywood box barely capable of carrying one man. Life preservers would have been useless, because we were in the Labrador Current where the waters are so cold that a man cannot survive immersion in them for more than a few minutes.

By dint of furious pumping, Jack and I found we could almost hold the water level where it was, although we could not gain upon the inflow. And so we pumped. The engine thundered on. We pumped. The minutes stretched into hours and we pumped. The fog held off, which was one minor blessing, and we pumped. The engine roared and the heat became so intense that we were sweating almost as much water back into the bilges as we were pumping out. We pumped. The tidal current slackened and turned and began to help us on our way. We pumped.

Occasionally one of us crawled on deck to breathe and to rest his agonized muscles for a moment. At eight o'clock I stuck my head out of the companionway and saw the massive headland of Mistaken Point a mile or so to leeward. I glanced at Enos. He was staring straight ahead, his eyes half shut and his mouth pursed into a dark pit of despair. He had taken out his dentures, a thing he always did in moments of stress. When I called out to tell him we were nearly holding the leak he gave no sign of hearing but continued staring over the bow as if he beheld some bleak and terrible vision from which he could not take his attention for a moment. Not at all cheered I ducked back into the engine room.

And then the main pump jammed.

That pump was a fool of a thing that had no right to be aboard a boat. Its innards were a complicated mass of springs and valves that could not possibly digest the bits of flotsam, jetsam and codfish floating in the vessel's bilge. But, fool of a thing or not, it was our only hope.

It was dark by this time, so Jack held a flashlight while I unbolted the pump's faceplate. The thing contained ten small coil springs and all of them leapt for freedom the instant the plate came off. They ricocheted off the cabin sides like a swarm of manic bees and fell to sink below the surface of the water in the bilges.

It does not seem possible, but we found them all. It took twenty-five or thirty minutes of groping with numbed arms under oily, icy water, but we found them all, reinstalled them, put back the faceplate, and again began to pump.

Meanwhile, the water had gained four inches. It was now over the lower part of the flywheel and less than two inches below the top of the carburetor. The flywheel spun a niagara of spray onto the red-hot exhaust pipe, turning the dark and roaring engine room into a sauna bath. We pumped.

Jack crawled on deck for a breather and immediately gave a frantic yell. For a second I hesitated. I did not think I had the fortitude to face a new calamity—but a second urgent summons brought me out on deck. Enos was frozen at the helm and by the last light of day I could see he was steering straight toward a wall of rock which loomed above us, no more than three hundred yards away.

I leapt for the tiller, Enos did not struggle but meekly moved aside. His expression had changed and had become almost beatific. It may have been the rum that did it—Enos was at peace with himself and with the Fates.

"We'd best run her onto the rocks," he explained mildly, "than be drowned in the cold, cold water."

Jack went back to the pump, and I put the vessel on a course to skirt the threatening cliffs. We were not impossibly far from Trepassey Bay, and there still seemed to be a chance we could reach the harbor and beach the vessel on a nonlethal shore.

At about eleven o'clock I saw a flashing light ahead and steered for it. When I prodded him, Enos confirmed that it might be the buoy marking the entrance to Trepassey harbor. However, before we reached it the fog overtook us and the darkness became total. We felt our way past the light-buoy and across the surrounding shoals with only luck and the Old Man to guide us.

As we entered the black gut which we hoped was the harbor entrance, I did not need Jack's warning shout to tell me that our time had about run out. The bullgine had begun to cough and splutter. The water level had reached her carburetor and, tough as she was, she could not remain alive for long on a mixture of gasoline and salt seawater.

Within Trepassey harbor all was inky black. No lights could be seen on the invisible shore. I steered blindly ahead, knowing that sooner or later we must strike the land. Then the engine coughed, stopped, picked up again, coughed, and stopped for good. Silently, in that black night, the little ship ghosted forward.

Jack came tumbling out on deck, for there was no point in remaining below while the vessel floundered. He had, and I remember this with great clarity, a flashlight in his mouth and a bottle of rum in each hand. . . .

. . . At that moment *Happy Adventure*'s forefoot hit something. She jarred a little, made a strange sucking sound, and the motion went out of her.

"I t'inks," said Enos as he nimbly relieved Jack of one of the bottles, "I t'inks we's run'd ashore!"

Jack believes *Happy Adventure* has a special kind of homing instinct. He may be right. Certainly she is never happier than when she is lying snuggled up against a working fish plant. Perhaps she identifies fish plants with the natal womb, which is not so strange when one remembers she was built in a fish plant yard and that she spent the many months of her refit as a semi-permanent fixture in the fish plant slip at Muddy Hole.

In any event, when she limped into Trepassey she unerringly found her way straight to her spiritual home. Even before we began playing flashlights on our surroundings we knew this was so. The old stench rose all around us in its familiar miasma.

The flashlights revealed that we had run ashore on a gently shelving beach immediately alongside a massively constructed wharf. Further investigation had to be delayed because the tide was falling and the schooner was in danger of keeling over on her bilge. Jack made a jump and managed to scale the face of the wharf. He caught the lines I threw him and we rigged a spider web of ropes from our two masts to the wharf timbers to hold the vessel upright when all the water had drained away from her.

When she seemed secure I joined Jack on the dock and cautiously we went exploring. The fog was so thick that our lights were nearly useless, and we practically bumped into the first human being we encountered. He was the night watchman for Industrial Seafood Packers, a huge concern to whose dock we were moored. After we had convinced the watchman that we did not have a cargo of fish to unload, but were only mariners in distress, he came aboard.

He seemed genuinely incredulous to find we did not have a radar set. How, he asked, had we found our way into the harbor? How had we missed striking the several draggers anchored in the fairway? And how, in hell's own name (his words), had we found the plant and managed to come alongside the wharf without hitting the L-shaped end where the cod-oil factory stood in lonely grandeur?

Since we could not answer these questions we evaded them, leaving him with the suspicion, which spread rapidly around Trepassey, that we were possessed by an occult power. Witches and warlocks have not yet vanished from the outport scene in Newfoundland.

The watchman was a generous man and he told us we could stay at the wharf as long as we wished. He felt, however, that we might be happier if we moored a hundred feet farther to seaward.

"'Tis the poipe, ye know; the poipe what carries off the gurry from the plant. Ye've moored hard alongside o'she."

Happy Adventure had come home with a vengeance and, for all I know, it may have *been* vengeance at that.

from Treasure Island

by Robert Louis Stevenson

Robert Louis Stevenson (1850–1894) and his 12-year-old stepson Lloyd drew a map of an imaginary Treasure Island to pass a rainy day during an 1881 vacation in Scotland. The map inspired Stevenson to write a story about the island to amuse his family. That story became his most beloved novel. Here young Jim Hawkins meets his first pirate at the Admiral Benbow Inn.

I remember him as if it were yesterday, as he came plodding to the inn door, his sea-chest following behind him in a hand-barrow—a tall, strong, heavy, nut-brown man, his tarry pigtail falling over the shoulders of his soiled blue coat, his hands ragged and scarred, with black, broken nails, and the sabre cut across one cheek, a dirty, livid white. I remember him looking round the cove and whistling to himself as he did so, and then breaking out in that old sea-song that he sang so often afterwards:

> "Fifteen men on the dead man's chest—
> Yo-ho-ho, and a bottle of rum!"

in the high, old tottering voice that seemed to have been tuned and broken at the capstan bars. Then he rapped on the door with a bit of stick like a handspike that he carried, and when my father appeared, called roughly for a glass of rum. This, when it was brought to him, he drank slowly, like a connoisseur, lingering on the taste and still looking about him at the cliffs and up at our signboard.

"This is a handy cove," says he at length; "and a pleasant sittyated grog-shop. Much company, mate?"

My father told him no, very little company, the more was the pity.

"Well, then," said he, "this is the berth for me. Here you, matey," he cried to the man who trundled the barrow; "bring up alongside and help up my chest. I'll stay here a bit," he continued. "I'm a plain man; rum and bacon and eggs is what I want, and that head up there for to watch ships off. What you mought call me? You mought call me captain. Oh, I see what you're at—there"; and he threw down three or four gold pieces on the threshold. "You can tell me when I've worked through that," says he, looking as fierce as a commander.

And indeed bad as his clothes were and coarsely as he spoke, he had none of the appearance of a man who sailed before the mast, but seemed like a mate or skipper accustomed to be obeyed or to strike. The man who came with the barrow told us the mail had set him down the morning before at the Royal George, that he had inquired what inns there were along the coast, and hearing ours well spoken of, I suppose, and described as lonely, had chosen it from the others for his place of residence. And that was all we could learn of our guest.

He was a very silent man by custom. All day he hung round the cove or upon the cliffs with a brass telescope; all evening he sat in a corner of the parlour next the fire and drank rum and water very strong. Mostly he would not speak when spoken to, only look up sudden and fierce and blow through his nose like a fog-horn; and we and the people who came about our house soon learned to let him be. Every day when he came back from his stroll he would ask if any seafaring men had gone by along the road. At first we thought it was the want of company of his own kind that made him ask this question, but at last we began to see he was desirous to avoid them. When a seaman put up at the Admiral Benbow (as now and then some did, making by the coast road for Bristol), he would look in at him through the curtained door before he entered the parlour; and he was always sure to be as silent as a mouse when any such was present. For me, at least, there was no secret about the matter, for I was, in a way, a sharer in his alarms. He had taken me aside one day and promised me a silver fourpenny on the first of every month if I would only keep my "weather-eye open for a seafaring man with one leg" and let him know the moment he appeared. Often enough when the first of the month came round and I applied to him for my wage, he would only blow through his nose at me and stare me down, but before the week was out he was sure to think better of it, bring me my fourpenny piece, and repeat his orders to look out for "the seafaring man with one leg."

How that personage haunted my dreams, I need scarcely tell you. On stormy nights, when the wind shook the four corners of the house and the surf roared along the cove and up the cliffs, I would see him in a thousand forms, and with a thousand diabolical expressions. Now the leg would be cut off at the knee, now at the hip; now he was a monstrous kind of a creature who had never had but the one leg, and that in the middle of his body. To see him leap and run and pursue me over hedge and ditch was the worst of nightmares. And altogether I paid pretty dear for my monthly fourpenny piece, in the shape of these abominable fancies.

But though I was so terrified by the idea of the seafaring man with one leg, I was far less afraid of the captain himself than anybody else who knew him. There were nights when he took a deal more rum and water than his head would carry; and then he would sometimes sit and sing his wicked, old, wild sea-songs, minding nobody; but sometimes he would call for glasses round and force all the trembling company to listen to his stories or bear a chorus to his singing. Often I have heard the house shaking with "Yo-ho-ho, and a bottle of rum," all the neighbours joining in for dear life, with the fear of death upon them, and each singing louder than the other to avoid remark. For in these fits he was the most overriding companion ever known; he would slap his hand on the table for silence all round; he would fly up in a passion of anger at a question, or sometimes because none was put, and so he judged the company was not following his story. Nor would he allow anyone to leave the inn till he had drunk himself sleepy and reeled off to bed.

His stories were what frightened people worst of all. Dreadful stories they were—about hanging, and walking the plank, and storms at sea, and the Dry Tortugas, and wild deeds and places on the Spanish Main. By his own account he must have lived his life among some of the wickedest men that God ever allowed upon the sea, and the language in which he told these stories shocked our plain country people almost as much as the crimes that he described. My father was always saying the inn would be ruined, for people would soon cease coming there to be tyrannized over and put down, and sent shivering to their beds; but I really believe his presence did us good. People were frightened at the time, but on looking back they rather liked it; it was a fine excitement in a quiet country life, and there was even a party of the younger men who pretended to admire him, calling him a "true sea-dog" and a "real old salt" and such like names, and saying there was the sort of man that made England terrible at sea.

In one way, indeed, he bade fair to ruin us, for he kept on staying week after week, and at last month after month, so that all the money had been long exhausted, and still my father never plucked up the heart to insist on having more. If ever he mentioned it, the captain blew through his nose so loudly that you might say he roared, and stared my poor father out of the room. I have seen him wringing his hands after such a rebuff, and I am sure the annoyance and the terror he lived in must have greatly hastened his early and unhappy death.

All the time he lived with us the captain made no change whatever in his dress but to buy some stockings from a hawker. One of the cocks of his hat having fallen down, he let it hang from that day forth, though it was a great annoyance when it blew. I remember the appearance of his coat, which he patched himself upstairs in his room, and which, before the end, was nothing but patches. He never wrote or received a letter, and he never spoke with any but the neighbours, and with these, for the most part, only when drunk on rum. The great sea-chest none of us had ever seen open.

He was only once crossed, and that was towards the end, when my poor father was far gone in a decline that took him off. Dr. Livesey came late one afternoon to see the patient, took a bit of dinner from my mother, and went into the parlour to smoke a pipe until his horse should come down from the hamlet, for we had no stabling at the old Benbow. I followed him in, and I remember observing the contrast the neat, bright doctor, with his powder as white as snow and his bright, black eyes and pleasant manners, made with the coltish country folk, and above all, with that filthy, heavy, bleared scarecrow of a pirate of ours, sitting, far gone in rum, with his arms on the table. Suddenly he—the captain, that is—began to pipe up his eternal song:

> "Fifteen men on the dead man's chest—
> Yo-ho-ho, and a bottle of rum!
> Drink and the devil had done for the rest—
> Yo-ho-ho, and a bottle of rum!"

At first I had supposed "the dead man's chest" to be that identical big box of his upstairs in the front room, and the thought had been mingled in my nightmares with that of the one-legged seafaring man. But by this time we had all long ceased to pay any particular notice to the song; it was new, that night, to nobody but Dr. Livesey, and on him I observed it did not produce an agreeable effect, for he looked up for a moment quite angrily before he went on with his talk to old Taylor, the gardener, on a new cure for the rheumatics. In the meantime, the captain gradually brightened up at his own music, and at last flapped his hand upon the table before him in a way we all knew to mean silence. The voices stopped at once, all but Dr. Livesey's; he went on as before, speaking clear and kind and drawing briskly at his pipe between every word or two. The captain glared at him for a while, flapped his hand again, glared still harder, and at last broke out with a villainous, low oath, "Silence, there, between decks!"

"Were you addressing me, sir?" says the doctor; and when the ruffian had told him, with another oath, that this was so, "I have only one thing to say to you, sir," replies the doctor, "that if you keep on drinking rum, the world will soon be quit of a very dirty scoundrel!"

The old fellow's fury was awful. He sprang to his feet, drew and opened a sailor's clasp-knife, and balancing it open on the palm of his hand, threatened to pin the doctor to the wall.

The doctor never so much as moved. He spoke to him as before, over his shoulder and in the same tone of voice, rather high, so that all the room might hear, but perfectly calm and steady: "If you do not put that knife this instant in your pocket, I promise, upon my honour, you shall hang at the next assizes."

Then followed a battle of looks between them, but the captain soon knuckled under, put up his weapon, and resumed his seat, grumbling like a beaten dog.

"And now, sir," continued the doctor, "since I now know there's such a fellow in my district, you may count I'll have an eye upon you day and night. I'm not a doctor only; I'm a magistrate; and if I catch a breath of complaint against you, if it's only for a piece of incivility like tonight's, I'll take effectual means to have you hunted down and routed out of this. Let that suffice."

Soon after, Dr. Livesey's horse came to the door and he rode away, but the captain held his peace that evening, and for many evenings to come.

It was not very long after this that there occurred the first of the mysterious events that rid us at last of the captain, though not, as you will see, of his affairs. It was a bitter cold winter, with long, hard frosts and heavy gales; and it was plain from the first that my poor father was little likely to see the spring. He sank daily, and my mother and I had all the inn upon our hands, and were kept busy enough without paying much regard to our unpleasant guest.

It was one January morning, very early—a pinching, frosty morning—the cove all grey with hoar-frost, the ripple lapping softly on the stones, the sun still low and only touching the hilltops and shining far to seaward. The captain had risen earlier than usual and set out down the beach, his cutlass swinging under the broad skirts of the old blue coat, his brass telescope under his arm; his hat tilted back upon his head. I remember his breath hanging like smoke in his wake as he strode off, and the last sound I heard of him as he turned the big rock was a loud snort of indignation, as though his mind was still running upon Dr. Livesey.

Well, mother was upstairs with father and I was laying the breakfast-table against the captain's return when the parlour door opened and a man stepped in on whom I had never set my eyes before. He was a pale, tallowy creature, wanting two fingers of the left hand, and though he wore a cutlass, he did not look much like a fighter. I had always my eye open for seafaring men, with one leg or two, and I remember this one puzzled me. He was not sailorly, and yet he had a smack of the sea about him too.

I asked him what was for his service, and he said he would take rum; but as I was going out of the room to fetch it, he sat down upon a table and motioned me to draw near. I paused where I was, with my napkin in my hand.

"Come here, sonny," says he. "Come nearer here."

I took a step nearer.

"Is this here table for my mate Bill?" he asked with a kind of leer.

I told him I did not know his mate Bill, and this was for a person who stayed in our house whom we called the captain.

"Well," said he, "my mate Bill would be called the captain, as like as not. He has a cut on one cheek and a mighty pleasant way with him, particularly in drink, has my mate Bill. We'll put it, for argument like, that your captain has a cut on one cheek—and we'll put it, if you like, that that cheek's the right one. Ah, well! I told you. Now, is my mate Bill in this here house?"

I told him he was out walking.

"Which way, sonny? Which way is he gone?"

And when I had pointed out the rock and told him how the captain was likely to return, and how soon, and answered a few other questions, "Ah," said he, "this'll be as good as drink to my mate Bill."

The expression of his face as he said these words was not at all pleasant, and I had my own reasons for thinking that the stranger was mistaken, even supposing he meant what he said. But it was no affair of mine, I thought; and besides, it was difficult to know what to do. The stranger kept hanging about just inside the inn door, peering round the corner like a cat waiting for a mouse. Once I stepped out myself into the road, but he immediately called me back, and as I did not obey quick enough for his fancy, a most horrible change came over his tallowy face, and he ordered me in with an oath that made me jump. As soon as I was back again he returned to his former manner, half fawning, half sneering, patted me on the shoulder, told me I was a good boy and he had taken quite a fancy to me. "I have a son of my own," said he, "as like you as two blocks, and he's all the pride of my 'art. But the great thing for boys is discipline, sonny—discipline. Now, if you had sailed along of Bill, you wouldn't have stood there to be spoke to twice—not you. That was never Bill's way, nor the way of sich as sailed with him. And here, sure enough, is my mate Bill, with a spyglass under his arm, bless his old 'art, to be sure. You and me'll just go back into the parlour, sonny, and get behind the door, and we'll give Bill a little surprise—bless his 'art, I say again."

So saying, the stranger backed along with me into the parlour and put me behind him in the corner so that we were both hidden by the open door. I was very uneasy and alarmed, as you may fancy, and it rather added to my fears to observe that the stranger was certainly frightened himself. He cleared the hilt of his cutlass and loosened the blade in the sheath; and all the time we were waiting there he kept swallowing as if he felt what we used to call a lump in the throat.

At last in strode the captain, slammed the door behind him, without looking to the right or left, and marched straight across the room to where his breakfast awaited him.

"Bill," said the stranger in a voice that I thought he had tried to make bold and big.

The captain spun round on his heel and fronted us; all the brown had gone out of his face, and even his nose was blue; he had the look of a man who sees a ghost, or the evil one, or something worse, if anything can be; and upon my word, I felt sorry to see him in a moment turn so old and sick.

"Come, Bill, you know me; you know an old shipmate, Bill, surely," said the stranger.

The captain made a sort of gasp.

"And who else?" returned the other, getting more at his ease. "Black Dog as ever was, come for to see his old shipmate Billy, at the Admiral Benbow inn. Ah, Bill, Bill, we have seen a sight of times, us two, since I lost them two talons," holding up his mutilated hand.

"Now, look here," said the captain, "you've run me down; here I am; well, then, speak up; what is it?"

"That's you, Bill," returned Black Dog, "you're in the right of it, Billy. I'll have a glass of rum from this dear child here, as I've took such a liking to; and we'll sit down, if you please, and talk square, like old shipmates."

When I returned with the rum, they were already seated on either side of the captain's breakfast-table—Black Dog next to the door and sitting sideways so as to have one eye on his old shipmate and one, as I thought, on his retreat.

He bade me go and leave the door wide open. "None of your keyholes for me, sonny," he said; and I left them together and retired into the bar.

For a long time, though I certainly did my best to listen, I could hear nothing but a low gabbing; but at last the voices began to grow higher, and I could pick up a word or two, mostly oaths, from the captain.

"No, no, no, no; and an end of it!" he cried once. And again, "If it comes to swinging, swing all, say I."

Then all of a sudden there was a tremendous explosion of oaths and other noises—the chair and table went over in a lump, a clash of steel followed, and then a cry of pain, and the next instant I saw Black Dog in full flight, and the captain hotly pursuing, both with drawn cut-lasses, and the former streaming blood from the left shoulder. Just at the door the captain aimed at the fugitive one last tremendous cut, which would certainly have split him to the chin had it not been inter-cepted by our big signboard of Admiral Benbow. You may see the notch on the lower side of the frame to this day.

That blow was the last of the battle. Once out upon the road, Black

Dog, in spite of his wound, showed a wonderful clean pair of heels and disappeared over the edge of the hill in half a minute. The captain, for his part, stood staring at the signboard like a bewildered man. Then he passed his hand over his eyes several times and at last turned back into the house.

"Jim," says he, "rum"; and as he spoke, he reeled a little, and caught himself with one hand against the wall.

"Are you hurt?" cried I.

"Rum," he repeated. "I must get away from here. Rum! Rum!"

I ran to fetch it, but I was quite unsteadied by all that had fallen out, and I broke one glass and fouled the tap, and while I was still getting in my own way, I heard a loud fall in the parlour, and running in, beheld the captain lying full length upon the floor. At the same instant my mother, alarmed by the cries and fighting, came running downstairs to help me. Between us we raised his head. He was breathing very loud and hard, but his eyes were closed and his face a horrible colour.

"Dear, deary me," cried my mother, "what a disgrace upon the house! And your poor father sick!"

In the meantime, we had no idea what to do to help the captain, nor any other thought but that he had got his death-hurt in the scuffle with the stranger. I got the rum, to be sure, and tried to put it down his throat, but his teeth were tightly shut and his jaws as strong as iron. It was a happy relief for us when the door opened and Dr. Livesey came in, on his visit to my father.

"Oh, doctor," we cried, "what shall we do? Where is he wounded?"

"Wounded? A fiddle-stick's end!" said the doctor. "No more wounded than you or I. The man has had a stroke, as I warned him. Now, Mrs. Hawkins, just you run upstairs to your husband and tell him, if possible, nothing about it. For my part, I must do my best to save this fellow's trebly worthless life; Jim, you get me a basin."

When I got back with the basin, the doctor had already ripped up the captain's sleeve and exposed his great sinewy arm. It was tattooed in several places. "Here's luck," "A fair wind," and "Billy Bones his fancy," were very neatly and clearly executed on the forearm; and up near the

shoulder there was a sketch of a gallows and a man hanging from it—
done, as I thought, with great spirit.

"Prophetic," said the doctor, touching this picture with his finger.
"And now, Master Billy Bones, if that be your name, we'll have a look at
the colour of your blood. Jim," he said, "are you afraid of blood?"

"No, sir," said I.

"Well, then," said he, "you hold the basin"; and with that he took
his lancet and opened a vein.

A great deal of blood was taken before the captain opened his eyes
and looked mistily about him. First he recognized the doctor with an
unmistakable frown; then his glance fell upon me, and he looked
relieved. But suddenly his colour changed, and he tried to raise himself, crying, "Where's Black Dog?"

"There is no Black Dog here," said the doctor, "except what you have
on your own back. You have been drinking rum; you have had a stroke,
precisely as I told you; and I have just, very much against my own will,
dragged you headforemost out of the grave. Now, Mr. Bones—"

"That's not my name," he interrupted.

"Much I care," returned the doctor. "It's the name of a buccaneer of my
acquaintance; and I call you by it for the sake of shortness, and what I
have to say to you is this: one glass of rum won't kill you, but if you take
one you'll take another and another, and I stake my wig if you don't
break off short, you'll die—do you understand that?—die, and go to your
own place, like the man in the Bible. Come, now, make an effort. I'll help
you to your bed for once."

Between us, with much trouble, we managed to hoist him upstairs,
and laid him on his bed, where his head fell back on the pillow as if
he were almost fainting.

"Now, mind you," said the doctor, "I clear my conscience—the
name of rum for you is death."

And with that he went off to see my father, taking me with him by
the arm.

"This is nothing," he said as soon as he had closed the door. "I have
drawn blood enough to keep him quiet awhile; he should lie for a

week where he is—that is the best thing for him and you; but another stroke would settle him."

About noon I stopped at the captain's door with some cooling drinks and medicines. He was lying very much as we had left him, only a little higher, and he seemed both weak and excited.

"Jim," he said, "you're the only one here that's worth anything, and you know I've been always good to you. Never a month but I've given you a silver fourpenny for yourself. And now you see, mate, I'm pretty low, and deserted by all; and Jim, you'll bring me one noggin of rum, now, won't you, matey?"

"The doctor—" I began.

But he broke in cursing the doctor, in a feeble voice but heartily. "Doctors is all swabs," he said; "and that doctor there, why, what do he know about seafaring men? I been in places hot as pitch, and mates dropping round with Yellow Jack, and the blessed land a-heaving like the sea with earthquakes—what do the doctor know of lands like that?—and I lived on rum, I tell you. It's been meat and drink, and man and wife, to me; and if I'm not to have my rum now I'm a poor old hulk on a lee shore, my blood'll be on you, Jim, and that doctor swab"; and he ran on again for a while with curses. "Look, Jim, how my fingers fidges," he continued in the pleading tone. "I can't keep 'em still, not I. I haven't had a drop this blessed day. That doctor's a fool, I tell you. If I don't have a drain o' rum, Jim, I'll have the horrors; I seen some on 'em already. I seen old Flint in the corner there, behind you; as plain as print, I seen him; and if I get the horrors, I'm a man that has lived rough, and I'll raise Cain. Your doctor hisself said one glass wouldn't hurt me. I'll give you a golden guinea for a noggin, Jim."

He was growing more and more excited, and this alarmed me for my father, who was very low that day and needed quiet; besides, I was reassured by the doctor's words, now quoted to me, and rather offended by the offer of a bribe.

"I want none of your money," said I, "but what you owe my father. I'll get you one glass, and no more."

When I brought it to him, he seized it greedily and drank it out.

"Aye, aye," said he, "that's some better, sure enough. And now, matey, did that doctor say how long I was to lie here in this old berth?"

"A week at least," said I.

"Thunder!" he cried. "A week! I can't do that; they'd have the black spot on me by then. The lubbers is going about to get the wind of me this blessed moment; lubbers as couldn't keep what they got, and want to nail what is another's. Is that seamanly behaviour, now, I want to know? But I'm a saving soul. I never wasted good money of mine, nor lost it neither; and I'll trick 'em again. I'm not afraid on 'em. I'll shake out another reef, matey, and daddle 'em again."

As he was thus speaking, he had risen from bed with great difficulty, holding to my shoulder with a grip that almost made me cry out, and moving his legs like so much dead weight. His words, spirited as they were in meaning, contrasted sadly with the weakness of the voice in which they were uttered. He paused when he had got into a sitting position on the edge.

"That doctor's done me," he murmured. "My ears is singing. Lay me back."

Before I could do much to help him he had fallen back again to his former place, where he lay for a while silent.

"Jim," he said at length, "you saw that seafaring man today?"

"Black Dog?" I asked.

"Ah! Black Dog," says he. "*He's* a bad un; but there's worse that put him on. Now, if I can't get away nohow, and they tip me the black spot, mind you, it's my old sea-chest they're after; you get on a horse—you can, can't you? Well, then, you get on a horse, and go to—well, yes, I will!—to that eternal doctor swab, and tell him to pipe all hands—magistrates and sich—and he'll lay 'em aboard at the Admiral Benbow—all old Flint's crew, man and boy, all on 'em that's left. I was first mate, I was, old Flint's first mate, and I'm the on'y one as knows the place. He gave it me at Savannah, when he lay a-dying, like as if I was to now, you see. But you won't peach unless they get the black spot on me, or unless you see that Black Dog again or a seafaring man with one leg, Jim—him above all."

"But what is the black spot, captain?" I asked.

"That's a summons, mate. I'll tell you if they get that. But you keep your weather-eye open, Jim, and I'll share with you equals, upon my honour."

He wandered a little longer, his voice growing weaker; but soon after I had given him his medicine, which he took like a child, with the remark, "If ever a seaman wanted drugs, it's me," he fell at last into a heavy, swoonlike sleep, in which I left him. What I should have done had all gone well I do not know. Probably I should have told the whole story to the doctor, for I was in mortal fear lest the captain should repent of his confessions and make an end of me. But as things fell out, my poor father died quite suddenly that evening, which put all other matters on one side. Our natural distress, the visits of the neighbours, the arranging of the funeral, and all the work of the inn to be carried on in the meanwhile kept me so busy that I had scarcely time to think of the captain, far less to be afraid of him.

He got downstairs next morning, to be sure, and had his meals as usual, though he ate little and had more, I am afraid, than his usual supply of rum, for he helped himself out of the bar, scowling and blowing through his nose, and no one dared to cross him. On the night before the funeral he was as drunk as ever; and it was shocking, in that house of mourning, to hear him singing away at his ugly old sea-song; but weak as he was, we were all in the fear of death for him, and the doctor was suddenly taken up with a case many miles away and was never near the house after my father's death. I have said the captain was weak, and indeed he seemed rather to grow weaker than regain his strength. He clambered up and down stairs, and went from the parlour to the bar and back again, and sometimes put his nose out of doors to smell the sea, holding on to the walls as he went for support and breathing hard and fast like a man on a steep mountain. He never particularly addressed me, and it is my belief he had as good as forgotten his confidences; but his temper was more flighty, and allowing for his bodily weakness, more violent than ever. He had an alarming way now when he was drunk of drawing his cutlass and laying it bare before him on the table. But with all that, he minded people less and seemed shut up in his own thoughts and rather wandering. Once, for instance, to our extreme wonder, he piped up to a different air, a kind of country love-song that he must have learned in his youth before he had begun to follow the sea.

So things passed until, the day after the funeral, and about three o'clock of a bitter, foggy, frosty afternoon, I was standing at the door for a moment, full of sad thoughts about my father, when I saw someone drawing slowly near along the road. He was plainly blind, for he tapped before him with a stick and wore a great green shade over his eyes and nose; and he was hunched, as if with age or weakness, and wore a huge old tattered sea-cloak with a hood that made him appear positively deformed. I never saw in my life a more dreadful-looking figure. He stopped a little from the inn, and raising his voice in an odd sing-song, addressed the air in front of him, "Will any kind friend inform a poor blind man, who has lost the precious sight of his eyes in the gracious defence of his native country, England—and God bless King George!—where or in what part of this country he may now be?"

"You are at the Admiral Benbow, Black Hill Cove, my good man," said I.

"I hear a voice," said he, "a young voice. Will you give me your hand, my kind young friend, and lead me in?"

I held out my hand, and the horrible, soft-spoken, eyeless creature gripped it in a moment like a vise. I was so much startled that I struggled to withdraw, but the blind man pulled me close up to him with a single action of his arm.

"Now, boy," he said, "take me in to the captain."

"Sir," said I, "upon my word I dare not."

"Oh," he sneered, "that's it! Take me in straight or I'll break your arm."

And he gave it, as he spoke, a wrench that made me cry out.

"Sir," said I, "it is for yourself I mean. The captain is not what he used to be. He sits with a drawn cutlass. Another gentleman—"

"Come, now, march," interrupted he; and I never heard a voice so cruel, and cold, and ugly as that blind man's. It cowed me more than the pain, and I began to obey him at once, walking straight in at the door and towards the parlour, where our sick old buccaneer was sitting, dazed with rum. The blind man clung close to me, holding me in one iron fist and leaning almost more of his weight on me than I could carry. "Lead me straight up to him, and when I'm in view, cry out, 'Here's a friend for you, Bill.' If you don't, I'll do this," and with that he gave me a twitch that I thought would have made me faint. Between this and that, I was so utterly terrified of the blind beggar that I forgot my terror of the captain, and as I opened the parlour door, cried out the words he had ordered in a trembling voice.

The poor captain raised his eyes, and at one look the rum went out of him and left him staring sober. The expression of his face was not so much of terror as of mortal sickness. He made a movement to rise, but I do not believe he had enough force left in his body.

"Now, Bill, sit where you are," said the beggar. "If I can't see, I can hear a finger stirring. Business is business. Hold out your left hand. Boy, take his left hand by the wrist and bring it near to my right."

We both obeyed him to the letter, and I saw him pass something from the hollow of the hand that held his stick into the palm of the captain's, which closed upon it instantly.

"And now that's done," said the blind man; and at the words he suddenly left hold of me, and with incredible accuracy and nimbleness, skipped out of the parlour and into the road, where, as I still stood motionless, I could hear his stick go tap-tap-tapping into the distance.

It was some time before either I or the captain seemed to gather our senses, but at length, and about at the same moment, I released his wrist, which I was still holding, and he drew in his hand and looked sharply into the palm.

"Ten o'clock!" he cried. "Six hours. We'll do them yet," and he sprang to his feet.

Even as he did so, he reeled, put his hand to his throat, stood swaying for a moment, and then, with a peculiar sound, fell from his whole height face foremost to the floor.

I ran to him at once, calling to my mother. But haste was all in vain. The captain had been struck dead by thundering apoplexy. It is a curious thing to understand, for I had certainly never liked the man, though of late I had begun to pity him, but as soon as I saw that he was dead, I burst into a flood of tears. It was the second death I had known, and the sorrow of the first was still fresh in my heart.

I lost no time, of course, in telling my mother all that I knew, and per-haps should have told her long before, and we saw ourselves at once in a difficult and dangerous position. Some of the man's money—if he had any—was certainly due to us, but it was not likely that our cap-tain's shipmates, above all the two specimens seen by me, Black Dog and the blind beggar, would be inclined to give up their booty in pay-ment of the dead man's debts. The captain's order to mount at once and ride for Dr. Livesey would have left my mother alone and unpro-tected, which was not to be thought of. Indeed, it seemed impossible for either of us to remain much longer in the house; the fall of coals in the kitchen grate, the very ticking of the clock, filled us with alarms. The neighbourhood, to our ears, seemed haunted by approaching foot-steps; and what between the dead body of the captain on the parlour floor and the thought of that detestable blind beggar hovering near at hand and ready to return, there were moments when, as the saying goes, I jumped in my skin for terror. Something must speedily be resolved upon, and it occurred to us at last to go forth together and seek help in the neighbouring hamlet. No sooner said than done. Bare-headed as we were, we ran out at once in the gathering evening and the frosty fog.

The hamlet lay not many hundred yards away, though out of view, on the other side of the next cove; and what greatly encouraged me, it was in an opposite direction from that whence the blind man had made his appearance and whither he had presumably returned. We were not many minutes on the road, though we sometimes stopped to lay hold of each other and hearken. But there was no unusual sound—nothing but the low wash of the ripple and the croaking of the inmates of the wood.

It was already candle-light when we reached the hamlet, and I shall never forget how much I was cheered to see the yellow shine in doors and windows; but that, as it proved, was the best of the help we were likely to get in that quarter. For—you would have thought men would have been ashamed of themselves—no soul would consent to return with us to the Admiral Benbow. The more we told of our troubles, the more—man, woman, and child—they clung to the shelter of their houses. The name of Captain Flint, though it was strange to me, was well enough known to some there and carried a great weight of terror. Some of the men who had been to field-work on the far side of the Admiral Benbow remembered, besides, to have seen several strangers on the road, and taking them to be smugglers, to have bolted away; and one at least had seen a little lugger in what we called Kitts Hole. For that matter, anyone who was a comrade of the captain's was enough to frighten them to death. And the short and the long of the matter was, that while we could get several who were willing enough to ride to Dr. Livesey's, which lay in another direction, not one would help us to defend the inn.

They say cowardice is infectious; but then argument is, on the other hand, a great emboldener; and so when each had said his say, my mother made them a speech. She would not, she declared, lose money that belonged to her fatherless boy; "If none of the rest of you dare," she said, "Jim and I dare. Back we will go, the way we came, and small thanks to you big, hulking, chicken-hearted men. We'll have that chest open, if we die for it. And I'll thank you for that bag, Mrs. Crossley, to bring back our lawful money in."

Of course I said I would go with my mother, and of course they all cried out at our foolhardiness, but even then not a man would go along with us. All they would do was to give me a loaded pistol lest we were attacked, and to promise to have horses ready saddled in case we were pursued on our return, while one lad was to ride forward to the doctor's in search of armed assistance.

My heart was beating finely when we two set forth in the cold night upon this dangerous venture. A full moon was beginning to rise and peered redly through the upper edges of the fog, and this increased our haste, for it was plain, before we came forth again, that all would be as bright as day, and our departure exposed to the eyes of any watchers. We slipped along the hedges, noiseless and swift, nor did we see or hear anything to increase our terrors, till, to our relief, the door of the Admiral Benbow had closed behind us.

I slipped the bolt at once, and we stood and panted for a moment in the dark, alone in the house with the dead captain's body. Then my mother got a candle in the bar, and holding each other's hand, we advanced into the parlour. He lay as we had left him, on his back, with his eyes open and one arm stretched out.

"Draw down the blind, Jim," whispered my mother; "they might come and watch outside. And now," said she when I had done so, "we have to get the key off *that*; and who's to touch it, I should like to know!" and she gave a kind of sob as she said the words.

I went down on my knees at once. On the floor close to his hand there was a little round of paper, blackened on the one side. I could not doubt that this was the *black spot*; and taking it up, I found written on the other side, in a very good, clear hand, this short message: "You have till ten tonight."

"He had till ten, mother," said I; and just as I said it, our old clock began striking. This sudden noise startled us shockingly; but the news was good, for it was only six.

"Now, Jim," she said, "that key."

I felt in his pockets, one after another. A few small coins, a thimble, and some thread and big needles, a piece of pigtail tobacco bitten away at the end, his gully with the crooked handle, a pocket compass, and a tinder box were all that they contained, and I began to despair.

"Perhaps it's round his neck," suggested my mother.

Overcoming a strong repugnance, I tore open his shirt at the neck, and there, sure enough, hanging to a bit of tarry string, which I cut with his own gully, we found the key. At this triumph we were filled with hope and hurried upstairs without delay to the little room where he had slept so long and where his box had stood since the day of his arrival.

It was like any other seaman's chest on the outside, the initial "B" burned on the top of it with a hot iron and the corners somewhat smashed and broken as by long, rough usage.

"Give me the key," said my mother; and though the lock was very stiff, she had turned it and thrown back the lid in a twinkling.

A strong smell of tobacco and tar rose from the interior, but nothing was to be seen on the top except a suit of very good clothes, carefully brushed and folded. They had never been worn, my mother said. Under that, the miscellany began—a quadrant, a tin canikin, several sticks of tobacco, two brace of very handsome pistols, a piece of bar silver, an old Spanish watch and some other trinkets of little value and mostly of foreign make, a pair of compasses mounted with brass, and five or six curious West Indian shells. I have often wondered since why he should have carried about these shells with him in his wandering, guilty, and hunted life.

In the meantime, we had found nothing of any value but the silver and the trinkets, and neither of these were in our way. Underneath there was an old boat-cloak, whitened with sea-salt on many a harbour-bar. My mother pulled it up with impatience, and there lay before us, the last things in the chest, a bundle tied up in oilcloth, and looking like papers, and a canvas bag that gave forth, at a touch, the jingle of gold.

"I'll show these rogues that I'm an honest woman," said my mother. "I'll have my dues, and not a farthing over. Hold Mrs. Crossley's bag." And she began to count over the amount of the captain's score from the sailor's bag into the one that I was holding.

It was a long, difficult business, for the coins were of all countries and sizes—doubloons, and louis d'ors, and guineas, and pieces of eight, and I know not what besides, all shaken together at random. The guineas, too, were about the scarcest, and it was with these only that my mother knew how to make her count.

When we were about half-way through, I suddenly put my hand upon her arm, for I had heard in the silent frosty air a sound that brought my heart into my mouth—the tap-tapping of the blind man's stick upon the frozen road. It drew nearer and nearer, while we sat holding our breath. Then it struck sharp on the inn door, and then we could hear the handle being turned and the bolt rattling as the wretched being tried to enter; and then there was a long time of silence both within and without. At last the tapping recommenced, and, to our indescribable joy and gratitude, died slowly away again until it ceased to be heard.

"Mother," said I, "take the whole and let's be going," for I was sure the bolted door must have seemed suspicious and would bring the whole hornet's nest about our ears, though how thankful I was that I had bolted it, none could tell who had never met that terrible blind man.

But my mother, frightened as she was, would not consent to take a fraction more than was due to her and was obstinately unwilling to be content with less. It was not yet seven, she said, by a long way; she knew her rights and she would have them; and she was still arguing with me when a little low whistle sounded a good way off upon the hill. That was enough, and more than enough, for both of us.

"I'll take what I have," she said, jumping to her feet.

"And I'll take this to square the count," said I, picking up the oilskin packet.

Next moment we were both groping downstairs, leaving the candle by the empty chest; and the next we had opened the door and were in full retreat. We had not started a moment too soon. The fog was rapidly dispersing; already the moon shone quite clear on the high ground on either side; and it was only in the exact bottom of the dell and round the tavern door that a thin veil still hung unbroken to conceal the first steps of our escape. Far less than half-way to the hamlet, very little beyond the bottom of the hill, we must come forth into the moonlight.

Nor was this all, for the sound of several footsteps running came already to our ears, and as we looked back in their direction, a light tossing to and fro and still rapidly advancing showed that one of the newcomers carried a lantern.

"My dear," said my mother suddenly, "take the money and run on. I am going to faint."

This was certainly the end for both, of us, I thought. How I cursed the cowardice of the neighbours; how I blamed my poor mother for her honesty and her greed, for her past foolhardiness and present weakness! We were just at the little bridge, by good fortune; and I helped her, tottering as she was, to the edge of the bank, where, sure enough, she gave a sigh and fell on my shoulder. I do not know how I found the strength to do it at all, and I am afraid it was roughly done, but I managed to drag her down the bank and a little way under the arch. Farther I could not move her, for the bridge was too low to let me do more than crawl below it. So there we had to stay—my mother almost entirely exposed and both of us within earshot of the inn.

My curiosity, in a sense, was stronger than my fear, for I could not remain where I was, but crept back to the bank again, whence, sheltering my head behind a bush of broom, I might command the road before our door. I was scarcely in position ere my enemies began to arrive, seven or eight of them, running hard, their feet beating out of time along the road and the man with the lantern some paces in front. Three men ran together, hand in hand; and I made out, even through the mist, that the middle man of this trio was the blind beggar. The next moment his voice showed me that I was right.

"Down with the door!" he cried.

"Aye, aye, sir!" answered two or three; and a rush was made upon the Admiral Benbow, the lantern-bearer following; and then I could see them pause, and hear speeches passed in a lower key, as if they were surprised to find the door open. But the pause was brief, for the blind man again issued his commands. His voice sounded louder and higher, as if he were afire with eagerness and rage.

"In, in, in!" he shouted, and cursed them for their delay.

Four or five of them obeyed at once, two remaining on the road with the formidable beggar. There was a pause, then a cry of surprise, and then a voice shouting from the house, "Bill's dead."

But the blind man swore at them again for their delay.

"Search him, some of you shirking lubbers, and the rest of you aloft and get the chest," he cried.

I could hear their feet rattling up our old stairs, so that the house must have shook with it. Promptly afterwards, fresh sounds of astonishment arose; the window of the captain's room was thrown open with a slam and a jingle of broken glass, and a man leaned out into the moonlight, head and shoulders, and addressed the blind beggar on the road below him.

"Pew," he cried, "they've been before us. Someone turned the chest out alow and aloft."

"Is it there?" roared Pew.

"The money's there."

The blind man cursed the money.

"Flint's fist, I mean," he cried.

"We don't see it here nohow," returned the man.

"Here, you below there, is it on Bill?" cried the blind man again.

At that another fellow, probably him who had remained below to search the captain's body, came to the door of the inn. "Bill's been overhauled a'ready," said he; "nothin' left."

"It's these people of the inn—it's that boy. I wish I had put his eyes out!" cried the blind man, Pew. "They were here no time ago—they had the door bolted when I tried it. Scatter, lads, and find 'em."

"Sure enough, they left their glim here," said the fellow from the window.

"Scatter and find 'em! Rout the house out!" reiterated Pew, striking with his stick upon the road.

Then there followed a great to-do through all our old inn, heavy feet pounding to and fro, furniture thrown over, doors kicked in, until the very rocks re-echoed and the men came out again, one after another, on the road, and declared that we were nowhere to be found. And just then the same whistle that had alarmed my mother and myself over the dead captain's money was once more clearly audible through the night, but this time twice repeated. I had thought it to be the blind man's trumpet, so to speak, summoning his crew to the assault, but I now found that it was a signal from the hillside towards the hamlet, and from its effect upon the buccaneers, a signal to warn them of approaching danger.

"There's Dirk again," said one. "Twice! We'll have to budge, mates."

"Budge, you skulk!" cried Pew. "Dirk was a fool and a coward from the first—you wouldn't mind him. They must be close by; they can't be far; you have your hands on it. Scatter and look for them, dogs! Oh, shiver my soul," he cried, "if I had eyes!"

This appeal seemed to produce some effect, for two of the fellows began to look here and there among the lumber, but half-heartedly, I thought, and with half an eye to their own danger all the time, while the rest stood irresolute on the road.

"You have your hands on thousands, you fools, and you hang a leg! You'd be as rich as kings if you could find it, and you know it's here, and you stand there skulking. There wasn't one of you dared face Bill, and I did it—a blind man! And I'm to lose my chance for you! I'm to be a poor, crawling beggar, sponging for rum, when I might be rolling in a coach! If you had the pluck of a weevil in a biscuit you would catch them still."

"Hang it, Pew, we've got the doubloons!" grumbled one.

"They might have hid the blessed thing," said another. "Take the Georges, Pew, and don't stand here squalling."

Squalling was the word for it; Pew's anger rose so high at these objections till at last, his passion completely taking the upper hand, he struck at them right and left in his blindness and his stick sounded heavily on more than one.

These, in their turn, cursed back at the blind miscreant, threatened him in horrid terms, and tried in vain to catch the stick and wrest it from his grasp.

This quarrel was the saving of us, for while it was still raging, another sound came from the top of the hill on the side of the hamlet—the tramp of horses galloping. Almost at the same time a pistol-shot, flash and report, came from the hedge side. And that was plainly the last signal of danger, for the buccaneers turned at once and ran, separating in every direction, one seaward along the cove, one slant across the hill, and so on, so that in half a minute not a sign of them remained but Pew. Him they had deserted, whether in sheer panic or out of revenge for his ill words and blows I know not; but there he remained behind, tapping up and down the road in a frenzy, and groping and calling for his comrades. Finally he took the wrong turn and ran a few steps past me, towards the hamlet, crying, "Johnny, Black Dog, Dirk," and other names, "you won't leave old Pew, mates—not old Pew!"

Just then the noise of horses topped the rise, and four or five riders came in sight in the moonlight and swept at full gallop down the slope.

At this Pew saw his error, turned with a scream, and ran straight for the ditch, into which he rolled. But he was on his feet again in a second and made another dash, now utterly bewildered, right under the nearest of the coming horses.

The rider tried to save him, but in vain. Down went Pew with a cry that rang high into the night; and the four hoofs trampled and spurned him and passed by. He fell on his side, then gently collapsed upon his face and moved no more.

I leaped to my feet and hailed the riders. They were pulling up, at any rate, horrified at the accident; and I soon saw what they were. One, tailing out behind the rest, was a lad that had gone from the hamlet to Dr. Livesey's; the rest were revenue officers, whom he had met by the way, and with whom he had had the intelligence to return at once. Some news of the lugger in Kitt's Hole had found its way to Supervisor Dance and set him forth that night in our direction, and to that circumstance my mother and I owed our preservation from death.

Pew was dead, stone dead. As for my mother, when we had carried her up to the hamlet, a little cold water and salts and that soon brought her back again, and she was none the worse for her terror, though she still continued to deplore the balance of the money. In the meantime the supervisor rode on, as fast as he could, to Kitt's Hole; but his men had to dismount and grope down the dingle, leading, and sometimes supporting, their horses, and in continual fear of ambushes; so it was no great matter for surprise that when they got down to the Hole the lugger was already under way, though still close in. He hailed her. A voice replied, telling him to keep out of the moonlight or he would get some lead in him, and at the same time a bullet whistled close by his arm. Soon after, the lugger doubled the point and disappeared. Mr. Dance stood there, as he said, "like a fish out of water," and all he could do was to dispatch a man to B—— to warn the cutter. "And that," said he, "is just about as good as nothing. They've got off clean, and there's an end. Only," he added, "I'm glad I trod on Master Pew's corns," for by this time he had heard my story.

I went back with him to the Admiral Benbow, and you cannot imagine a house in such a state of smash; the very clock had been thrown down by these fellows in their furious hunt after my mother and myself; and though nothing had actually been taken away except the captain's money-bag and a little silver from the till, I could see at once that we were ruined. Mr. Dance could make nothing of the scene.

"They got the money, you say? Well, then, Hawkins, what in fortune were they after? More money, I suppose?"

"No, sir; not money, I think," replied I. "In fact, sir, I believe I have the thing in my breast pocket; and to tell you the truth, I should like to get it put in safety."

"To be sure, boy; quite right," said he. "I'll take it, if you like."

"I thought perhaps Dr. Livesey—" I began.

"Perfectly right," he interrupted very cheerily, "perfectly right—a gentleman and a magistrate. And, now I come to think of it, I might as well ride round there myself and report to him or squire. Master Pew's dead, when all's done; not that I regret it, but he's dead, you see, and people will make it out against an officer of His Majesty's revenue, if make it out they can. Now, I'll tell you, Hawkins, if you like, I'll take you along."

I thanked him heartily for the offer, and we walked back to the hamlet where the horses were. By the time I had told mother of my purpose they were all in the saddle.

"Dogger," said Mr. Dance, "you have a good horse; take up this lad behind you."

As soon as I was mounted, holding on to Dogger's belt, the supervisor gave the word, and the party struck out at a bouncing trot on the road to Dr. Livesey's house.

We rode hard all the way till we drew up before Dr. Livesey's door. The house was all dark to the front.

Mr. Dance told me to jump down and knock, and Dogger gave me a stirrup to descend by. The door was opened almost at once by the maid.

"Is Dr. Livesey in?" I asked.

No, she said, he had come home in the afternoon but had gone up to the hall to dine and pass the evening with the squire.

"So there we go, boys," said Mr. Dance.

This time, as the distance was short, I did not mount, but ran with Dogger's stirrup-leather to the lodge gates and up the long, leafless, moonlit avenue to where the white line of the hall buildings looked on either hand on great old gardens. Here Mr. Dance dismounted, and taking me along with him, was admitted at a word into the house.

The servant led us down a matted passage and showed us at the end into a great library, all lined with bookcases and busts upon the top of them, where the squire and Dr. Livesey sat, pipe in hand, on either side of a bright fire.

I had never seen the squire so near at hand. He was a tall man, over six feet high, and broad in proportion, and he had a bluff, rough-and-ready face, all roughened and reddened and lined in his long travels. His eyebrows were very black, and moved readily, and this gave him a look of some temper, not bad, you would say, but quick and high.

"Come in, Mr. Dance," says he, very stately and condescending.

"Good evening, Dance," says the doctor with a nod. "And good evening to you, friend Jim. What good wind brings you here?"

The supervisor stood up straight and stiff and told his story like a lesson; and you should have seen how the two gentlemen leaned forward and looked at each other, and forgot to smoke in their surprise and interest. When they heard how my mother went back to the inn, Dr. Livesey fairly slapped his thigh, and the squire cried "Bravo!" and broke his long pipe against the grate. Long before it was done, Mr. Trelawney (that, you will remember, was the squire's name) had got up from his seat and was striding about the room, and the doctor, as if to hear the better, had taken off his powdered wig and sat there looking very strange indeed with his own close-cropped black poll.

At last Mr. Dance finished the story.

"Mr. Dance," said the squire, "you are a very noble fellow. And as for riding down that black, atrocious miscreant, I regard it as an act of virtue, sir, like stamping on a cockroach. This lad Hawkins is a trump, I perceive. Hawkins, will you ring that bell? Mr. Dance must have some ale."

"And so, Jim," said the doctor, "you have the thing that they were after, have you?"

"Here it is, sir," said I, and gave him the oilskin packet.

The doctor looked it all over, as if his fingers were itching to open it; but instead of doing that, he put it quietly in the pocket of his coat.

"Squire," said he, "when Dance has had his ale he must, of course, be off on His Majesty's service; but I mean to keep Jim Hawkins here to sleep at my house, and with your permission, I propose we should have up the cold pie and let him sup."

"As you will, Livesey," said the squire; "Hawkins has earned better than cold pie."

So a big pigeon pie was brought in and put on a side-table, and I made a hearty supper, for I was as hungry as a hawk, while Mr. Dance was further complimented and at last dismissed.

"And now, squire," said the doctor.

"And now, Livesey," said the squire in the same breath.

"One at a time, one at a time," laughed Dr. Livesey.

"You have heard of this Flint, I suppose?"

"Heard of him!" cried the squire. "Heard of him, you say! He was the bloodthirstiest buccaneer that sailed. Blackbeard was a child to Flint. The Spaniards were so prodigiously afraid of him that, I tell you, sir, I was sometimes proud he was an Englishman. I've seen his top-sails with these eyes, off Trinidad, and the cowardly son of a rum-puncheon that I sailed with put back—put back, sir, into Port of Spain."

"Well, I've heard of him myself, in England," said the doctor. "But the point is, had he money?"

"Money!" cried the squire. "Have you heard the story? What were these villains after but money? What do they care for but money? For what would they risk their rascal carcasses but money?"

"That we shall soon know," replied the doctor. "But you are so confoundedly hot-headed and exclamatory that I cannot get a word in. What I want to know is this: Supposing that I have here in my pocket some clue to where Flint buried his treasure, will that treasure amount to much?"

"Amount, sir!" cried the squire. "It will amount to this: If we have the clue you talk about, I fit out a ship in Bristol dock, and take you and Hawkins here along, and I'll have that treasure if I search a year."

"Very well," said the doctor. "Now, then, if Jim is agreeable, we'll open the packet"; and he laid it before him on the table.

The bundle was sewn together, and the doctor had to get out his instrument case and cut the stitches with his medical scissors. It contained two things—a book and a sealed paper.

"First of all we'll try the book," observed the doctor.

The squire and I were both peering over his shoulder as he opened it, for Dr. Livesey had kindly motioned me to come round from the side-table, where I had been eating, to enjoy the sport of the search. On the first page there were only some scraps of writing, such as a man with a pen in his hand might make for idleness or practice. One was the same as the tattoo mark, "Billy Bones his fancy"; then there was "Mr. W. Bones, mate," "No more rum," "Off Palm Key he got itt," and some other snatches, mostly single words and unintelligible. I could not help wondering who it was that had "got itt," and what "itt" was that he got. A knife in his back as like as not.

"Not much instruction there," said Dr. Livesey as he passed on.

The next ten or twelve pages were filled with a curious series of entries. There was a date at one end of the line and at the other a sum of money, as in common account-books, but instead of explanatory writing, only a varying number of crosses between the two. On the 12th of June, 1745, for instance, a sum of seventy pounds had plainly become due to someone, and there was nothing but six crosses to explain the cause. In a few cases, to be sure, the name of a place would be added, as "Offe Caraccas," or a mere entry of latitude and longitude, as, "62° 17°, 20°, 19° 2° 40°."

The record lasted over nearly twenty years, the amount of the separate entries growing larger as time went on, and at the end a grand total had been made out after five or six wrong additions, and these words appended, "Bones, his pile."

"I can't make head or tail of this," said Dr. Livesey.

"The thing is as clear as noonday," cried the squire. "This is the black-hearted hound's account-book. These crosses stand for the names of ships or towns that they sank or plundered. The sums are the scoundrel's share, and where he feared an ambiguity, you see he added something clearer. 'Offe Caraccas,' now; you see, here was some unhappy vessel boarded off that coast. God help the poor souls that manned her—coral long ago."

"Right!" said the doctor. "See what it is to be a traveller. Right! And the amounts increase, you see, as he rose in rank."

There was little else in the volume but a few bearings of places noted in the blank leaves towards the end and a table for reducing French, English, and Spanish moneys to a common value.

"Thrifty man!" cried the doctor. "He wasn't the one to be cheated."

"And now," said the squire, "for the other."

The paper had been sealed in several places with a thimble by way of seal; the very thimble, perhaps, that I had found in the captain's pocket. The doctor opened the seals with great care, and there fell out the map of an island, with latitude and longitude, soundings, names of hills and bays and inlets, and every particular that would be needed to bring a ship to a safe anchorage upon its shores. It was about nine miles long and five across, shaped, you might say, like a fat dragon standing up, and had two fine land-locked harbours, and a hill in the centre part marked "The Spy-glass." There were several additions of a later date, but above all, three crosses of red ink—two on the north part of the island, one in the southwest—and beside this last, in the same red ink, and in a small, neat hand, very different from the captain's tottery characters, these words: "Bulk of treasure here."

Over on the back the same hand had written this further information:

> Tall tree, Spy-glass shoulder, bearing a point to the N. of N.N.E.
> Skeleton Island E.S.E. and by E.
> Ten feet.
> The bar silver is in the north cache; you can find it by the trend of the east hummock, ten fathoms south of the black crag with the face on it.
> The arms are easy found, in the sand-hill, N. point of north inlet cape, bearing E. and a quarter N.
>
> —J. F.

That was all; but brief as it was, and to me incomprehensible, it filled the squire and Dr. Livesey with delight.

"Livesey," said the squire, "you will give up this wretched practice at once. Tomorrow I start for Bristol. In three weeks' time—three weeks!—two weeks—ten days—we'll have the best ship, sir, and the choicest crew in England. Hawkins shall come as cabin-boy. You'll make a famous cabin-boy, Hawkins. You, Livesey, are ship's doctor; I am admiral. We'll take Redruth, Joyce, and Hunter. We'll have favourable winds, a quick passage, and not the least difficulty in finding the spot, and money to eat, to roll in, to play duck and drake with ever after."

"Trelawney," said the doctor, "I'll go with you; and I'll go bail for it, so will Jim, and be a credit to the undertaking. There's only one man I'm afraid of."

"And who's that?" cried the squire. "Name the dog, sir!"

"You," replied the doctor; "for you cannot hold your tongue. We are not the only men who know of this paper. These fellows who attacked the inn tonight—bold, desperate blades, for sure—and the rest who stayed aboard that lugger, and more, I dare say, not far off, are, one and all, through thick and thin, bound that they'll get that money. We must none of us go alone till we get to sea. Jim and I shall stick together in the meanwhile; you'll take Joyce and Hunter when you ride to Bristol, and from first to last, not one of us must breathe a word of what we've found."

"Livesey," returned the squire, "you are always in the right of it. I'll be as silent as the grave."

Philip Ashton's Own Account
by Philip Ashton

Marblehead, Massachusetts fisherman Philip Ashton (1703–1746) was 19 years old when pirate captain Ned Low captured him off Nova Scotia. Low was among the most vicious of pirates. He once made a Nantucket whaling captain eat his own ears—salted—before killing him.

Upon Friday the 15th of June, 1722, after being out some time in a schooner with four men and a boy off Cape Sable, I stood in for Port Rossaway, designing to lie there all Sunday. Having arrived at four in the afternoon, we saw, among other vessels which had reached the port before us, a brigantine supposed to be inward bound from the West Indies. After remaining three or four hours at anchor, a boat from the brigantine came alongside with four hands, who leaped on deck and, suddenly drawing out pistols and brandishing cutlasses, demanded the surrender both of ourselves and our vessel. All remonstrance was vain; nor indeed, had we known who they were before boarding us, could we have made any effectual resistance, being only five men and a boy; and were thus under the necessity of submitting at discretion. We were not single in misfortune, as thirteen or fourteen fishing vessels were in like manner surprised the same evening.

When carried on board the brigantine I found myself in the hands of Ned Low, an infamous pirate, whose vessel had two great guns, four swivels and about forty-two men. I was strongly urged to sign the articles of agreement among the pirates and to join their number, which I steadily refused, and suffered much bad usage in consequence. At length, being conducted along with five of the prisoners to the quarterdeck, Low came up to us with pistols in his hand and loudly demanded, "Are any of you married men?"

This unexpected question added to the sight of the pistol, struck us all speechless. We were alarmed lest there was some secret meaning in his words and that he would proceed to extremities; therefore none could reply. In a violent passion he cocked a pistol and, clapping it to my head, cried out, "You dog, why don't you answer?" swearing vehemently at the same time that he would shoot me through the head. I was sufficiently terrified by his threats and fierceness, but rather than lose my life in so trifling a matter I ventured to pronounce, as loud as I durst speak, that I was not married. Hereupon he seemed to be somewhat pacified and turned away.

It appeared that Low was resolved to take no married men whatever, which often seemed surprising to me until I had been a considerable time with him. But his own wife had died lately before he became a pirate, and he had a young child at Boston for whom he entertained such tenderness, on every lucid interval from drinking and reveling, that, on mentioning it, I have seen him sit down and weep plentifully. Thus I concluded that his reason for taking only single men was probably that they might have no ties such as wives and children to divert them from his service and render them desirous of returning home.

The pirates, finding force of no avail in compelling us to join them, began to use persuasion instead of it. They tried to flatter me into compliance by setting before me the share I should have in their spoils and the riches which I should become master of; and all the time eagerly importuned me to drink along with them. But I still continued to resist their proposals, whereupon Low, with equal fury as before, threatened to shoot me through the head; and though I earnestly entreated my release he and his people wrote my name and that of my companions in their books.

On the 19th of June the pirates changed the privateer, as they called their vessel, and went into a new schooner belonging to Marblehead, which they had captured. They then put all the prisoners whom they designed sending home on board of the brigantine and sent her to Boston, which induced me to make another unsuccessful attempt for liberty; but though I fell on my knees to Low he refused to let me go. Thus I saw the brigantine depart with all the captives excepting myself and seven more.

A very short time before she departed I had nearly effected my escape; for a dog belonging to Low being accidentally left on shore, he ordered some hands into a boat to bring it off. Thereupon two young men, captives, both belonging to Marblehead, readily leapt into the boat, and I, considering that if I could once get on shore means might be found of effecting my escape, endeavored to go along with them. But the quartermaster, called Russel, catching hold of my shoulder, drew me back. As the young men did not return he thought I was privy to their plot and, with the most outrageous oaths, snapped his pistol on my denying all knowledge of it. The pistol missing fire, however, only served to enrage him the more. He snapped it three times again, and as often it missed fire; on which he held it overboard and then it went off. Russel on this drew his cutlass and was about to attack me in the utmost fury, when I leapt down into the hold and saved myself.

Off St. Michael's the pirates took a large Portuguese pink, laden with wheat, coming out of the road; and, she being a good sailer and carving fourteen guns, transferred their company into her. It afterwards became necessary to careen her, whence they made three islands, called the Triangles, lying about forty leagues to the eastward of Surinam.

In heaving down the pink, Low had ordered so many men to the shrouds and yards that the ports, by her heeling, got under water and, the sea rushing in, she overset. He and the doctor were then in the cabin, and as soon as he observed the water gushing in he leaped out of one of the stern ports while the doctor attempted to follow him. But the violence of the sea repulsed the latter, and he was forced back into the cabin. Low, however, contrived to thrust his arm into the port and, dragging him out, saved his life. Meanwhile the vessel completely overset. Her keel turned out of the water but as the hull filled she sank, in the depth of about six fathoms.

The yardarms, striking the ground, forced the masts somewhat above the water. As the ship overset, the people got from the shrouds and yards upon the hull and as the hull went down they again resorted to the rigging, rising a little out of the sea.

Being an indifferent swimmer, I was reduced to great extremity; for, along with other light lads, I had been sent up to the main top-gallant yard; and the people of a boat who were now occupied in preserving the men refusing to take me in, I was compelled to attempt reaching the buoy. This I luckily accomplished and as it was large secured myself there until the boat approached. I once more requested the people to take me in but they still refused, as the boat was full. I was uncertain whether they designed leaving me to perish in the situation. However, the boat, being deeply laden, made way very slowly, and one of my own comrades, captured at the same time with myself, calling to me to forsake the buoy and swim towards her, I assented, and, reaching the boat, he drew me on board. Two men, John Bell and Zana Gourdon, were lost in the pink.

Though the schooner in company was very near at hand, her people were employed mending their sails under an awning and knew nothing of the accident until the boat, full of men, got alongside.

The pirates, having thus lost their principal vessel and the greatest part of their provisions and water, were reduced to great extremities for want of the latter. They were unable to get a supply at the Triangles nor, on account of calms and currents, could they make the island of Tobago. Thus they were forced to stand for Grenada, which they reached after being on short allowance for sixteen days together.

Grenada was a French settlement, and Low, on arriving, after having sent below all his men except a sufficient number to maneuver the vessel, said he was from Barbadoes, that he had lost the water on board and was obliged to put in here for a supply.

The people entertained no suspicion of his being a pirate, but afterwards, supposing him a smuggler, thought it a good opportunity to make a prize of his vessel. Next day, therefore, they equipped a large sloop of seventy tons and four guns, with about thirty hands, as sufficient for the capture, and came alongside, while Low was quite unsuspicious of their design. But this being evidently betrayed by their number and actions, he quickly called ninety men on deck and, having eight guns mounted, the French sloop became an easy prey.

Provided with these two vessels, the pirates cruised about in the West Indies, taking seven or eight prizes, and at length arrived at the island of Santa Cruz, where they captured two more. While lying there Low thought he stood in need of a medicine chest and in order to procure one sent four Frenchmen in a ship he had taken to St. Thomas', about twelve leagues distant, with money to purchase it, promising them liberty and the return of all their vessels for the service. But he declared, at the same time, if it proved otherwise he would kill the rest of the men and burn the vessels. In little more than twenty-four hours the Frenchmen returned with the object of their mission, and Low punctually performed his promise by restoring the vessels.

Having sailed for the Spanish American settlements, the pirates described two large ships about halfway between Carthagena and Portobello, which proved to be the Mermaid, an English man-of-war, and a Guineaman. They approached in chase until discovering the man-of-war's great range of teeth, when they immediately put about and made the best of their way off. The man-of-war then commenced the pursuit and gained upon them apace, and I confess that my terrors were now equal to any that I had previously suffered; for I concluded that we should certainly be taken and that I should no less certainly be hanged for company's sake; so true are the words of Solomon, "A companion of fools shall be destroyed." But the two pirate vessels, finding themselves outsailed, separated; and Farrington Spriggs, who commanded the schooner in which I was, stood in for the shore. The Mermaid, observing the sloop with Low himself to be the larger of the two, crowded all sail and continued gaining still more, indeed until her shot flew over; but one of the sloop's crew showed Low a shoal which he could pass, and in the pursuit the man-of-war grounded. Thus the pirates escaped hanging on this occasion.

Spriggs and one of his chosen companions, dreading the consequences of being captured and brought to justice, laid their pistols beside them in the interval and, pledging a mutual oath in a bumper of liquor, swore if they saw no possibility of escape to set foot to foot and blow out each other's brains. But, standing towards the shore, they made Pickeroon Bay and escaped the danger.

Next we repaired to a small island called Utilla, about seven or eight leagues to leeward of the island of Roatan, in the Bay of Honduras, where the bottom of the schooner was cleaned. There were now twenty-two persons on board, and eight of us engaged in a plot to overpower our masters and make our escape. Spriggs proposed sailing for New England in quest of provisions and to increase his company; and we intended, on approaching the coast, when the rest had indulged freely in liquor and fallen sound asleep, to secure them under the hatches and then deliver ourselves up to government.

Although our plot was carried on with all possible privacy Spriggs had somehow or other got intelligence of it; and, having fallen in with Low on the voyage, went on board his ship to make a furious declaration against us. But Low made little account of his information, otherwise it might have been fatal to most of our number. Spriggs, however, returned raging to the schooner, exclaiming that four of us should go forward to be shot, and to me in particular be said, "You dog Ashton, you deserve to be hanged up to the yardarm for designing to cut us off." I replied that I had no intention of injuring any man on board but I should be glad if they would allow me to go away quietly. At length this flame was quenched and through the goodness of God I escaped destruction.

Roatan harbor, as all about the Bay of Honduras, is full of small islands which pass under the general name of keys; and, having got in here, Low with some of his chief men landed on a small island which they called Port Royal Key. There they erected huts and continued carousing, drinking and firing, while the different vessels of which they now had possession were repairing.

On Saturday the 9th of March, 1723, the cooper, with six hands, was going ashore for water; and, coming alongside of the schooner, I requested to be of the party. Seeing him hesitate, I urged that I had never hitherto been ashore and thought it hard to be so closely confined, when everyone besides had the liberty of landing as there was occasion. Low had before told me, on requesting to be sent away in some of the captured vessels which he dismissed, that I should go home when he did and swore that I should never previously set my foot on land. But now I considered if I could possibly once get on terra firma, though in ever such bad circumstances, I should account it a happy deliverance, and resolved never to embark again.

The cooper at length took me into the longboat while Low and his chief people were on a different island from Roatan, where the watering place lay. My only clothing was a frock and trousers, a milled cap, but neither shirt, shoes, stockings nor anything else.

When we first landed I was very active in assisting to get the casks out of the boat and in rolling them to the watering place. Then, taking a hearty draught of water, I strolled along the beach, picking up stones and shells; but on reaching the distance of a musketshot from the party, I began to withdraw towards the skirts of the woods. In answer to a question by the cooper of whither I was going I replied. "for coconuts," as some coco trees were just before me; and as soon as I was out of sight of my companions I took to my heels, running as fast as the thickness of the bushes and my naked feet could admit. Notwithstanding I had got a considerable way into the woods, I was still so near as to hear the voices of the party if they spoke loud, and I lay close in a thicket where I knew they could not find me.

After my comrades had filled their casks and were about to depart the cooper called on me to accompany them; however, I lay snug in the thicket and gave him no answer, though his words were plain enough.

At length, after hallooing, I could hear them say to one another, "the dog is lost in the woods and cannot find the way out again." Then they hallooed once more and cried, "He has run away and won't come to us," and the cooper observed that had he known my intentions he would not have brought me ashore. Satisfied of their inability to find me among the trees and bushes, the cooper at last, to show his kindness, exclaimed, "If you do not come away presently I shall go off and leave you alone." Nothing, however, could induce my to discover myself; and my comrades, seeing it vain to wait any longer, put off without me.

Thus I was left on a desolate island, destitute of all help and remote from the track of navigators; but, compared with the state and society I had quitted, I considered the wilderness hospitable and the solitude interesting.

When I thought they were all gone I emerged from my thicket and came down to a small run of water about a mile from the place where our casks were filled and there sat down to observe the proceedings of the pirates. To my great joy, in five days their vessel sailed, and I saw the schooner part from them to shape a different course.

I then began to reflect on myself and my present condition. I was on an island which I had no means of leaving; I knew of no human being within many miles; my clothing was scanty and it was impossible to procure a supply. I was altogether destitute of provision, nor could tell how my life was to be supported. This melancholy prospect drew a copious flood of tears from my eyes; but, as it had pleased God to grant my wishes in being liberated from those whose occupation was devising mischief against their neighbors, I resolved to account every hardship light. Yet Low would never suffer his men to work on the Sabbath, which was more devoted to play; and I have even seen some of them sit down to read in a good book.

In order to ascertain how I was to live in time to come I began to range over the island, which proved ten or eleven leagues long and lay in about sixteen degrees, thirty minutes north latitude. But I soon found that my only companions would be the beasts of the earth and fowls of the air; for there were no indications of any habitations on the island, though every now and then I found some shreds of earthenware scattered in a lime walk, said by some to be the remains of Indians formerly dwelling here.

The island was well watered, full of high hills and deep valleys. Numerous fruit trees, such as figs, vines and coconuts, are found in the latter; and I found a kind larger than an orange, oval-shaped, of a brownish color without and red within. Though many of these had fallen under the trees I could not venture to take them until I saw the wild hogs feeding with safety, and then I found them very delicious fruit.

Store of provisions abounded here, though I could avail myself of nothing but the fruit; for I had no knife or iron implement, either to cut up a tortoise on turning it, or weapon wherewith to kill animals, nor had I any means of making a fire to cook my capture even if I were successful.

Sometimes I entertained thoughts of digging pits and covering them over with small branches of trees for the purpose of taking hogs or deer; but I wanted a shovel and every substitute for the purpose and I was soon convinced that my hands were insufficient to make a cavity deep enough to retain what should fall into it. Thus I was forced to rest satisfied with fruit, which was to be esteemed very good provision for anyone in my condition.

In process of time, while poking among the sand with a stick in quest of tortoise's eggs, which I had heard were laid in the sand, part of one came up adhering to it; and, on removing the sand, I found nearly a hundred and fifty, which had not lain long enough to spoil. Therefore, taking some, I ate them and strung others on a strip of palmetto, which, being hung up in the sun, became thick and somewhat hard, so that they were more palatable. After all they were not very savory food, though one who had nothing but what fell from the trees behoved to be content. Tortoises lay their eggs in the sand in holes about a foot or a foot and a half deep, and smooth the surface over them so that there is no discovering where they lie. According to the best of my observation the young are hatched in eighteen or twenty days and then immediately take to the water.

Many serpents are on this and the adjacent islands; one, about twelve or fourteen feet long, is as large as a man's waist but not poisonous. When lying at length they look like old trunks of trees covered with short moss, though they more usually assume a circular position. The first time I saw one of these serpents I had approached very near before discovering it to be a living creature. It opened its mouth wide enough to have received a hat and breathed on me. A small black fly creates such annoyance that even if a person possessed ever so many comforts his life would be oppressive to him unless for the possibility of retiring to some small quay, destitute of wood and bushes, where multitudes are dispersed by the wind.

To this place, then, was I confined during nine months without seeing a human being. One day after another was lingered out, I know not how, void of occupation or amusement except collecting food, rambling from hill to hill and from island to island and gazing on sky and water. Although my mind was occupied by many regrets I had the reflection that I was lawfully employed when taken, so that I had no hand in bringing misery on myself. I was also comforted to think that I had the approbation and consent of my parents in going to sea, and I trusted that it would please God in his own time and manner to provide for my return to my father's house. Therefore I resolved to submit patiently to my misfortune.

It was my daily practice to ramble from one part of the island to another, though I had a more special home near the waterside. Here I built a hut to defend me against the heat of the sun by day and the heavy dews by night. Taking some of the best branches that I could find fallen from the trees, I contrived to fit them against a low-hanging bough by fastening them together with split palmetto leaves. Next I covered the whole with some of the largest and most suitable leaves that I could get. Many of those huts were constructed by me generally near the beach, with the open part fronting the sea, to have the better look-out and the advantage of the sea breeze, which both the heat and the vermin required.

But the insects were so troublesome that I thought of endeavoring to get over to some of the adjacent keys in hopes of enjoying rest. However, I was, as already said, a very indifferent swimmer. I had no canoe nor any means of making one. At length, having got a piece of bamboo, which is hollow like a reed and light as cork, I ventured, after frequent trials with it under my breast and arms, to put off for a small key about a gunshot distant, which I reached in safety.

My new place of refuge was only about three or four hundred feet in circuit, being very low, and clear of woods and brush. From exposure to the wind it was quite free of vermin, and I seemed to have got into a new world, where I lived infinitely more at ease. Hither I retired, therefore, when the heat of the day rendered the insect tribe most obnoxious; yet I was obliged to be much on Roatan to procure food and water, and at night on account of my hut.

When swimming back and forward between the two islands I used to bind my frock and trousers about my head and, if I could have carried over wood and leaves whereof to make a hut with equal facility, I should have passed more of my time on the smaller one.

Yet these excursions were not unattended with danger. Once, I remember, when passing from the larger island, the bamboo, before I was aware, slipped from under me, and the tide or current set down so strong that it was with great difficulty I could reach the shore. At another time, when swimming over to the small island, a shovel-nosed shark, which, as well as alligators, abound in those seas, struck me in the thigh, just as my foot could reach the bottom, and grounded itself from the shallowness of the water, as I suppose, so that its mouth could not get round towards me. The blow I felt some hours after making the shore. By repeated practice I at length became a pretty dexterous swimmer and amused myself by passing from one island to another among the keys.

I suffered very much from being barefoot. So many deep wounds were made in my feet from traversing the woods, where the ground was covered with sticks and stones, and on the hot beach over sharp broken shells, that I was scarce able to walk at all. Often, when treading with all possible caution, a stone or shell on the beach or a pointed stick in the woods would penetrate the old wound and the extreme anguish would strike me down as suddenly as if I had been shot. Then I would remain for hours together with tears gushing from my eyes from the acuteness of the pain. I could travel no more than absolute necessity compelled me in quest of subsistence and I have sat, my back leaning against a tree, looking out for a vessel during a complete day.

Once, while faint from such injuries, as well as smarting under the gain of them, a wild boar rushed towards me. I knew not what to do, for I had not strength to resist his attack. Therefore as he drew nearer I caught the bough of a tree and half suspended myself by means of it. The boar tore away part of my ragged trousers with tusks and then left me. This, I think, was the only time that I was attacked by any wild beast, and I considered myself to have had a very great deliverance.

As my weakness continued to increase I often fell to the ground insensible and then, as also when I laid myself to sleep, I thought I should never awake again, or rise in life. Under this affliction I first lost count of the days of the week. I could not distinguish Sunday, and as my illness became more aggravated I became ignorant of the month also.

All this time I had no healing balsam for my feet nor any cordial to revive my drooping spirits. My utmost efforts could only now and then procure some figs and grapes. Neither had I fire; for, though I had heard of a way to procure it by rubbing two sticks together, my attempts in this respect, continued until I was tired, proved abortive, The rains having come on, attended with chill winds, I suffered exceedingly.

While passing nine months in this lonely, melancholy and irksome condition my thoughts would sometimes wander to my parents; and I reflected that, notwithstanding it would be consolatory to myself if they knew where I was, it might be distressing to them. The nearer my prospect of death, which I often expected, the greater my penitence became.

Sometime in November 1723 I descried a small canoe approaching with a single man. But the sight excited little emotion. I kept my seat on the beach, thinking I could not expect a friend and knowing that I had no enemy to fear nor was I capable of resisting one. As the man approached he betrayed many signs of surprise; he called me to him and I told him he might safely venture ashore, for I was alone and almost expiring. Coming close up, he knew not what to make of my garb and my countenance seemed so singular that he looked wild with astonishment. He started back a little and surveyed me more thoroughly; but, recovering himself again, came forward and, taking me by the hand, expressed his satisfaction at seeing me.

This stranger proved to be a native of North Britain. He was well advanced in years, of a grave and venerable aspect and of a reserved temper. His name I never knew; he did not disclose it and I had not inquired during the period of our acquaintance. But he informed me he had lived twenty-two years with the Spaniards, who now threatened to burn him though I know not for what crime. Therefore he had fled hither as a sanctuary, bringing his dog, gun and ammunition, as also a small quantity of pork, along with him. He designed spending the remainder of his days on the island, where he could support himself by hunting.

I experienced much kindness from the stranger. He was always ready to perform any civil offices and assist me in whatever he could, though he spoke little; and he gave me a share of his pork.

On the third day after his arrival he said he would make an excursion in his canoe among the neighboring islands for the purpose of killing wild hogs and deer, and wished me to accompany him. Though my spirits were somewhat recruited by his society, the benefit of the fire, which I now enjoyed, and dressed provisions, my weakness and the soreness of my feet precluded me; therefore he set out alone, saying he would return in a few hours. The sky was serene and there was no prospect of any danger during a short excursion, seeing he had come nearly twelve leagues in safety in his canoe. But, when he had been absent about an hour, a violent gust of wind and rain arose, in which he probably perished, as I never heard of him more.

Thus, after having the pleasure of a companion almost three days, I was reduced to my former lonely state as unexpectedly as I had been relieved from it. Yet, through God's goodness, I was myself preserved from having been unable to accompany him, and I was left in better circumstances than those in which he had found me; for now I had about five pounds of pork, a knife, a bottle of gunpowder, tobacco, tongs, and flint, by which means my life could be rendered more comfortable. I was enabled to have fire, extremely requisite at this time, being the rainy months of winter. I could cut up a tortoise and have a delicate broiled meal. Thus, by the help of the fire and dressed provisions, through the blessing of God I began to recover strength, though the soreness of my feet remained. But I had, beside; the advantage of being able now and then to catch a dish of crayfish which, when roasted, proved good eating. To accomplish this I made up a small bundle of old broken sticks, nearly resembling pitch-pine or candlewood; and having lighted one end, waded with it in my hand up to the waist in water. The crayfish, attracted by the light, would crawl to my feet and lie directly under it; when, by means of a forked stick, I could toss them ashore.

Between two and three months after the time of losing my companion I found a small canoe while ranging along the shore. The sight of it revived my regret for his loss, for I judged that it had been his canoe; and from being washed up here, a certain proof of his having been lost in the tempest. But, on examining it more narrowly, I satisfied myself that it was one which I had never seen before.

Master of this little vessel, I began to think myself admiral of the neighboring seas as well as sole possessor and chief commander of the islands. Profiting by its use, I could transport myself to the places of retreat more conveniently than by my former expedient of swimming.

In process of time I projected an excursion to some of the larger and more distant islands, partly to learn how they were stored or inhabited and partly for the sake of amusement. Laying in a stock of figs and grapes, therefore, as also some tortoise to eat, and carrying my implements for fire, I put off to steer for the island of Bonacco, which is about four or five leagues long and situated five or six from Roatan.

In the course of the voyage, observing a sloop at the east end of the island, I made the best of my way to the west, designing to travel down by land, both because a point of rocks ran far into the sea, beyond which I did not care to venture in the canoe, as was necessary to come ahead of the sloop, and because I wished to ascertain something concerning her people before I was discovered. Even in my worst circumstances I never could brook the thoughts of returning on board of my piratical vessel, and resolved rather to live and die in my present situation. Hauling up the canoe and making it fast as well as I was able, I set out on the journey. My feet were yet in such a state that two days and the best part of two nights were occupied in it. Sometimes the woods and the bushes were so thick that it was necessary to crawl half a mile together on my hands and knees, which rendered my progress very slow.

When within a mile or two of the place where I supposed the sloop might lie I made for the water side and approached the sea gradually, that I might not too soon disclose myself to view; however, on reaching the beach, there was no appearance of the sloop, whence I judged that she had sailed during the time spent by me in traveling.

Being much fatigued with the journey, I rested myself against the stump of a tree with my face towards the sea, where sleep overpowered me. But I had not slumbered long before I was suddenly awakened by the noise of firing. Starting up in affright, I saw nine periaguas or large canoes full of men firing upon me from the sea; whence I soon turned about and ran among the bushes as fast as my sore feet would allow, while the men, who were Spaniards, cried after me, "O Englishman, we will give you good quarter." However, my astonishment was so great and I was so suddenly roused from sleep that I had no self-command to listen to their offers of quarter, which, it may be, at another time, in my cooler moments, I might have done. Thus I made into the woods, and the strangers continued firing after me to the number of 150 bullets at least, many of which cut small twigs of the bushes close by my side. Having gained an extensive thicket beyond reach of the shot, I lay close several hours until, observing by the sound of their oars that the

Spaniards were departing, I crept out. I saw the sloop under English colors sailing away with the canoes in tow, which induced me to suppose she was an English vessel which had been at the Bay of Honduras and taken there by the Spaniards.

Next day I returned to the tree where I had been so nearly surprised, and was astonished to find six or seven shot in the trunk within a foot or less of my head. Yet through the wonderful goodness of God, though having been as a mark to shoot at, I was preserved.

After this I traveled to recover my canoe at the western end of the island, which I reached in three days, but suffering severely from the soreness of my feet and the scantiness of provision. This island is not so plentifully stored as Roatan, so that during the five or six days of my residence I had difficulty in procuring subsistence. And the insects were, besides, infinitely more numerous and harassing than at my old habitation. These circumstances deterred me from further exploring the island; and, having reached the canoe very tired and exhausted, I put off for Roatan, which was a royal palace to me compared with Bonacco, and arrived at night in safety.

Here I lived, if it may be called living, alone for about seven months after losing my North British companion. My time was spent in the usual manner, hunting for food and ranging among the islands.

Sometime in June 1724, while on the small quay, whither I often retreated to be free from the annoyance of insects, I saw two canoes making for the harbor. Approaching nearer, they observed the smoke of a fire which I had kindled and, at a loss to know what it meant, they hesitated on advancing. What I had experienced at Bonacco was still fresh in my memory and, loath to run the risk of such another firing, I withdrew to my canoe, lying behind the quay, not above 100 yards distant, and immediately rowed over to Roatan. There I had places of safety against an enemy and sufficient accommodation for any ordinary number of friends.

The people in the canoes observed me cross the sea to Roatan, the passage not exceeding a gunshot over; and, being as much afraid of pirates as I was of Spaniards, approached very cautiously towards the shore. I then came down to the beach, showing myself openly; for their conduct led me to think that they could not be pirates, and I resolved, before being exposed to the danger of their shot, to inquire who they were. If they proved such as I did not like, I could easily retire. But before I spoke, they, as full of apprehension as I could be, lay on their oars and demanded who I was and whence I came. To which I replied that I was an Englishman and had run away from pirates. On this they drew somewhat nearer, inquiring who was there, besides myself, when I assured them in return that I was alone. Next, according to my original purpose, having put similar questions to them, they said they had come from the Bay of Honduras. Their words encouraged me to bid them row ashore, which they did accordingly, though at some distance; and one man landed, whom I advanced to meet. But he started back at the sight of a poor, ragged, wild, forlorn, miserable object so near him. Collecting himself, however, he took me by the hand and we began embracing each other, he from surprise and wonder and I from a sort of ecstasy of joy. When this was over he took me in his arms and carried me down to the canoes, where all his comrades were struck with astonishment at my appearance; but they gladly received me and I experienced great tenderness from them.

I gave the strangers a brief account of my escape from Low and my lonely residence for sixteen months, the hardships I had suffered and the dangers to which I had been exposed. They stood amazed at the recital. They wondered I was alive and expressed much satisfaction at being able to relieve me. Observing me very weak and depressed, they gave me about a spoonful of rum to recruit my fainting spirits. But even this small quantity, from my long disuse of strong liquors, threw me into violent agitation and produced a kind of stupor, which at last ended in privation of sense. Some of the party, perceiving a state of insensibility come on, would have administered more rum, which those better skilled among them prevented; and, after lying a short time in a fit, I revived.

Then I ascertained that the strangers were eighteen in number, the chief of them named John Hope, an old man called Father Hope by his companions, and John Ford, and all belonging to the Bay of Honduras. The cause of their coming hither was an alarm for an attack from the sea by the Spaniards while the Indians should make descent by land and cut off the Bay; thus they had fled for safety. On a former occasion the two persons above named had for the like reason taken shelter among these islands and lived four years at a time on a small one named Barbarat, about two leagues from Roatan. There they had two plantations, as they called them; and now they brought two barrels of flour, with other provisions, firearms, dogs for hunting and nets for tortoises; and also an Indian woman to dress their provisions. Their principal residence was a small key about a quarter of a mile round lying near to Barbarat and named by them the Castle of Comfort, chiefly because it was low and clear of woods and bushes, so that the free circulation of the wind could drive away the pestiferous mosquitoes and other insects. Hence they sent to the surrounding islands for wood, water and materials to build two houses, such as they were, for shelter.

I now had the prospect of a much more agreeable life than I had spent during the sixteen months past. For besides having company, the strangers treated me with a great deal of civility in their way. They clothed me and gave me a large wrapping gown as a defense against the nightly dews until their houses were covered; and there was plenty of provisions. Yet after all they were bad society; and, as to their common conversation, there was little difference between them and pirates. However, it did not appear that they were now engaged in any such evil design as rendered it unlawful to join them or be found in their company.

In process of time and with the assistance afforded by my companions I gathered so much strength as sometimes to be able to hunt along with them. The islands abounded with wild hogs, deer and tortoise; and different ones were visited in quest of game. This was brought home, where instead of being immediately consumed it was hung up to dry in smoke, so as to be a ready supply at all times.

I now considered myself beyond the reach of danger from an

enemy; for, independent of supposing that nothing could bring anyone here, I was surrounded by a number of men with arms constantly in their hands. Yet, at the very time that I thought myself most secure, I was very nearly again falling into the hands of pirates.

Six or seven months after the strangers joined me, three of them, along with myself, took a four-oared canoe for the purpose of hunting and killing tortoise on Bonacco. During our absence the rest repaired their canoes and prepared to go over to the Bay of Honduras to examine how matters stood there and bring off their remaining effects in case it were dangerous to return. But before they had departed we were on our voyage homewards, having a full load of pork and tortoise, as our object was successfully accomplished. While entering the mouth of the harbor, in a moonlight evening we saw a great flash and heard a report much louder than that of a musket proceed from a large periagua, which we observed near the Castle of Comfort. This put us in extreme consternation and we knew not what to consider; but in a minute or two we heard a volley from eighteen or twenty small arms discharged towards the shore and also some returned from it. Satisfied that an enemy, either Spaniards or pirates, was attacking our people, and being intercepted from them by periaguas lying between us and the shore, we thought the safest plan was trying to escape. Therefore, taking down our little mast and sail, that they might not betray us, we rowed out of the harbor as fast as possible towards an island about a mile and a half distant, trusting to retreat undiscovered. But the enemy, having either seen us before lowering our sail or heard the noise of the oars, followed with all speed in an eight- or ten-oared periagua. Observing her approach and fast gaining on us, we rowed with all our might to make the nearest shore. However, she was at length enabled to discharge a swivel, the shot from which passed over our canoe. Nevertheless we contrived to reach the shore before being completely within the range of small arms, which our pursuers discharged on us while landing.

They were now near enough to cry aloud that they were pirates and not Spaniards and that we need not dread them, as we should get good quarter; thence supposing that we should be the easier induced to surrender. Yet nothing could have been said to discourage me more from putting myself in their power. I had the utmost dread of a pirate; and my original aversion was now enhanced by the apprehension of being sacrificed by my former desertion. Thus, concluding to keep as clear of them as I could, and the Honduras Bay men having no great inclination to do otherwise, we made the best of our way to the woods. Our pursuers carried off the canoe with all its contents, resolving, if we would not go to them, to deprive us as far as possible of all means of subsistence where we were. But it gave me, who had known both want and solitude, little concern now that I had company and there were arms among us to procure provision and also fire wherewith to dress it.

Our assailants were some men belonging to Spriggs, my former commander, who had thrown off his allegiance to Low, and set up for himself at the head of a gang of pirates, with a good ship of twenty-four guns and a sloop of twelve, both presently lying in Roatan harbor. He had put in for fresh water and to refit at the place where I first escaped; and, having discovered my companions at the small island of their retreat, sent a periagua full of men to take them. Accordingly they carried all ashore, as also a child and an Indian woman, the last of whom they shamefully abused. They killed a man after landing and, throwing him into one of the canoes containing tar, set it on fire and burnt his body in it. Then they carried the people on board of their vessels, where they were barbarously treated. One of them turned pirate, however, and told the others that John Hope had hid many things in the woods; therefore they beat him unmercifully to make him disclose his treasure, which they carried off with them.

After the pirates had kept these people five days on board of their vessels they gave them a flat of five or six tons to carry them to the Bay of Honduras, but no kind of provision for the voyage: and further, before dismissal, compelled them to swear that they would not come near me and my party, who had escaped to another island.

While the vessels rode in the harbor we kept a good lookout but were exposed to some difficulties from not daring to kindle a fire to dress our victuals, lest our residence should be betrayed. Thus we lived for five days on raw provisions. As soon as they sailed, however, Hope, little regarding the oath extorted from him, came and informed us of what had passed; and I could not, for my own part, be sufficiently grateful to Providence for escaping the hands of the pirates, who would have put me to a cruel death.

Hope and all his people except John Symonds now resolved to make their way to the Bay. . . . Symonds urged me to stay and bear him company, and gave several reasons why I should more likely obtain a passage from the Jamaica men to New England than by the Bay of Honduras. As this seemed a fairer prospect of reaching my home, which I was extremely anxious to do, I assented; and, having thanked Hope and his companions for their civilities, I took leave of them and they departed. . . .

We spent two or three months after the usual manner, ranging from island to island, but the prevalence of the winter rains precluded us from obtaining more game than we required.

When the season for the Jamaica traders approached, Symonds proposed repairing to some other island to obtain a quantity of tortoise-shell, which he could exchange for clothes and shoes; and, being successful in this respect, we next proceeded to Bonacco, which lies nearer the main, that we might thence take a favorable opportunity to run over.

Having been a short time at Bonacco, a furious tempest arose and continued for three days, when we saw several vessels standing in for the harbor. The largest of them was anchored at a great distance, but a brigantine came over the shoals opposite to the watering place and sent her boat ashore with casks. Recognizing three people who were in the boat by their dress and appearance for Englishmen, I concluded they were friends and showed myself openly on the beach before them. They ceased rowing immediately on observing me and, after answering their inquiries of who I was, I put the same question, saying they might come ashore with safety. They did so and a happy meeting it was for me.

I now found that the vessels were a fleet under convoy of the Diamond, man-of-war, bound for Jamaica; but many ships had parted company in the storm. The Diamond had sent in the brigantine to get water here, as the sickness of her crew had occasioned a great consumption of that necessary article.

Symonds, who had kept at a distance lest the three men might hesitate to come ashore, at length approached to participate in my joy, though at the same time testifying considerable reluctance at the prospect of my leaving him. The brigantine was commanded by Captain Dove, with whom I was acquainted, and she belonged to Salem, within three miles of my father's house. Captain Dove not only treated me with great civility and engaged to give me a passage home, but took me into pay, having lost a seaman, whose place he wanted me to supply. Next day, the Diamond having sent her longboat ashore with casks for water, they were filled; and, after taking leave of Symonds, who shed tears at parting, I was carried on board of the brigantine.

We sailed along with the Diamond, which was bound for Jamaica, in the latter end of March 1725, and kept company until the first of April. By the providence of Heaven we passed safely through the gulf of Florida and reached Salem Harbor on the first of May, two years, ten months and fifteen days after I was first taken by pirates, and two years and nearly two months after making my escape from them on Roatan Island. That same evening I went to my father's house, where I was received as one risen from the dead.

from Run Silent, Run Deep
by Edward L. Beach

Edward L. Beach (born 1918) was the son of a career naval officer. The younger Beach graduated from Annapolis, earned the Navy Cross during World War II as executive officer of the submarine USS Tirante, and later served as naval aide to President Eisenhower. Beach's war experience lends authority to this account of submarine combat from his best-selling 1955 novel.

Our stay in Midway was no different from the previous one, but the island itself had undergone considerable change since the last time any of us had seen it. There was a big new pier constructed in the lagoon, and one of our great seagoing submarine tenders, the *Sperry*, was moored there to increase the refit capacity of the island base. Instead of one submarine, there were four in various stages of refit between patrols at the atoll, *Walrus* becoming the fifth.

There seemed to be at least twice as many men on the island as before, twice as many planes, and four times as much work being done. Midway did its best for us, receiving us with a brass band when we warped alongside the *Sperry*, dumping a load of mail on our decks, plus ice cream and a crate of fruit, and we were carted off almost immediately to the old Pan-American Hotel, now known as the Gooneyville Lodge, to begin our two weeks' rest and recuperation. During the ensuing time we did our best to avoid boredom. We threw a ship's party, complete with huge steaks and all the trimmings, and we organized fishing parties, baseball games, and other diversions.

Naturally, it was not enough, and no one pretended it was. More and more our crew spent their free time down in the ship, watching her get ready for our next run, and more and more we speculated where it would be. The only thing which could be counted to keep most of us away from the ship, for a time at least, was the receipt of mail, which arrived three times a week from Pearl. I never ceased to wonder at the efficiency of the San Francisco post office, which somehow always knew where to send mail so that it would be waiting for us when we arrived and kept it coming until we left. Then apparently, the mail would be allowed to accumulate somewhere—probably in Pearl Harbor—until our next port of call.

Jim, as usual, received the lion's share of mail in our group and somehow also seemed to be able to view it with greater detachment. For the rest of *Walrus'* crew, and for all of Midway, for that matter, arrival of the mail plane and the unavoidable, aggravating wait while the Midway mail clerks swiftly parceled out the different bags, had assumed the proportions of a ritual. The reception committee at the airfield, for instance, merely to see the mail plane arrive, grew so unwieldy that a notice over the signature of the Island Commander was issued requesting the practice be terminated and promising utmost dispatch in sorting and handling.

And, with little else to occupy their spare time, our crew became prolific letter writers. This added a burden to Hugh, Dave, and Jerry, who were required to censor every piece of outgoing mail. After giving them a hand once or twice, which all the officers did when the pile grew excessively large, I could readily understand their often-repeated reassurance to the crew that they did not remember what they had read. But I did carry away the impression that some of our letter writers were certainly unabashed, if not adept, at putting their thoughts and yearnings down on paper.

ComSubPac's endorsement to our patrol report, when at last it came in, was of course of consuming interest to Jim, Keith, and me.

We were credited with two ships sunk and two probables, which was what we had expected, but the comment of most importance was the one which simply stated, "The reports of torpedo failure during this patrol are important additions to the growing body of evidence in this regard, and to the remedy of which active steps are in hand."

Two days later a bulky package labeled "Secret" arrived in the mail, addressed to "The Commanding Officer, USS *Walrus*." It was from ComSubPac and contained our Operation Order. We were to return to AREA SEVEN, the scene of our first patrol.

And three days after that, a newly painted *Walrus*, now gray instead of black, refitted, repaired, and cleaned up—and her bridge even more cut down than before—pointed her lean prow once again to the western sky. She was no longer the brand-new submarine we had brought out from New London the previous year. The miles she had steamed and the battles she had fought had taken their toll on her appearance. Over a hundred depth charges had left their marks, both internally and externally, as well as the chance hit by a Japanese shell. The changes brought about by time and use, the modifications required by ComSubPac, and our own realization of our needs to do the job—more plotting equipment, more bunks, more food stowage, a bigger crew—were equally marked.

Walrus' bridge was now a low, streamlined structure, with a bare steel skeleton bracing the periscope supports. It looked a little strange compared with the sleek, rounded bridges and elongated conical shears of the newer subs beginning to arrive from the States, but it was roomier, and did the job as efficiently. Around the bridge were welded several foundations for 50-caliber machine guns, and on its forward and aft parts we now carried two double 20-millimeter gun mounts, with watertight stowage alongside for the four guns when not needed.

On our main deck the torpedo reload equipment had been removed entirely. The large steel mast and boom originally stepped in the main deck forward had been demounted and left in Pearl. Our old three-inch antiaircraft gun which had been mounted aft of the bridge was gone. In its place, but mounted forward in the area of the torpedo loading mast, was a broadside-firing four-incher, exactly like the gun the old *S-16* had carried and very likely lifted from one of her sisters.

Down below, the interior of the ship looked somewhat different too. Much new equipment had been added, welded to the steel skin of the ship or bolted to the deck. The smooth cork lining of the interior of the pressure hull was now pocked with spots where it had to be removed for welding and had been less attractively patched. New instruments had been installed: an automatic plotter, which required two men to keep pointers matched with our course and speed, and forced us to move Jerry Cohen's plotting position down into the control room; a gadget which measured the temperature of the sea at different depths; an improved SJ radar, using much more power, and producing longer detection ranges; and more air-conditioning, required not only for the increased heat output of our new gear but also for the increased crew we carried as a partial consequence.

And as we got under way for the coast of Kyushu once more, changes again had been made in our crew. Fifteen men had to be left behind to fill the insatiable demands of new construction, and to provide continuity for the rotation program. Eighteen new hands, all graduates of the submarine school but otherwise entirely new to submarine duty, took their places. The loss which affected the wardroom most was good old steady Tom Schultz, whose orders detaching him and ordering him to the submarine school as instructor had arrived in our first mail. Hugh Adams had moved into his shoes as Engineer, not without some trepidation, and two new Ensigns had reported aboard.

We held a special wake for Tom in Gooneyville Lodge, and he promised to look up our mothers, wives, and relatives back in the States. Not that any of the rest of us was married except Jim, who shook his head when Tom offered to carry any special trinket or message to Laura for him.

The crew also tried hard to show Tom how well he was liked, presenting him with a gold wristwatch they purchased at the Ship's Service, and Tom, in his turn, insisted upon personally handling all our lines from the dock when we got under way.

The changes left Keith, now a seasoned submariner and a full Lieutenant, the third officer in rank aboard, next after Jim. Hugh was
fourth, and Dave Freeman, his junior by only a few numbers, fifth,
now serving as Keith's understudy as well as Communications Officer.
Jerry Cohen, keeping his job as Plotting Officer during battle stations,
became Hugh's assistant in the engineering department. Our two new
Ensigns, who were named Patrick Donnelly and Cecil Throop, would,
like Jerry during the previous patrol, be given general assignments
under instruction.

One disadvantage of this new setup, so far as I was concerned, was
that I now had to share my room with someone, since *Walrus* was not
fitted with the extra accommodations in the wardroom "country" that
some of the later submarines carried. Throop, who drew the unpopular
assignment of sleeping in the bunk newly installed above mine, proved
to be a very sound sleeper, and a very loud one. As we made our way
west, I began to wonder how long I would be able to stand it when the
irregular hours on station began to take their toll.

One thing which it was unnecessary to burden the others with, at
the moment at any rate, was the following special entry in the Operation Order pamphlet, which I pulled out before handing the pamphlet
over to Jim to read:

> *Particular caution is enjoined with regard to an old destroyer of*
> *the* Akikaze *class operating out of the Bungo Suido. This vessel*
> *had been unusually successful in antisubmarine work, and*
> *prefers the astern position when escorting. You will under no cir-*
> *cumstances seek combat with it except under conditions of special*
> *advantage.*

I read and reread the words. There must be some important reason
behind them—and add to this the remembered conversation with
Captain Blunt months before. Of specific information as to Bungo's
activities I had heard very little, though there had been stories circu-
lating about Bungo Pete and his abilities as a depth-charge launcher for

some time. "He even seems to know the names of his victims," I remembered Captain Blunt saying.

The fact that we had been warned against him was understandable; the restriction not to attack him except under conditions of "special advantage" could only mean that we were to stay clear of him unless fate practically delivered him into our hands. But what were we to do if a convoy turned up with Bungo Pete as one of the escorts? For that matter, there was more than one *Akikaze*-class destroyer in the Jap Navy. How, then, to tell them apart? I studied her in the book of recognition photos until I could have recognized her, or one of her many sisters, through the periscope, from the bridge on a dark night, or anywhere else we might be likely to run into her. But if we ran into an *Akikaze*, it could be any one of fully thirty-four nearly identical tincans.

My final evaluation was the only one possible. Bungo had an *Akikaze*, he liked to escort from astern, and he operated in AREA SEVEN. Therefore we would avoid tangling with any destroyer of this type occupying such a position while convoying—at least of our own volition. But if he knew of our presence and general position, he would carry the fight to us anyhow, and in this case we might as well do as well as we could for ourselves if we got the chance.

Another portion of the Operation Order dealt with the possibility of encountering Japanese submarines, and this Jim, Keith, and I discussed at length. There were indications (unspecified) that Jap submersibles were being used for antisubmarine work, perhaps ordered out to wait for U. S. boats going or coming on patrol. We might therefore be apt to encounter one of them almost anywhere.

Daily drills en route to our operation areas had seemed a simple matter of keeping at the peak of training, and they had been an accepted part of our daily routine. Now, with the two special problems *Walrus* might run into, one of which only I knew about, I directed that the drills be doubled in frequency. We concentrated on two things: on detection and avoidance of an enemy submarine torpedo, calculating the quickest ways of dodging it in the various possible situations; and on swiftly changing fire-control problems, with emphasis on flexibility in setting the new data into the TDC and the angle solver and getting off an answering shot.

Most important from the self-protection angle, of course, were measures to avoid enemy torpedoes. First came the absolute imperativeness of seeing the torpedo as it came at us, or of spotting the enemy sub's periscope. To confound his approach, Jim and Rubinoffski cooked up a special zigzag plan of our own which consisted of steering either side of the base course line—never on it—and following an indefinite zigzag while so doing. Once taught to our helmsmen, the plan took care of itself. It sent us all over the ocean and we hoped it would force the enemy boat to use his periscope more often and thus increase our chances for spotting it. The need for alert lookouts we dinned into the ears of our new men, and our old ones too, with never-ceasing emphasis; it was up to them to see the telltale wake or periscope soon enough to enable something to be done about it. On that simple requirement our salvation depended. Once sighted, we could turn forward or away, or even line up for a torpedo shot in return. Given enough time, we knew we could get clear.

All the way out to Kyushu we drilled on the possibilities, and when we got there we were as ready for them as we could be. Keith, already an expert on the TDC, became adept at switching his inputs virtually instantaneously at my snapped command. Jim, hovering as backer-up for both of us, found it possible to speed things up by making certain of the settings for him when he had both hands otherwise engaged. And I realized that in Jim one of the sub force's best TDC operators had never been developed, for it seemed to be nearly second nature to him.

We varied the procedure and the personnel, too, so that our abilities did not depend on who happened to be on watch when the emergency came. About the time we passed through the Nanpo Shoto our crew was so tuned to the problem that from a standing start, with only the cruising watch at their stations, we could get our torpedoes on their way within thirty seconds. Our battle-stations personnel could shoot a salvo at a destroyer going by at high speed, thirty knots, shift target to a submerged submarine at three knots on a different bearing, make the necessary changes in torpedo gyro angle, depth, setting, firing bearing, and get a second salvo of torpedoes on its way—all within ten seconds by stop watch.

Perhaps our great emphasis on preparation also led me to expect something out of the ordinary as soon as we entered AREA SEVEN, just as we had on our first patrol, so long ago. Subconsciously I had nerved myself to having a Jap sub fire at us somewhere during the trip across the Pacific, and to finding Bungo Pete waiting for us at the other end. Neither eventuality came to pass. The patrol began with the most prosaic of beginnings—a week on station, within close sight of land, without any sign whatsoever of enemy activity except for an occasional airplane, and numbers of small fishing smacks with groups of straw-hatted Japanese out for a day's fishing.

During the early part of our second week a big old-fashioned freighter, heavily laden, crawled up the coast pouring smoke from a large stack nearly as tall as his masts. He wasn't making much speed and disdained to zigzag, probably figuring he wasn't fast enough for it to do any good. There was plenty of time for both Jim and Keith to get a look at him before we sank him; he went down belching smoke and dirt. A great expanse of filthy water, studded with floating junk and debris of all kinds plus a number of round black objects which slowly clustered together, marked his grave.

Two days later we trapped another single ship not far from where we had sunk the first, this time shortly after we had surfaced for the night. The approach was entirely by radar, for it was so dark that we did not see the target until just before firing. He never knew what hit him, either. We fired three torpedoes at short range, and all three exploded with thunderous detonations, one forward, one amidships, one at the stern. The ship went down like a rock, still on an even keel, leaving at least three boatloads of survivors. They must have been living in the lifeboats!

This was when Jim had an idea and, acting upon it, we ran south at full speed the rest of the night, moved close in to the coast in a totally new spot by next morning. Two ships sunk in the same vicinity would be sure to bring trouble instead of more targets, as he put it, and if we could move closer to where our victims came from—they had both been heading north—we might nab one before he was diverted.

He was right, too, for the very next day a small tanker happened by. I told Jim that this was entirely his own ship, that he had found it, and that therefore he had the right to do it the necessary honors while I took over his job as backer-upper and general understudy.

Jim needed no urging or second suggestion. He grabbed the periscope eagerly, took over command as though born to it, and the conduct of the approach was beyond criticism. He even swung at the last minute to use the stern tubes instead of bow tubes, thus equalizing our torpedo expenditure; and there was that same unholy exhilaration in his face as he gave the final command, "Shoot!" I wished old Blunt could have seen it—in any event I would see that he heard about it.

The only criticism I might have made was that instead of lowering the periscope after firing and getting it back up in time to see his torpedoes hit, Jim left it up the whole time the torpedoes ran toward the target, and watched the doomed ship's hopeless last-minute efforts to evade with positive glee.

It took it twenty minutes to sink, with one torpedo amidships which blew part of his side off. Jim gave everyone in the conning tower and several from the control room a chance to get a look at the death agonies.

Three ships in four days, and not a depth charge in return! We felt pretty cocky as we stood out into the center of AREA SEVEN to let our "hot spots" cool off a little. We had not even experienced much trouble with our torpedoes, though one of the odd *"pwhyunng"* noises had been reported during each of the first and last attacks. After a day we moved into one of our old positions on an enemy probable course line drawn from the mouth of the Bungo Suido.

Another week went by. We changed our position several times, went close into the coast once more, then back out to the original position again, all to no avail. The Japanese were simply refusing to cooperate, we decided.

And then one night, after the surfaced routine for the night had become well established, Kohler rushed to the bridge hatch, called up to me: "Captain! They're calling us on the radio!"

There was something strange about this, I felt, as I hastily put on a pair of red goggles and climbed below. Kohler preceded me down the ladder, but he went right by the radio room, led me into the crew's mess compartment immediately aft of it. A crowd of our men were gathered around the entertainment radio mounted above one of the mess tables. Several were hastily clothed, some merely in their underwear, one man, I saw, half-shaven with lather drying on his face. Dave was there, looking grave, and so was Pat Donnelly. A woman's voice was coming over the loud-speaker.

" . . . American submarine sailors," she was saying, "we regret to have to do this to you, but you have brought it upon yourselves. Japan did not make war upon you; you brought killing and wanton destruction to us. You have violated our waters, killed our toilers on the sea whose only crime is that they sought to travel our own home waters, which you have unjustly invaded. For this you have merited death, and death you shall have." Her voice lilting, she kept on: "While you are awaiting your last moments, perhaps this recording from home may make the thought of the future easier to face with equanimity." The melodious voice stopped and the strains of a popular dance tune filled the crowded compartment.

"Who the hell is that?" I interjected angrily.

Dave turned, seeing me for the first time. "Haven't you heard her before, Captain? The men call her 'Tokyo Rose.'"

Kohler nodded. "Yessir, we've had her on a couple of times before this. Usually she just plays music and hands out a load of baloney. Tonight, though, she was different."

"Dammit, Kohler!" I blazed, "I don't want anyone to listen to her again! I'll have the radio disconnected until we leave the area if you do!" Her words had been disturbing enough to me; who knew what their effect could be on some of our less experienced sailors?

"But she called us by name, Captain!"

"What!"

"That's what I tried to you tell you, sir! She was telling that to us—to the *Walrus!*"

Dave nodded. "I heard it too, sir. She said she had a special message for the crew of the U. S. submarine *Walrus*. She said she knew we were here, not far from the Bungo Suido, and that we had sunk some ships, but those were the last ones we'd ever sink." Several solemn faces nodded in corroboration.

The music stopped. "Men of the *Walrus*," the limpid voice said sweetly, "enjoy yourselves while you can, for eternity is a long, long time. Think of your loved ones, but don't bother to write because you'll never be able to mail the letters. Just think of all the thoughts they will be wasting on you, and the unanswered letters your wives and sweethearts will write—those who do think of you, and who do write!" She ended in a loud titter, almost a giggle. I had never heard anything quite so evil in my life.

"Turn that Goddamed radio off! Kohler, remember what I told you!" I stamped furiously away and climbed back on the bridge, more upset in mind than I could admit anyone to see. I needed to think.

No one on Midway—for that matter no one in the ship, either, except Jim—had known of our destination until after we had left the island out of sight. But somehow the Japanese propaganda ministry had full knowledge that *Walrus* was the submarine currently off Kyushu. Captain Blunt already had hinted that he was worried about some of the uncannily accurate information Bungo Pete seemed to possess; now I could see why. There could be only one explanation: espionage at Pearl Harbor!

For that matter, only Captain Blunt, ComSubPac himself, and one or two others on his staff knew where we had been sent, and even if others had guessed, how could they have predicted our movements so accurately? It had to be more specific than guesswork. No, unless some rational explanation presented itself, there must be a security leak back in Pearl. It was a horrid conclusion, yet inescapable. Then another thought presented itself: We had not yet gotten to the bottom of the torpedo troubles. Could there, somehow, be some connection? Could those, also, be the result of sabotage or espionage? I paced back and forth on the cigarette deck, puzzling over the few facts at my disposal, feeling the cool breeze of the night on my forehead, feeling anything but cool inside.

Despite premonitions I could not put down, nothing of note occurred the rest of the night, nor during the next day, but I had done some heavy thinking. When next we surfaced there was one significant change in our routine. Our garbage contained several carefully prepared scraps of paper bearing the name USS *Octopus*, some official in appearance, some apparently from personal mail. Quin, entering into the spirit of it, had even made, by hand, a very creditable reproduction of a large rubber stamp of the name. And all vestiges of the name *Walrus* had been carefully removed.

The garbage sacks were thrown overboard as usual, and as usual they floated aft into our wake, slowly becoming water-logged. As I had suspected, and found to be so upon investigation, some of them were not so well weighted as others. There was a good possibility that some of them might remain afloat for an appreciable time.

There was no longer a submarine in our navy named the *Octopus*. Choice of that name for our stratagem had been made for that reason, and out of pure sentiment. It was a good joke through the ship that the skipper had decided to change the name of *Walrus* to that of his first boat, the old *Octopus*.

And I told no one that my regular nightly visits to the radio room, which became a habit at about this time, were for the sole purpose of plugging a pair of earphones into the extra receiver and surreptitiously listening to Tokyo Rose's program.

She several times made me speechless with rage, but she never mentioned the *Octopus*, nor, for that matter, did she refer to the *Walrus* again. The whole thing began to look like a great waste of time and effort, for our men had to go over everything they put into the garbage very carefully, and every day Quin had to prepare more natural-looking paper with *Octopus* on it. But we kept it up during the rest of our time in the area.

There wasn't much time left, as a matter of fact. A few days more than a week, and our "bag" of three ships was beginning to look like the total for that patrol. The week passed. We sighted nothing but air- craft and a number of fishing boats. Then, only two nights before we were due to leave the area, the radar got a contact. It was a rough night, dark, overcast, raining intermittently, with a high, uneasy sea running. It was warm, too, unseasonably so, and the ship was bouncing uncom- fortably with no regular pattern as we slowly cruised along, two engines droning electricity back into our battery.

"Radar contact!" O'Brien happened to have the radar watch, and it was his high-pitched voice which sounded the call to action. "Looks like a convoy!" he added.

"Man tracking stations!" responded Keith, muffled in oilskins on the forward part of the bridge. Pat Donnelly, standing watch with Keith as Assistant OOD, was aft on the cigarette deck, as was I. I was beside Keith in a second.

"What's the bearing?"

"I've got the rudder over. We'll have it dead astern in a minute!" A main engine belched and sputtered; then another, and we had four half-submerged exhaust ports blowing engine vapor, water, and a thin film of smoke alternately above and under the waves.

"True bearing is nearly due north, Captain!" Keith was doing my thinking for me. "We're steadying up on course south right now, still making one-third speed."

I went aft again, searching the ocean astern. Nothing could be seen through the binoculars, not even the faint lightening of the murk which would indicate where water and sky met to form the far-distant and unseen horizon. *Walrus* pitched erratically, and a sudden gust of warm wet wind whipped my sodden clothes around my body. I spread my feet apart and leaned into it with my knees slightly bent, adjusting to the jerky motion of the ship. Holding my binoculars to my eyes, I made a deliberate search all around the horizon, or where I imagined the horizon to be. Nearly completed, I was startled by a small black object which abruptly intruded into my field of view, relaxed as quickly. It was only the stern light fixture, mounted on top of our stern chock where, for over a year, it had been a useless appendage.

"Keith, have the radar search all around!" I called. It wouldn't do for us to become so interested in our contact that something else, an escort vessel perhaps, or some as-yet-undetected section of the convoy, could happen unexpectedly upon us.

"Nothing on the radar, sir! Just the original contact!" Keith had anticipated that, too. I moved back to the forward part of the bridge, almost collided with Hugh Adams, who chose that instant to come jumping out of the hatch. He was rubbing his eyes.

"Take me a few minutes to relieve you, Keith," he gasped. "I'm not night-adapted—I was sound asleep when you called tracking stations."

"I've been up here. I can see fine," I broke in. "Keith, I'll take over that part of it. You go below and take over the TDC so that Jim can organize the approach."

Both of them nodded gratefully, and delaying only long enough to make the turnover of essential details to Hugh, Keith swung himself below.

Jim's voice came over the announcing system: "Captain, it's a good-sized convoy. Looks like a dozen ships, maybe more. At least two of them are escorts—maybe more of them, too. Course one-six-zero, speed about ten!"

"Steer one-six-zero!" I told the helmsman. Not Oregon—he would not come on until battle stations was sounded. "All ahead two thirds." Then raising my voice, "Maneuvering, make turns for ten knots!" The conning-tower messenger would relay the word to the maneuvering room via telephone. In a moment I could feel our speed pick up, a slightly more determined manner with which *Walrus* thrust her snout into the seas. Some of them began to come aboard over the bow, running aft on the deck, partially washing down through it, smothering our new four-inch gun and breaking in a shower of spray on the forward part of the bridge beneath the 20-millimeter gun platform.

We ran on thus for several more minutes. Jim's voice again: "Recommend course one-six-five, speed twelve."

I gave the necessary orders without comment. No doubt that was the convoy course and speed according to more extensive plotting data.

Several more minutes. "Captain, we've got eleven big ships, three or four smaller ones. Possibly one other astern, also small. They're zigzagging around base course one-six-five, speed fourteen knots, making good about twelve down the course line. We're almost dead ahead of them. Range to nearest ship, the leading escort, is ten thousand yards."

"What's the range to the stern escort?" These fellows had come out of the Bungo, all right, and that stern escort must be nobody else but Bungo Pete himself. At least he was keeping to Bungo's old favorite position, astern, the clean-up spot. Bungo would have figured that after an attack the submarine was most apt to wind up astern of the convoy, and out of torpedoes, too, until a reload could be effected. It was not a bad analysis. It would almost unquestionably be true for a submerged attack, very likely so for a surfaced one as well. Captain Blunt had wondered whether any German liaison officers might have been helping him—here I caught my breath as an idea rose, full blown, in my brain: Bungo might most likely be a Japanese submariner himself! He would be one of their old-timers, no doubt, working on the problem for all he was worth and making, thereby, his own contribution to the war effort of his country! Just as Captain Sammy Sams was doing in the role relegated to him!

As such he was doubly dangerous, though I couldn't hate him quite so much as before. And if this, indeed, was Bungo himself, cruising along in his *Akikaze*-class tincan behind the convoy, we were in for an interesting night of it.

"Range to stern escort—we can hardly make him out—he's fading in and out of the radar scope—about fifteen thousand yards." Jim fell silent for a minute. "Zig! The convoy has zigged to his left. Now on course one-three-zero!"

We followed suit. "Keep plotting and checking his zigs, Jim," I said. "When we get them down pat we'll start in." I began to weigh the various factors of the problem. Bungo was astern, and he was by far the most dangerous of the many destroyers and antisubmarine escorts. Instead of turning toward the rear of the convoy, which would be the natural thing to do after shooting our torpedoes, maybe we should turn back toward the head.

This would keep us clear of Bungo for a while. If we could count on a bit of confusion on the part of the Japs, perhaps overdependence on Bungo's sweeping-up operation, we might get away with it. One thing we would have to be careful to avoid, however, was the temptation to dive. If we dived, we became virtually stationary, and that was what Bungo Pete wanted us to do. Plodding along astern of the convoy, having had ample time to be fully alerted to our presence, he would be upon us immediately and subject us to another one of those silent, thorough, unhurried, and practically lethal creeping attacks, or perhaps something else, even better, which he might have thought of since. That, above everything, we had to keep away from.

"Another zig, right, this time! Course now one-six-five! Recommend increase speed to fourteen knots!"

"All ahead standard!" I ordered. "Sound the general alarm. Jim, will you come up to the bridge for a moment?"

"We're already practically at battle stations, skipper," said Jim a second later. The musical chimes were still sounding. "Just a couple of men haven't taken over their regular battle stations yet." He looked at me questioningly.

"Jim," I told him, "I want to avoid tangling with that last ship. It's no doubt a tincan, and it might even be the one that nearly sank us on our first run here."

"How do you know that?"

"I'll tell you all about it later. Should have before this. Besides that, we mustn't dive unless it's absolutely an emergency. I want to try to stay on the surface, and if we have to we'll take our chances with any of the other escorts. But if they make us dive, that fellow astern will come on up and take over, and we can figure on having a hell of a time!"

My voice was clipped and short. Jim didn't bother to question further. "I've got it," he breathed.

"Just as soon as they zig once more and give us an angle on either bow, we'll swing with them and go on in. We'll need full power, so as to have plenty of speed for maneuvering if we get into a tight spot."

"Aye, aye, sir!" Jim disappeared.

"Hugh," I said, "did you get all that?"

"Yessir!" in a taut voice.

"We might be getting gunfire on the bridge. If I order everyone below, you go too. You can be the last one down, but if we have to dive, you're our last hope. We can't take a chance on your being knocked out."

"Yessir!" again.

"All right. Now, have all the bridge guns mounted. Get all the twenty millimeters up, with two extra men to man each mount, and all four of the bridge fifties. Get plenty of ammunition, too." Hugh leaned to the hatch to give the orders. "Bring up both BAR's also. You and I might as well have something to shoot too."

In a few moments a veritable arsenal was handed up the bridge hatch and the lookouts busied themselves setting the guns in place. The 20's, stowed in pressure-proof containers, had to be lifted out and placed in their mounts. The 50's came up from below, were set in their sockets, and the BAR's we leaned in an out-of-the-way corner. Near each gun we made a neat pile of extra ammunition, belts for the 50's, bandoliers of clips for the BAR's, and a half-dozen round magazines for each of the 20-millimeters. If we should have to dive it would all be lost, but that didn't matter.

Two of the extra men were detailed forward of the OOD's platform for the forward mount, the other two aft on the cigarette deck. The 50's could be handled by the lookouts, one to each, with Hugh and me helping with the ammunition belts and firing our own BAR's in between. Preparations were completed just about the time the enemy convoy zigged again.

"Zig, to his right! Angle on the bow, port thirty-five!" Jim's voice in the bridge speaker. It was time to make our move.

"Right full rudder! All ahead flank!" The diesels groaned with the suddenly increased load. Their exhaust spewed forth with doubled vigor. The ship leaned to port, the two port mufflers choking and splashing, and our stern skidded across the sea, half under and half over the water. Big waves leaped high on to our decks, spraying great patterns of shredded white clouds to half-conceal our stern. A semi-transparent mist rose over the deck, whipped by the wind into the cloud pouring out of the starboard muffler pipes, trailed off to starboard and aft, lying low in the tossing, dirty sea.

It was dark, lampblack dark. Only the faintest hint of gray above the water and in the sky. No telling where the horizon was—it all combined into the same dullness, the sea rising right up into the sky. It had stopped raining and the atmosphere felt oppressive, warm, humid. I could smell the odor of sweat mixed with salt spray.

A sea mounted our bow, came straight aft, smothered the gun, and broke in a tall shower at the base of the bridge. Hugh and I ducked, got only a bucketful or two on our backs. The two men standing by the forward 20 were drenched, water streaming down from their hair and off their faces.

"Come on back here!" I yelled. Gratefully they climbed over the bulwark separating us. "Stay here until you're needed," I told them.

"Bridge! Recommend course three-one-zero!" That was Jim. I cupped my hands over the bridge gyro repeater, took a careful look, had to wipe out the accumulation of water before I could read it. We were already nearing due west, two-seven-oh.

"Steady on three-one-zero!" I shouted down the hatch. The rudder began to come off, and *Walrus* straightened up.

Now her speed increased even more, and she pitched and bucked like a wild thing. The wind whistled in my hair, the salt droplets battered my face. No longer rising to the sea, she simply disregarded it, smashed through it. Great clouds of spray were thrown to either side, rising to bridge height as we raced by. Sea after sea rolled over her bullnose, pounded against our bridge front beneath the 20-millimeter gun with a repetitive, drumming hollowness, cast more spume and water into the air.

It started to rain again. The fresh water felt good, washing some of the salt from my face and out of my eyes. It and the spray were bad for the binoculars, though, for the droplets would mar our vision. "Hugh!" I said urgently, "Lens paper! Lots of it!"

Hugh handed me a wadded-up hunk, leaned to the hatch to call for more.

"Range!" I shouted into the mike.

"Five thousand, leading ship!"

"Where's the nearest tincan!"

"Four thousand, thirty degrees on our port bow!" answered Jim.

"How about the other one on this side?"

"Sixty-five hundred yards, sixty relative!"

Jim had gotten us into the best position possible. We were going in astern of the leading escort, which was maintaining station more or less dead ahead of the convoy, and were well clear and ahead of the port-flanking tincan.

"How much farther to go?"

"I figure to start shooting at two thousand. They're all pretty well bunched. We'll shoot a spread of six fish forward, then swing for the stern tubes, shoot them, and in the meantime reload the four torpedoes left forward. Then if we get a chance we can let go with those four. That will leave us only one fish, in the after torpedo room."

"Good," I said into the mike. "What's the range now?"

"Four thousand! We're all ready, except for opening the outer doors. We'll start opening them at three thousand yards!"

I felt curiously detached and emotionless. The die had been cast the moment I directed the rudder be put right. Now it was merely the matter of riding it on out to a finish. The reload would be a problem, because of the motion on the ship, and I was glad that back in New London Keith had insisted on the installation of special pad-eyes for extra securing tackle. We had also carried out special reload drill while on the surface, against just such an eventuality as was now before us.

The ship, of course, carried only twenty-four torpedoes in all, sixteen in the forward torpedo room and eight in the after room. Having attacked with three fish twice out of the forward tube nest and once out of the after nest, we had fifteen fish left: ten forward and five aft. It would be worthwhile to reload the four left after the first salvo forward and try to get them off, but hardly so for the single left aft.

"What's the range now?" I had been searching for the targets, was still unable to see them. We were racing to destroy some men and some ships I had never seen. Perhaps I never would see them—I could tell their approximate bearing by looking up at the angle swept by the parabolic radar reflector whenever, from the motion of the mast behind me, I knew it was taking a bearing. They had been slightly on the starboard bow; now the leading ship bore several degrees on the port bow.

"Three-three-double-oh! Recommend change course to two-nine-oh! We're starting to open outer doors now—with this speed it may take us a little time!"

The newer boats had hydraulically operated outer torpedo tube doors, but not *Walrus*, already outdated. Ours had to be cranked open by hand, one by one, against the water pressure built up by our speed.

"Left to two-nine-zero!"

The rudder indicator went left a little, came back to center. Oregon's voice: "Steady on two-nine-oh!"

Out of nothing they popped into view. "Targets!" I bawled. I flung my binoculars into the TBT bracket, twisted it violently both ways, taking it all in. A solid mass of ships, dead ahead and to starboard. Well to port, a single smaller vessel, the leading escort. No need to worry about him. To starboard, far to starboard, a single tiny shape—the port flanker. He would be a problem soon.

But the ships ahead—we couldn't miss! There must be three columns at least, solid black against a lowering grayness. Eleven ships in all, Jim had said.

"Range, Jim!" I said into the mike. "I've got the TBT on the leading ship—looks like a tanker!"

"Two-five-double-oh! Do you see the escorts, Captain?"

"I see them! We're all right! Keep the ranges coming!"

"Range, two-four-double-oh! Outer doors are open, sir! Two-three-double-oh! Two-two-double-oh! Taking a radar sweep—clear all around—Range two-one-double-oh!"

"TBT is on the leading ship, Jim," I said into the mike. "Angle on the bow is large, around port ninety."

Hanging on to *Walrus'* careening bridge, I kept my binoculars rigidly fixed on the leading ship. *Walrus* rolled spasmodically from side to side, pitched her bows under—her bows, where six bronze warheads needed only the word from me to send them on their deadly mission. A sea roared up to the bridge; instinctively I ducked. *Walrus* heaved and pounded. It had stopped raining. Somehow the sky looked just a bit less dark, the gray less pronounced. Our targets were outlined distinctly for me now. Two tankers in the near column. Maybe more beyond. A large freighter bringing up the rear of the nearest column. All big ships, big and fast.

"Two thousand yards!" Jim's voice carried a finality, a defiance to it.

I risked a quick glance to starboard—the port-flanking tincan was still clear, much nearer. We had a couple of minutes to go, to be deliberate with. Now that we had got there, as Captain Blunt used to say, TAKE YOUR TIME AND MAKE EVERY FISH COUNT!

"Stand by forward!" Into the mike. "I'm on the leading ship, Jim! Let me know as each one goes out!—Shoot!"

"Fire!" Jim had been holding the announcing system button down as he gave the command. I felt nothing. No jolt, no jerk as three thousand pounds, a ton and a half, was expelled.

"One's away," blared the bridge speaker. A pregnant pause. "Two's away!" More time. I took my glasses off the TBT, swung around to inspect the nearing destroyer. "Three's away!" Jim was shooting a spread, would need no further TBT bearings from me. "Four's away!" I looked forward, reaching out to see the white wakes, impossible in the heaving black water. "Five's away!" The oncoming tincan was looming larger all the time. Wonder if he's seen anything yet? "Number six away! All torpedoes expended forward! Range to target, one-three-double-oh!"

"Left full rudder!" I yelled the order. *Walrus* scudded around, the starboard mufflers roaring their choked protest.

"Recommend course zero-nine-zero!"

"No!" I shouted, then recollecting myself, grabbed the mike: "No good, Jim. Too close to the port-flanking tincan!" I tried to speak calmly. "How about one-seven-zero with a left ninety gyro for the stern tubes?"

"Roger!"

"Oregon, steady on one-seven-zero!" He had heard the colloquy with Jim, and the rudder had already eased a few degrees in anticipation. But, disciplined helmsman that he was, he had to have the order.

"Steady on one-seven-zero!" No question about Oregon's steering ability. He gently eased the rudder off and the ship lunged ahead, the lubber's line right on the marker.

I picked up the mike, ran to the after TBT, plugged it in. "Stand by aft! After TBT!" I said into the mike. I had to push Pat Donnelly aside to give me a clear shot for sighting.

The after bridge speaker: "Standing by aft! We're all set below, Captain! Range one-two-five-oh!"

"Shoot!" I had the TBT aimed right between the first and second ships of the near column, at another ship in the second column whose black silhouette completely filled the space between them.

"Seven's away! Eight's away!" Another look at the destroyer. We were running nearly right away from him, gaining, with our temporary speed advantage. "Nine away! Ten away! All torpedoes expended, Captain! We're reloading forward."

Ten torpedoes—we were lighter by better than thirty thousand pounds, and about seventy thousand dollars' worth of complicated mechanism was out there running in the ocean.

And we were in something of a box, too. Any change in course would increase the approaching destroyer's chances of catching us, make it easier for him to see us.

"Range to the near escort, dead astern!" I called the inquiry into the mike, leaning against the periscope supports with my feet braced in front of me. In this location I could not feel the radar mast rotate, but I could sense it going around, sweeping aft. *Walrus'* motion was no different on the new course. Seas were still sweeping her with regularity, leaping higher than her radio antenna stanchions—higher than a man's height—

splattering all over the deck aft, sometimes virtually submerging it. Steam, from our hot mufflers under the deck, boiled up through the wooden slats, drifted faintly away. It would be suicide to walk aft there.

"Range to escort, one-nine-double-oh!" He WAS close!

Something had happened in the direction of the convoy. I turned—a flash as though of light, but bigger than any light, and yellower. It lasted only a fraction of a second. Then another, and another! No sound—there couldn't be any sound, with all the natural noises of wind and sea going on. I looked harder. Could that be the suspicion of yet another flash in the second column? These were all torpedo hits, of that there could be no doubt, and probably from our bow salvo at that. Our stern shots would be a minute or so later getting there.

Back to the escort: "What's the range now?" He didn't look any different, but in the dim visibility it would be hard to tell anyhow. Still bows on, still coming, no indication of having seen anything out of the ordinary.

"Range to escort, one-nine-five-oh!" That was not good. We should be making twenty knots to his fourteen, should be pulling ahead faster than that.

Flash! Another hit! And then, flash-flash—two, almost together. Some notice at last from the convoy. Now it was evident that it was breaking up. Ships were turning every which way. Suddenly it was no longer an entity, a constant you could think of as a single thing; it had disintegrated, almost in an instant, into eleven different ships. It was as though they were being driven by some inner compulsion. Dark forms outlined against the slightly less dark sky seemed to be motivated by only one emotion, one heedless, reckless, awful necessity: to get away from the convoy center.

"Good God!" The outburst came without conscious volition. A violent cone of flame, white-hot with fringes of yellow and orange, screamed into the heavens! It towered over the convoy, towered over us too, cast everything into pitiless relief, turned the night into broad daylight!

In the insane light of the explosion the leading tanker was visible, broken in half, bow and stern floating idiotically with nothing between them. The second tanker seemed all right; so did the third ship in that column. The one which had blown up must have been one of those in the middle column. As I watched, fascinated, the masts of the freighter, last in the near column of ships, grew shorter, his stack disappeared—and I was looking at his bottom.

Then the noise of it reached us, a horrible, sudden, all-gone crash, a detonation of a million pounds of TNT, a complete, unutterable holocaust! It could only have been an ammunition ship. No wonder the ships of the convoy had been trying to get away!

"Captain! What is it!" Jim's voice on the bridge speaker.

"I'm OK—come on up here!" Jim arrived in time to see the second tanker burst into flames. His comment was identical to mine:

"Good God! Did we do that?"

"Yes, Jim." I silently pointed out the tincan on our tail. "He can't miss seeing us now, unless he's too interested in what's going on over there to tend to his business."

"We'll have to watch for our chance, now, old man." I said. "Most of those ships have escaped the blast, though we can probably scratch four of them. Get back on the radar and give me a picture of how it looks."

Jim ran down the hatch. His voice came in a couple of seconds: "Convoy has scattered. We have only nine pips on the scope left. One seems to have fallen behind"—that would be the capsized freighter—"they're really in a mess there, all right."

"What's the range to the tincan?"

"Near destroyer—one-seven-double-oh!"

He was closing to look us over. There was no doubt about it: we were in trouble. Normally we should dive. Only one other thing to do.

"Range to convoy?"

"Convoy—nearest ship one-five-double-oh. The rest on up to three-oh-double-oh!"

That settled it. The convoy had at least one fleeing ship nearer to us than the destroyer, coming in more or less on our beam. Presumably he would be jittery, scared, not, at all events, a ship-of-war.

"Right full rudder!" I ran back to the fore part of the bridge. "All right, boys! Man those guns!" They jumped to them with alacrity. "When we go by this ship, put everything you have into his bridge! Never mind anything else, just his bridge!"

I took a bearing, gave Oregon a course so as to pass starboard to starboard at about a quarter of a mile. This would put the Jap ship between us and the escort. As the rudder went over, Jim informed me that our torpedo reload had been completed. We were ready for business again, with four fish forward and one aft.

The range closed swiftly at our combined speeds. Larger and larger loomed the blunt, black bow of the ship. I don't think they even saw us. At point-blank range—it was more like four hundred than five hundred yards when we got abeam—we opened up with everything we had, swept his bridge. It was grim work holding the 20's on, especially for the two men forward who were half under water a good part of the time, but they kept to it. I could see the tracer bullets arching into the enemy's bridge area, disappearing into the square-windowed pilot-house, as we swept on.

I shot a quick glance across his stern. The pursuing destroyer had not changed course yet, was still heading more or less for the bow of the ship behind which we had disappeared. It was dark again, the flare of the explosion having gone, but the lights of two big fires in two of the convoy reflected from the hulls of both ships behind us. We, by contrast, must be in the shadow, unless unlucky enough to become silhouetted. The freighter we had raked wavered in his course. Perhaps we had gotten the steersman—he swung off to the left, toward the onrushing tincan, his swing increasing rapidly. The destroyer saw it too, put his rudder hard over, barely avoided colliding. This gave us an opening:

"Range to destroyer!" I yelled into the mike. "Stand by aft! Angle on the bow, starboard ninety!" It was greater, but he would surely turn again. "Shift to after TBT!" I ran aft, plugged in the mike.

"Range eight hundred!" said the speaker.

"Give him twenty knots!" I waited an age, it seemed to me. It could not have been more than ten seconds.

"Set!"

"Shoot!" I shouted. There was only one torpedo left aft, but it might do some good, if we had luck. I reached for the mike, tugged at it to unplug it, when the whole side of the destroyer blossomed in red and orange. Heedless, I ran forward as the tearing crack of several shells passed close overhead. There was a screaming of machine-gun bullets and several dull thuds, followed by the characteristic wavering whines of a ricochet or two. In the midst of this came the twin chatter of the after mount; Pat Donnelly and the two men detailed to the after 20-millimeter were holding it steady into the black hull of the destroyer.

And then, cataclysmically, a mushroom of white water burst in the middle of the other ship, hoisted him up amidships, his back broken, bow and stern sagging deep into the water. His guns stopped, except for one small one on the bridge which kept going for several seconds longer until the black ocean closed over it.

Up ahead, chaos. Two ships on fire, one black hull still not under, but bottom up, showing red in the flame. Other ships, one minus a stack, probably as a result of the explosion of the ammunition ship close aboard, cutting madly in all directions. Too close, now, to change course again. Keep going. Have to keep going. We aimed our course to go between the two burning ships. Just beyond we found another, all alone, making off to the west. We drew up alongside, less than a mile away, keeping out of the light of the fires. We turned toward.

Angle on the bow, port eighty, range fifteen hundred—Fire! Two fish. Two left. We put our rudder right, ran past him on the opposite course, saw both torpedoes hit, saw the splash as the air flasks of both blew up. I raved with impotent fury at the sight, forgetting that we should instead be thankful that the single torpedo we had fired aft, less than three minutes before, had functioned properly.

Nothing to do but come around again. We left the rudder full right, turned madly in a full circle, lined him up again—Fire! That did it. One torpedo hit and exploded and he sagged down by the bow. Maybe he'd sink, maybe not, but we had no more fish to make sure.

Another tearing, ripping noise overhead. Then another, and a third and fourth. Two ships shooting: Bungo, racing up from his position astern to join the fight, and someone else, either the starboard flanker or the lead escort. We were trapped—we'd have to dive. They were too far away for effective reply with our automatic small-caliber weapons, and there was no question of our trying our own four-inch gun in reply, even if we could stand on deck to use it.

"All hands below!" I yelled. Hugh wavered as the lookouts and Pat dashed past us. I motioned impatiently to the hatch. He dropped below.

"Rudder amidships—all ahead emergency!" I yelled to Oregon. I aimed for the narrow space between the two flaming ships again. If we could get between them once more—I knew there was no escort vessel on *that* side—that would force the two destroyers to slow down and maneuver to avoid their own ships. That might be our chance.

I pushed the bridge speaker button for the general announcing system: "*Maneuvering, give it everything you've got!*" They did, too. Clouds of blue-white smoke poured out of our exhaust. Our speed picked up perceptibly. *Walrus* arrowed for the hole, slipped through it, headed eastward at full speed, leaving the wrecked ships behind and a cloud of diesel smoke to obscure our passage. The two destroyers, shadowy figures at fairly long range, were cut off, had to shoot over them. Both were firing continuously, the one from the convoy's rear particularly well. From his position that must be Bungo, and he was using salvo fire with methodical precision. The shells were still tearing overhead, closer, if anything, than before, despite the obstruction in the range. One or two dropped close alongside, kicked up great spouts of water. No question about it. Old Bungo was a good naval officer and ran a taut, tough ship. His destroyer—*Akikaze* class, all right—was shooting at least two to the other's one, and accurately, despite the weather.

I picked up the mike. "They're going to have to slow down because what's left of their convoy is in the way," I said. "Take a sweep around with the radar . . ."

Another salvo from Bungo. I could see all four flashes from his guns.

He would have to hold back on the next salvo or two, now, because of the ships in the way.

There was a blinding flash. The whole world turned kaleidoscopic. Stars and pinwheels and fireballs whirled about me, all emanating from a round, sunlike face emitting rays of white-hot fire—the face of Bungo Pete. He looked benign, friendly, despite the fireballs . . . surprisingly like Sammy Sams.

The wheels were still spinning when I opened my eyes. I was lying in my own bunk, and there was the smell of medicine all around. Cecil Throop's bunk springs and mattress, which had been slung above mine, were gone. Jim and Keith were standing beside my bunk, smiling at me, bracing themselves against the gentle heave of the ship.

"What happened?" I managed to say. "What about Bungo . . . ?" I gripped the sides of the bunk, tried to raise myself. My whole right side shot excruciating pain through my body.

"Take it easy, skipper, everything's fine. We're through the Nanpo Shoto, and we're on our way back to Pearl Harbor. Right now it's broad daylight and we're riding on the surface on three engines, making excellent time. Now that you're feeling better, everything's jake." Jim's face was wreathed in a happy grin.

"What happened?" I asked again.

"Nothing much. You just stopped a Jap four-inch shell all by yourself and have been out for three days, that's all. And your right leg's broken, so don't try to get up." I fumbled for it. The cast felt as if it occupied half the bunk.

"How did I get down here?"

"We heard the shell hit—you were talking on the mike, remember? And you were still holding the button down after you were knocked out. Rubinoffski and I found you lying there, out cold. We hauled you down below and dived, and we've been running ever since. We had to lay you out on the wardroom table to set your leg and sew you up."

"How badly hurt am I?" I knew part of the answer without asking. The strain of what little talking I had already done was telling, and it was an effort to keep my voice from dropping to a whisper. Jim and Keith began to edge for the door.

"The Pharmacist's Mate says you'll be fine, skipper," said Keith. "You had a bad concussion and a couple of bad cuts besides the break, but nothing that won't mend in time."

A wave of pain hit me as the two lifted the green curtain and passed out into the passageway. I tried to call out, but couldn't. The bulkheads receded, wobbled, blended into a dull ivory from their original white and gray. Someone came through the curtain—I hardly noticed the jab of the needle.

Despite Jim's and Keith's assurances, and the number of smiling well-wishers who came to see me during the latter stages of our trip, I was far from being in good shape when we put in to Pearl. I don't remember much of the first part of the trip, or whether anything out of the ordinary happened during it. Once in a while, it seemed to me, we dived—whether for drill or for real I could not tell, and cared less. Later on there was a discussion of having a plane meet us near Midway to take me off. I remember becoming violently upset at the idea, as well as the following suggestion, in a few days, that *Walrus* put in there to leave me. I became more lucid rapidly then and was able to think of some of the things lying ahead for all of us. One thing was obvious, though everyone avoided the subject until I brought it up. I was through as skipper of *Walrus*.

from Pincher Martin
by William Golding

Nobel laureate William Golding (1911–1993) served in Great Britian's Royal Navy during World War II, participating in the Normandy invasion and the sinking of the German battleship Bismarck. *His later work drew upon that experience to explore human behavior under duress.*

He was struggling in every direction, he was the centre of the writhing and kicking knot of his own body. There was no up or down, no light and no air. He felt his mouth open of itself and the shrieked word burst out,

"Help!"

When the air had gone with the shriek, water came in to fill its place—burning water, hard in the throat and mouth as stones that hurt. He hutched his body towards the place where air had been but now it was gone and there was nothing but black, choking welter. His body let loose its panic and his mouth strained open till the hinges of his jaw hurt. Water thrust in, down, without mercy. Air came with it for a moment so that he fought in what might have been the right direction. But the water reclaimed him and spun so that knowledge of where the air might be was erased completely. Turbines were screaming in his ears and green sparks flew out from the centre like tracer. There was a piston engine too, racing out of gear and making the whole universe shake. Then for a moment there was air like a cold mask against his face and he bit into it. Air and water mixed, dragged down into his body like gravel. Muscles, nerves and blood, struggling lungs, a machine in the head, they worked for one moment in an ancient pattern. The lumps of hard water jerked in the gullet, the lips came together and parted, the tongue arched, the brain lit a neon track.

"Moth——"

But the man lay suspended behind the whole commotion, detached from his jerking body. The luminous pictures that were shuffled before him were drenched in light but he paid no attention to them. Could he have controlled the nerves of his face, or could a face have been fashioned to fit the attitude of his consciousness where it lay suspended between life and death that face would have worn a snarl. But the real jaw was contorted down and distant, the mouth was slopped full. The green tracer that flew from the centre began to spin into a disc. The throat at such a distance from the snarling man vomited water and drew it in again. The hard lumps of water no longer hurt. There was a kind of truce, observation of the body. There was no face but there was a snarl.

A picture steadied and the man regarded it. He had not seen such a thing for so many years that the snarl became curious and lost a little intensity. It examined the picture.

The jam jar was standing on a table, brightly lit from O.P. It might have been a huge jar in the centre of a stage or a small one almost touching the face, but it was interesting because one could see into a little world there which was quite separate but which one could control. The jar was nearly full of clear water and a tiny glass figure floated upright in it. The top of the jar was covered with a thin membrane— white rubber. He watched the jar without moving or thinking while his distant body stilled itself and relaxed. The pleasure of the jar lay in the fact that the little glass figure was so delicately balanced between opposing forces. Lay a finger on the membrane and you would compress the air below it which in turn would press more strongly on the water. Then the water would force itself farther up the little tube in the figure, and it would begin to sink. By varying the pressure on the membrane you could do anything you liked with the glass figure which was wholly in your power. You could mutter,—sink now! And down it would go, down, down; you could steady it and relent. You could let it struggle towards the surface, give it almost a bit of air then send it steadily, slowly, remorselessly down and down.

The delicate balance of the glass figure related itself to his body. In a moment of wordless realization he saw himself touching the surface of the sea with just such a dangerous stability, poised between floating and going down. The snarl thought words to itself. They were not articulate, but they were there in a luminous way as a realization.

Of course. My lifebelt.

It was bound by the tapes under that arm and that. The tapes went over the shoulders—and now he could even feel them—went round the chest and were fastened in front under the oilskin and duffle. It was almost deflated as recommended by the authorities because a tightly blown-up belt might burst when you hit the water. Swim away from the ship then blow up your belt.

With the realization of the lifebelt a flood of connected images came back—the varnished board on which the instructions were displayed, pictures of the lifebelt itself with the tube and metal tit threaded through the tapes. Suddenly he knew who he was and where he was. He was lying suspended in the water like the glass figure; he was not struggling but limp. A swell was washing regularly over his head.

His mouth slopped full and he choked. Flashes of tracer cut the darkness. He felt a weight pulling him down. The snarl came back with a picture of heavy seaboots and he began to move his legs. He got one toe over the other and shoved but the boot would not come off. He gathered himself and there were his hands far off but serviceable. He shut his mouth and performed a grim acrobatic in the water while the tracer flashed. He felt his heart thumping and for a while it was the only point of reference in the formless darkness. He got his right leg across his left thigh and heaved with sodden hands. The seaboot slipped down his calf and he kicked it free. Once the rubber top had left his toes he felt it touch him once and then it was gone utterly. He forced his left leg up, wrestled with the second boot and got it free. Both boots had left him. He let his body uncoil and lie limply.

His mouth was clever. It opened and shut for the air and against the water. His body understood too. Every now and then it would clench its stomach into a hard knot and sea water would burst out over his tongue. He began to be frightened again—not with animal panic but with deep fear of death in isolation and long drawn out. The snarl came back but now it had a face to use and air for the throat. There was something meaningful behind the snarl which would not waste the air on noises. There was a purpose which had not yet had time and experience to discover how relentless it was. It could not use the mechanism for regular breathing but it took air in gulps between the moments of burial.

He began to think in gulps as he swallowed the air. He remembered his hands again and there they were in the darkness, far away. He brought them in and began to fumble at the hard stuff of his oilskin. The button hurt and would hardly be persuaded to go through the hole. He slipped the loop off the toggle of his duffle. Lying with little movement of his body he found that the sea ignored him, treated him as a glass figure of a sailor or as a log that was almost ready to sink but would last a few moments yet. The air was regularly in attendance between the passage of the swells.

He got the rubber tube and drew it through the tapes. He could feel the slack and uninflated rubber that was so nearly not holding him up. He got the tit of the tube between his teeth and unscrewed with two fingers while the others sealed the tube. He won a little air from between swells and fuffed it through the rubber tube. For uncounted numbers of swell and hollow he taxed the air that might have gone into his lungs until his heart was staggering in his body like a wounded man and the green tracer was flicking and spinning. The lifebelt began to firm up against his chest but so slowly that he could not tell when the change came. Then abruptly the swells were washing over his shoulders and the repeated burial beneath them had become a wet and splashing slap in the face. He found he had no need to play catch-as-catch-can for air. He blew deeply and regularly into the tube until the lifebelt rose and strained at his clothing. Yet he did not stop blowing at once. He played with the air, letting a little out and then blowing again as if frightened of stopping the one positive action he could take to help himself. His head and neck and shoulders were out of the water now for long intervals. They were colder than the rest of his body. The air stiffened them. They began to shake.

He took his mouth from the tube.

"Help! Help!"

The air escaped from the tube and he struggled with it. He twisted the tit until the air was safe. He stopped shouting and strained his eyes to see through the darkness but it lay right against his eyeballs. He put his hand before his eyes and saw nothing. Immediately the terror of blindness added itself to the terror of isolation and drowning. He began to make vague climbing motions in the water.

"Help! Is there anybody there? Help! Survivor!"

He lay shaking for a while and listened for an answer but the only sound was the hissing and puddling of the water as it washed round him. His head fell forward.

He licked salt water off his lips.

"Exercise."

He began to tread water gently. His mouth mumbled.

"Why did I take my sea boots off? I'm no better off than I was." His head nodded forward again.

"Cold. Mustn't get too cold. If I had those boots I could put them on and then take them off and then put them on——"

He thought suddenly of the boots sinking through water towards a bottom that was still perhaps a mile remote from them. With that, the whole wet immensity seemed to squeeze his body as though he were sunk to a great depth. His chattering teeth came together and the flesh of his face twisted. He arched in the water, drawing his feet up away from the depth, the slopping, glutinous welter.

"Help! Help——!"

He began to thresh with his hands and force his body round. He stared at the darkness as he turned but there was nothing to tell him when he had completed the circle and everywhere the darkness was grainless and alike. There was no wreckage, no sinking hull, no struggling survivors but himself, there was only darkness lying close against the balls of the eyes. There was the movement of water.

He began to cry out for the others, for anyone.

"Nat! Nathaniel! For Christ's sake! Nathaniel! Help!"

His voice died and his face untwisted. He lay slackly in his lifebelt, allowing the swell to do what it would. His teeth were chattering again and sometimes this vibration would spread till it included his whole body. His legs below him were not cold so much as pressed, squeezed mercilessly by the sea so that the feeling in them was not a response to temperature but to weight that would crush and burst them. He searched for a place to put his hands but there was nowhere that kept the ache out of them. The back of his neck began to hurt and that not gradually but with a sudden stab of pain so that holding his chin away from his chest was impossible. But this put his face into the sea so that he sucked it into his nose with a snoring noise and a choke. He spat and endured the pain in his neck for a while. He wedged his hands between his lifebelt and his chin and for a swell or two this was some relief but then the pain returned. He let his hands fall away and his face dipped in the water. He lay back, forcing his head against the pain so that his eyes if they had been open would have been looking at the sky. The pressure on his legs was bearable now. They were no longer flesh, but had been transformed to some other substance, petrified and comfortable. The part of his body that had not been invaded and wholly subdued by the sea was jerking intermittently. Eternity, inseparable from pain was there to be examined and experienced. The snarl endured. He thought. The thoughts were laborious, disconnected but vital.

Presently it will be daylight.

I must move from one point to another.

Enough to see one move ahead.

Presently it will be daylight.

I shall see wreckage.

I won't die.

I can't die.

Not me——

Precious.

He roused himself with a sudden surge of feeling that had nothing to do with the touch of the sea. Salt water was coming fast out of his eyes. He snivelled and gulped.

"Help, somebody—help!"

His body lifted and fell gently.

If I'd been below I might have got to a boat even. Or a raft. But it had to be my bloody watch. Blown off the bloody bridge. She must have gone on perhaps to starboard if he got the order in time, sinking or turning over. They'll be there in the darkness somewhere where she sank asking each other if they're down-hearted, knots and stipples of heads in the water and oil and drifting stuff. When it's light I must find them, Christ I must find them. Or they'll be picked up and I'll be left to swell like a hammock. Christ!

"Help! Nathaniel! Help——!"

And I gave the right order too. If I'd done it ten seconds earlier I'd be a bloody hero—Hard a-starboard for Christ's sake!

Must have hit us bang under the bridge. And I gave the right order. And I get blown to buggery.

The snarl fixed itself, worked on the wooden face till the upper lip was lifted and the chattering teeth bared. The little warmth of anger flushed blood back into the tops of the cheeks and behind the eyes. They opened.

Then he was jerking and splashing and looking up. There was a difference in the texture of the darkness; there were smears and patches that were not in the eye itself. For a moment and before he remembered how to use his sight the patches lay on the eyeballs as close as the darkness had been. Then he firmed the use of his eyes and he was inside his head, looking out through the arches of his skull at random formations of dim light and mist. However he blinked and squinted they remained there outside him. He bent his head forward and saw, fainter than an afterimage, the scalloped and changing shape of a swell as his body was lifted in it. For a moment he caught the inconstant outline against the sky, then he was floating up and seeing dimly the black top of the next swell as it swept towards him. He began to make swimming motions. His hands were glimmering patches in the water and his movements broke up the stony weight of his legs. The thoughts continued to flicker.

We were travelling north-east. I gave the order. If he began the turn she might be anywhere over there to the east. The wind was westerly. That's the east over there where the swells are running away down hill.

His movements and his breathing became fierce. He swam a sort of clumsy breast-stroke, buoyed up on the inflated belt. He stopped and lay wallowing. He set his teeth, took the tit of the lifebelt and let out air till he was lying lower in the water. He began to swim again. His breathing laboured. He stared out of his arches intently and painfully at the back of each swell as it slunk away from him. His legs slowed and stopped; his arms fell. His mind inside the dark skull made swimming movements long after the body lay motionless in the water.

The grain of the sky was more distinct. There were vaporous changes of tone from dark to gloom, to grey. Near at hand the individual hillocks of the surface were visible. His mind made swimming movements.

Pictures invaded his mind and tried to get between him and the urgency of his motion towards the east. The jam jar came back but robbed of significance. There was a man, a brief interview, a desk-top so polished that the smile of teeth was being reflected in it. There was a row of huge masks hung up to dry and a voice from behind the teeth that had been reflected in the desk spoke softly.

"Which one do you think would suit Christopher?"

There was a binnacle-top with the compass light just visible, there was an order shouted, hung up there for all heaven and earth to see in neon lighting.

"Hard a-starboard, for Christ's sake!"

Water washed into his mouth and he jerked into consciousness with a sound that was half a snore and half a choke. The day was inexorably present in green and grey. The seas were intimate and enormous. They smoked. When he swung up a broad, hilly crest he could see two other smoking crests then nothing but a vague circle that might be mist or fine spray or rain. He peered into the circle, turning himself, judging direction by the run of the water until he had inspected every part. The slow fire of his belly, banked up to endure, was invaded. It lay defenceless in the middle of the clothing and sodden body.

"I won't die! I won't!"

The circle of mist was everywhere alike. Crests swung into view on that side, loomed, seized him, elevated him for a moment, let him down and slunk off, but there was another crest to take him, lift him so that he could see the last one just dimming out of the circle. Then he would go down again and another crest would loom weltering towards him.

He began to curse and beat the water with the flat of his white hands. He struggled up the swells. But even the sounds of his working mouth and body were merged unnoticed in the thin innumerable sounds of travelling water. He hung still in his belt, feeling the cold search his belly with its fingers. His head fell on his chest and the stuff slopped weakly, persistently over his face. Think. My last chance. Think what can be done.

She sank out in the Atlantic. Hundreds of miles from land. She was alone, sent north-east from the convoy to break WT silence. The U-boat may be hanging round to pick up a survivor or two for questioning. Or to pick off any ship that comes to rescue survivors. She may surface at any moment, breaking the swell with her heavy body like a half-tide rock. Her periscope may sear the water close by, eye of a land-creature that has defeated the rhythm and necessity of the sea. She may be passing under me now, shadowy and shark-like, she may be lying down there below my wooden feet on a bed of salty water as on a cushion while her crew sleeps. Survivors, a raft, the whaler, the dinghy, wreckage may be jilling about only a swell or two away hidden in the mist and waiting for rescue with at least bully and perhaps a tot.

He began to rotate in the water again, peering blearily at the mist, he squinted at the sky that was not much higher than a roof; he searched the circle for wreckage or a head. But there was nothing. She had gone as if a hand had reached up that vertical mile and snatched her down in one motion. When he thought of the mile he arched in the water, face twisted, and began to cry out.

"Help, curse you, sod you, bugger you—Help!"

Then he was blubbering and shuddering and the cold was squeezing him like the hand that had snatched down the ship. He hiccupped slowly into silence and started to rotate once more in the smoke and green welter.

One side of the circle was lighter than the other. The swell was shouldering itself on towards the left of this vague brightness; and where the brightness spread the mist was even more impenetrable than behind him. He remained facing the brightness not because it was of any use to him but because it was a difference that broke the uniformity of the circle and because it looked a little warmer than anywhere else. He made swimming movements again without thought and as if to follow in the wake of that brightness was an inevitable thing to do. The light made the sea-smoke seem solid. It penetrated the water so that between him and the very tops of the restless hillocks it was bottle green. For a moment or two after a wave had passed he could see right into it but the waves were nothing but water—there was no weed in them, no speck of solid, nothing drifting, nothing moving but green water, cold, persistent idiot water. There were hands to be sure and two forearms of black oilskin and there was the noise of breathing, gasping. There was also the noise of the idiot stuff, whispering, folding on itself, tripped ripples running tinkling by the ear like miniatures of surf on a flat beach; there were sudden hisses and spats, roars and incompleted syllables and the soft friction of wind. The hands were important under the bright side of the circle but they had nothing to seize on. There was an infinite drop of the soft, cold stuff below them and under the labouring, dying body.

The sense of depth caught him and he drew his dead feet up to his belly as if to detach them from the whole ocean. He arched and gaped, he rose over the chasm of deep sea on a swell and his mouth opened to scream against the brightness.

It stayed open. Then it shut with a snap of teeth and his arms began to heave water out of the way. He fought his way forward.

"Ahoy—for Christ's sake! Survivor! Survivor! Fine on your starboard bow!"

He threshed with his arms and legs into a clumsy crawl. A crest overtook him and he jerked himself to the chest out of water.

"Help! Help! Survivor! For God's sake!"

The force of his return sent him under but he struggled up and shook the wave from his head. The fire of his belly had spread and his heart was thrusting the sluggish blood painfully round his body. There was a ship in the mist to port of the bright patch. He was on her starboard bow—or—and the thought drove him to foam in the water—he was on her port quarter and she was moving away. But even in his fury of movement he saw how impossible this was since then she would have passed by him only a few minutes ago. So she was coming towards, to cut across the circle of visibility only a few yards from him.

Or stopped.

At that, he stopped too, and lay in the water. She was so dull a shape, little more than a looming darkness that he could not tell both her distance and her size. She was more nearly bows on than when he had first seen her and now she was visible even when he was in a trough. He began to swim again but every time he rose on a crest he screamed.

"Help! Survivor!"

But what ship was ever so lop-sided? A carrier? A derelict carrier, deserted and waiting to sink? But she would have been knocked down by a salvo of torpedoes. A derelict liner? Then she must be one of the Queens by her bulk—and why lop-sided? The sun and the mist were balanced against each other. The sun could illumine the mist but not pierce it. And darkly in the sun-mist loomed the shape of a not-ship where nothing but a ship could be.

He began to swim again, feeling suddenly the desperate exhaustion of his body. The first, fierce excitement of sighting had burned up the fuel and the fire was low again. He swam grimly; forcing his arms through the water, reaching forward under his arches with sight as though he could pull himself into safety with it. The shape moved. It grew larger and not clearer. Every now and then there was something like a bow-wave at the forefoot. He ceased to look at her but swam and screamed alternately with the last strength of his body. There was green force round him, growing in strength to rob, there was mist and glitter over him; there was a redness pulsing in front of his eyes—his body gave up and he lay slack in the waves and the shape rose over him. He heard through the rasp and thump of his works the sound of waves breaking. He lifted his head and there was rock stuck up in the sky with a sea-gull poised before it. He heaved over in the sea and saw how each swell dipped for a moment, flung up a white hand of foam then disappeared as if the rock had swallowed it. He began to think swimming motions but knew now that his body was no longer obedient. The top of the next swell between him and the rock was blunted, smoothed curiously, then jerked up spray. He sank down, saw without comprehension that the green water was no longer empty. There was yellow and brown. He heard not the formless mad talking of uncontrolled water but a sudden roar. Then he went under into a singing world and there were hairy shapes that flitted and twisted past his face, there were sudden notable details close to of intricate rock and weed. Brown tendrils slashed across his face, then with a destroying shock he hit solidity. It was utter difference, it was under his body, against his knees and face, he could close fingers on it, for an instant he could even hold on. His mouth was heedlessly open and his eyes so that he had a moment of close and intent communion with three limpets, two small and one large that were only an inch or two from his face. Yet this solidity was terrible and apocalyptic after the world of inconstant wetness. It was not vibrant as a ship's hull might be but merciless and mother of panic. It had no business to interrupt the thousands of miles of water going about their purposeless affairs and therefore the world sprang here into sudden war. He felt himself picked up and away from the limpets, reversed, tugged, thrust down into weed and darkness. Ropes held him, slipped and let him go. He saw light, got a mouthful of air and foam. He glimpsed a riven rock face with trees of spray growing up it and the sight of this rock floating in mid-Atlantic was so dreadful that he wasted his air by screaming as if it had been a wild beast. He went under into a green calm, then up and was thrust sideways. The sea no longer played with him. It stayed its wild movement and held him gently, carried him with delicate and careful motion like a retriever with a bird. Hard things touched him about the feet and knees. The sea laid him down gently and retreated. There were hard things touching his face and chest, the side of his forehead. The sea came back and fawned round his face, licked him. He thought movements that did not happen. The sea came back and he thought the movements again and this time they happened because the sea took most of his weight. They moved him forward over the hard things. Each wave and each movement moved him forward. He felt the sea run down to smell at his feet then come back and nuzzle under his arm. It no longer licked his face. There was a pattern in front of him that occupied all the space under the arches. It meant nothing. The sea nuzzled under his arm again.

He lay still.

The pattern was white and black but mostly white. It existed in two layers, one behind the other, one for each eye. He thought nothing, did nothing while the pattern changed a trifle and made little noises. The hardnesses under his cheek began to insist. They passed through pressure to a burning without heat, to a localized pain. They became vicious in their insistence like the nag of an aching tooth. They began to pull him back into himself and organize him again as a single being.

Yet it was not the pain nor the white and black pattern that first brought him back to life, but the noises. Though the sea had treated

him so carefully, elsewhere it continued to roar and thump and col-
lapse on itself. The wind too, given something to fight with other than
obsequious water was hissing round the rock and breathing gustily
in crevices. All these noises made a language which forced itself into
the dark, passionless head and assured it that the head was somewhere, somewhere—and then finally with the flourish of a gull's cry over
the sound of wind and water, declared to the groping consciousness:
wherever you are, you are here!

Then he was there, suddenly, enduring pain but in deep communion with the solidity that held up his body. He remembered how eyes
should be used and brought the two lines of sight together so that the
patterns fused and made a distance. The pebbles were close to his face,
pressing against his cheek and jaw. They were white quartz, dulled and
rounded, a miscellany of potato-shapes. Their whiteness was qualified
by yellow stains and flocks of darker material. There was a whiter thing
beyond them. He examined it without curiosity, noting the bleached
wrinkles, the blue roots of nails, the corrugations at the finger-tips. He
did not move his head but followed the line of the hand back to an oilskin sleeve, the beginnings of a shoulder. His eyes returned to the pebbles and watched them idly as if they were about to perform some
operation for which he was waiting without much interest. The hand
did not move.

Water welled up among the pebbles. It stirred them slightly, paused,
then sank away while the pebbles clicked and chirruped. It swilled
down past his body and pulled gently at his stockinged feet. He
watched the pebbles while the water came back and this time the last
touch of the sea lopped into his open mouth. Without change of
expression he began to shake, a deep shake that included the whole of
his body. Inside his head it seemed that the pebbles were shaking
because the movement of his white hand forward and back was
matched by the movement of his body. Under the side of his face the
pebbles nagged.

The pictures that came and went inside his head did not disturb him
because they were so small and remote. There was a woman's body,

white and detailed, there was a boy's body; there was a box office, the bridge of a ship, an order picked out across a far sky in neon lighting, a tall, thin man who stood aside humbly in the darkness at the top of a companion ladder; there was a man hanging in the sea like a glass sailor in a jam jar. There was nothing to choose between the pebbles and the pictures. Sometimes one was uppermost, sometimes the other. The individual pebbles were no bigger than the pictures. Sometimes a pebble would be occupied entirely by a picture as though it were a window, a spy-hole into a different world or other dimension. Words and sounds were sometimes visible as shapes like the shouted order. They did not vibrate and disappear. When they were created they remained as hard enduring things like the pebbles. Some of these were inside the skull, behind the arch of the brow and the shadowy nose. They were right in the indeterminate darkness above the fire of hard-nesses. If you looked out idly, you saw round them.

There was a new kind of coldness over his body. It was creeping down his back between the stuffed layers of clothing. It was air that felt like slow fire. He had hardly noticed this when a wave came back and filled his mouth so that a choke interrupted the rhythm of shaking.

He began to experiment. He found that he could haul the weight of one leg up and then the other. His hand crawled round above his head. He reasoned deeply that there was another hand on the other side somewhere and sent a message out to it. He found the hand and worked the wrist. There were still fingers on it, not because he could move them but because when he pushed he could feel the wooden tips shifting the invisible pebbles. He moved his four limbs in close and began to make swimming movements. The vibrations from the cold helped him. Now his breath went in and out quickly and his heart began to race again. The inconsequential pictures vanished and there was nothing but pebbles and pebble noises and heart-thumps. He had a valuable thought, not because it was of immediate physical value but because it gave him back a bit of his personality. He made words to express this thought, though they did not pass the barrier of his teeth.

"I should be about as heavy as this on Jupiter."

At once he was master. He knew that his body weighed no more than it had always done, that it was exhausted, that he was trying to crawl up a little pebble slope. He lifted the dents in his face away from the pebbles that had made them and pushed with his knees. His teeth came together and ground. He timed the expansion of his chest against the pebbles, the slow shaking of his body till they did not hold up the leaden journey. He felt how each wave finished farther and farther down towards his feet. When the journey became too desperate he would wait, gasping, until the world came back. The water no longer touched his feet.

His left hand—the hidden one—touched something that did not click and give. He rolled his head and looked up under the arch. There was greyish yellow stuff in front of his face. It was pock-marked and hollowed, dotted with red lumps of jelly. The yellow tents of limpets were pitched in every hole. Brown fronds and green webs of weed hung over them. The white pebbles led up into a dark angle. There was a film of water glistening over everything, drops falling, tiny pools caught at random, lying and shuddering or leaking down among the weed. He began to turn on the pebbles, working his back against the rock and drawing up his feet. He saw them now for the first time, distant projections, made thick and bear-like by the white, seaboot stockings. They gave him back a little more of himself. He got his left hand down beneath his oar and began to heave. His shoulder lifted a little. He pushed with feet, pulled with hands. His back was edging into the angle where the pools leaked down. His head was high. He took a thigh in both hands and pulled it towards his chest and then the other. He packed himself into the angle and looked down at the pebbles over his knees. His mouth had fallen open again.

And after all, as pebbles go there were not very many of them. The length of a man or less would measure out the sides of the triangle that they made under the shadow of the rock. They filled the cleft and they were solid.

He took his eyes away from the pebbles and made them examine the water. This was almost calm in comparison with the open sea; and the reason was the rock round which the waves had whirled him. He could see the rock out there now. It was the same stuff as this, grey and creamy with barnacles and foam. Each wave tripped on it so that although the water ran and thumped on either side of the cleft, there was a few yards of green, clear water between him and the creamy rock. Beyond the rock was nothing but a smoking advance of sea with watery sunlight caught in it.

He let his eyes close and ignored the pictures that came and went behind them. The slow movement of his mind settled on a thought. There was a small fire in his body that was almost extinguished but incredibly was still smouldering despite the Atlantic. He folded his body consciously round that fire and nursed it. There was not more than a spark. The formal words and the pictures evolved themselves.

A seabird cried over him with a long sound descending down wind. He removed his attention from the spark of fire and opened his eyes again. This time he had got back so much of his personality that he could look out and grasp the whole of what he saw at once. There were the dark walls of rock on either side that framed the brighter light. There was sunlight on a rock with spray round it and the steady march of swells that brought their own fine mist along with them under the sun. He turned his head sideways and peered up.

The rock was smoother above the weeds and limpets and drew together. There was an opening at the top with daylight and the suggestion of cloud caught in it. As he watched, a gull flicked across the opening and cried in the wind. He found the effort of looking up hurt him and he turned to his body, examined the humps that were his knees under the oilskin and duffle. He looked closely at a button.

His mouth shut then opened. Sounds came out. He readjusted them and they were uncertain words.

"I know you. Nathaniel sewed you on. I asked him to. Said it was an excuse to get him away from the mess-deck for a bit of peace."

His eyes closed again and he fingered the button clumsily.

"Had this oilskin when I was a rating. Lofty sewed on the buttons before Nathaniel."

His head nodded on his knees.

"All the blue watch. Blue watch to muster."

The pictures were interrupted by the solid shape of a snore. The shiverings were less dramatic but they took power from his arms so that presently they fell away from his knees and his hands lay on the pebbles. His head shook. Between the snores the pebbles were hard to the feet, harder to the backside when the heels had slid slowly from under. The pictures were so confused that there was as much danger that they would destroy the personality as that the spark of fire would go out. He forced his way among them, lifted his eyelids and looked out.

The pebbles were wavering down there where the water welled over them. Higher up, the rock that had saved him was lathered and fringed with leaping strings of foam. There was afternoon brightness outside but the cleft was dripping, dank and smelly as a dockside latrine. He made quacking sounds with his mouth. The words that had formed in his mind were: Where is this bloody rock? But that seemed to risk something by insult of the dark cleft so that he changed them in his throat.

"Where the hell am I?"

A single point of rock, peak of a mountain range, one tooth set in the ancient jaw of a sunken world, projecting through the inconceivable vastness of the whole ocean—and how many miles from dry land? An evil pervasion, not the convulsive panic of his first struggles in the water, but a deep and generalized terror set him clawing at the rock with his blunt fingers. He even got half-up and leaned or crouched against the weed and the lumps of jelly.

"Think, you bloody fool, think."

The horizon of misty water stayed close, the water leapt from the rock and the pebbles wavered.

"Think."

He crouched, watching the rock, not moving but trembling continually. He noted how the waves broke on the outer rock and were tamed, so that the water before the cleft was sloppily harmless. Slowly, he settled back into the angle of the cleft. The spark was alight and the heart was supplying it with what it wanted. He watched the outer rock but hardly saw it. There was a name missing. That name was written on the chart, well out in the Atlantic, eccentrically isolated so that seamen who could to a certain extent laugh at wind and weather had made a joke of the rock. Frowning, he saw the chart now in his mind's eye but not clearly. He saw the navigating commander of the cruiser bending over it with the captain, saw himself as navigator's yeoman standing ready while they grinned at each other. The captain spoke with his clipped Dartmouth accent—spoke and laughed.

"I call that name a near miss."

Near miss whatever the name was. And now to be huddled on a near miss how many miles from the Hebrides? What was the use of the spark if it winked away in a crack of that ludicrous isolation? He spat his words at the picture of the captain.

"I am no better off than I was."

He began to slide down the rocks as his bones bent their hinges. He slumped into the angle and his head fell. He snored.

But inside, where the snores were external, the consciousness was moving and poking about among the pictures and revelations, among the shape-sounds and the disregarded feelings like an animal cease-lessly examining its cage. It rejected the detailed bodies of women, slowly sorted the odd words, ignored the pains and the insistence of the shaking body. It was looking for a thought. It found the thought, separated it from the junk, lifted it and used the apparatus of the body to give it force and importance.

"I am intelligent."

There was a period of black suspension behind the snores; then the right hand, so far away, obeyed a command and began to fumble and pluck at the oilskin. It raised a flap and crawled inside. The fingers found cord and a shut clasp-knife. They stayed there.

The eyes blinked open so that the arch of brows was a frame to green sea. For a while the eyes looked, received impressions without seeing them. Then the whole body gave a jump. The spark became a flame, the body scrambled, crouched, the hand flicked out of the oilskin pocket and grabbed rock. The eyes stared and did not blink.

As the eyes watched, a wave went clear over the outer rock so that they could see the brown weed inside the water. The green dance beyond the pebbles was troubled. A line of foam broke and hissed up the pebbles to his feet. The foam sank away and the pebbles chattered like teeth. He watched, wave after wave as bursts of foam swallowed more and more of the pebbles and left fewer visible when they went back. The outer rock was no longer a barrier but only a gesture of defence. The cleft was being connected more and more directly with the irresistible progress of the green, smoking seas. He jerked away from the open water and turned towards the rock. The dark, lavatorial cleft, with its dripping weed, with its sessile, mindless life of shell and jelly was land only twice a day by courtesy of the moon. It felt like solidity but it was a sea-trap, as alien to breathing life as the soft slop of the last night and the vertical mile.

A gull screamed with him so that he came back into himself, leaned his forehead against the rock and waited for his heart to steady. A shot of foam went over his feet. He looked down past them. There were fewer pebbles to stand on and those that had met his hands when he had been washed ashore were yellow and green beneath a foot of jumping water. He turned to the rock again and spoke out loud.

"Climb!"

He turned round and found handholds in the cleft. There were many to choose from. His hands were poor, sodden stuff against their wet projections. He leaned a moment against the rock and gathered the resources of his body together. He lifted his right leg and dropped the foot in an opening like an ash-tray. There was an edge to the ash-tray but not a sharp one and his foot could feel nothing. He took his forehead away from a weedy surface and heaved himself up until the right leg was straight. His left leg swung and thumped. He got the toes on a shelf and stayed so, only a few inches off the pebbles and spreadeagled. The cleft rose by his face and he looked at the secret drops of the stillicide in the dark angle as though he envied them their peace. Time went by drop by drop. The two pictures drifted apart.

The pebbles rattled below him and a last lick of water flipped into the crevice. He dropped his head and looked down over his lifebelt, through the open skirt of the oilskin to where the wetted pebbles lay in the angle of the cleft. He saw his seaboot stockings and thought his feet back into them.

"I wish I had my seaboots still."

He changed the position of his right foot cautiously and locked his left knee stiffly upright to bear his weight without effort. His feet were selective in a curious way. They could not feel rock unless there was sharpness. They only became a part of him when they were hurting him or when he could see them.

The tail end of a wave reached right into the angle and struck in the apex with a plop. A single string of spray leapt up between his legs, past the lifebelt and wetted his face. He made a sound and only then found how ruinous an extension of flesh he carried round him. The sound began in the throat, bubbled and stayed there. The mouth took no part but lay open, jaw lying slack on the hard oilskin collar. The bubbling increased and he made the teeth click. Words twisted out between them and the frozen stuff of his upper lip.

"Like a dead man!"

Another wave reached in and spray ran down his face. He began to labour at climbing. He moved up the intricate rock face until there were no more limpets nor mussels and nothing clung to the rock but his own body and tiny barnacles and green smears of weed. All the time the wind pushed him into the cleft and the sea made dispersed noises.

The cleft narrowed until his head projected through an opening, not much wider than his body. He got his elbows jammed on either side and looked up.

Before his face the rock widened above the narrowest part of the cleft into a funnel. The sides of the funnel were not very smooth; but they were smooth enough to refuse to hold a body by friction. They sloped away to the top of the rock like a roof angle. The track from his face to the cliff-like edge of the funnel at the top was nearly twice the length of a man. He began to turn his head, slowly, searching for handholds, but saw none. Only at about halfway there was a depression, but too shallow for a handhold. Blunted fingers would never be safe on the rounded edge.

There came a thud from the bottom of the angle. Solid water shot into the angle, burst and washed down again. He peered over his lifebelt, between his two feet. The pebbles were dimmed, appeared clearly for a moment, then vanished under a surge of green water. Spray shot up between his body and the rock.

He pulled himself up until his body from the waist was leaning forward along the slope. His feet found the holds where his elbows had been. His knees straightened slowly while he breathed in gasps and his right arm reached out in front of him. Fingers closed on the blunted edge of the depression. Pulled.

He took one foot away from a hold and edged the knee up. He moved the other.

He hung, only a few inches from the top of the angle, held by one hand and the friction of his body. The fingers of his right hand quivered and gave. They slipped over the rounded edge. His whole body slid down and he was back at the top of the crevice again. He lay still, not seeing the rock by his eyes and his right arm was stretched above him.

The sea was taking over the cleft. Every few seconds there came the thump and return of a wave below him. Heavy drops fell and trickled on the surface of the funnel before his face. Then a wave exploded and water cascaded over his legs. He lifted his face off the rock and the snarl wrestled with his stiff muscles.

"Like a limpet."

He lay for a while, bent at the top of the crevice. The pebbles no longer appeared in the angle. They were a wavering memory of themselves between bouts of spray. Then they vanished, the rock vanished with them and with another explosion the water hit him from head to foot. He shook it from his face. He was staring down at the crevice as though the water were irrelevant.

He cried out.

"Like a limpet!"

He put his feet down and felt for holds, lowered himself resolutely, clinging each time the water hit him and went back. He held his breath and spat when each wave left him. The water was no longer cold but powerful rather. The nearer he lowered his body to the pebbles the harder he was struck and the heavier the weight that urged him down at each return. He lost his hold and fell the last few inches and immediately a wave had him, thrust him brutally into the angle then tried to tear him away. Between waves when he staggered to his feet the water was knee-deep over the pebbles and they gave beneath him. He fell on all fours and was hidden in a green heap that hit the back of the angle and climbed up in a tree-trunk of spray. He staggered round the angle then gripped with both hands. The water tore at him but he held on. He got his knife free and opened the blade. He ducked down and immediately there were visions of rock and weed in front of his eyes. The uproar of the sea sank to a singing note in the ears. Then he was up again, the knife swinging free, two limpets in his hands and the sea knocked him down and stood him on his head. He found rock and clung against the backwash. When the waves left him for a moment he opened his mouth and gasped in the air as though he were winning territory. He found holds in the angle and the sea exploded, thrust him up so that now his effort was to stay down and under control. After each blow he flattened himself to escape the descent of the water. As he rose the seas lost their quality of leaden power but became more personal and vicious. They tore at his clothing, they beat him in the crutch, they tented up his oilskin till the skirt was crumpled above his waist. If he looked down the water came straight at his face, or hit him in the guts and thrust him up.

He came to the narrowest part and was shoved through. He opened his eyes after the water gushed back and breathed wetly as the foam streamed down his face. A lock of hair was plastered just to the bridge of his nose and he saw the end of it, double. The chute struck him again, the waterfall rushed back and he was still there, wedged by his weight in the narrowest part of the crevice where the funnel began and his body was shaking. He lay forward on the slope and began to straighten his legs. His face moved up against the rock and a torrent swept back over him. He began to fumble in the crumples of his oilskin. He brought out a limpet and set it on the rock by his waist. Water came again and went. He reversed his knife and tapped the limpet on the top with the haft. The limpet gave a tiny sideways lurch and sucked itself down against the rock. A weight pressed on him and the man and the limpet firmed down against the rock together.

His legs were straight and stiff and his eyes were shut. He brought his right arm round in a circle and felt above him. He found the blunted dent that was too smooth for a handhold. His hand came back, was inundated, fumbled in oilskin. He pulled it out and when the hand crawled round and up there was a limpet in the palm. The man was looking at the rock an inch or two from his face but without interest. What life was left was concentrated in the crawling right hand. The hand found the blunted hollow, and pitched the limpet beyond the edge. The body was lifted a few inches and lay motionless waiting for the return of the water. When the chute had passed the hand came back, took the knife, moved up and tapped blindly on rock. The fingers searched stiffly, found the limpet, hit with the haft of the knife.

He turned his face, endured another wave and considered the limpet above him gravely. His hand let the knife go, which slid and clattered and hung motionless by his waist. He took the tit of the lifebelt and unscrewed the end. The air breathed out and his body flattened a little in the funnel. He laid the side of his head down and did nothing. Before his mouth the wet surface of the rock was blurred a little and regularly the blur was erased by the return of the waterfall. Sometimes the pendant knife would clatter.

Again he turned his face and looked up. His fingers closed over the limpet. Now his right leg was moving. The toes searched tremulously for the first limpet as the fingers had searched for the second. They did not find the limpet but the knee did. The hand let go, came down to the knee and lifted that part of the leg. The snarl behind the stiff face felt the limpet, as a pain in the crook of the knee. The teeth set. The whole body began to wriggle; the hand went back to the higher limpet and pulled. The man moved sideways up the slope of the roof. The left leg came in and the seaboot stocking pushed the first leg away. The side of the foot was against the limpet. The leg straightened. Another torrent returned and washed down.

The man was lying with one foot on a limpet, held mostly by friction. But his foot was on one limpet and the second one was before his eyes. He reached up and there was a possible handhold that his fingers found, provided the other one still gripped the limpet by his face. He moved up, up, up and then there was an edge for his fingers. His right arm rose, seized. He pulled with both arms, thrust with both legs. He saw a trench of rock beyond the edge, glimpsed sea, saw whiteness on the rocks and jumble. He fell forward.

He was lying in a trench. He could see a weathered wall of rock and a long pool of water stretching away from his eye. His body was in some other place that had nothing to do with this landscape. It was splayed, scattered behind him, his legs in different worlds, neck twisted. His right arm was bent under his body and his wrist doubled. He sensed this hand and the hard pressure of the knuckles against his side but the pain was not intense enough to warrant the titanic effort of moving. His left arm stretched away along the trench and was half-covered in water. His right eye was so close to this water that he could feel a little pluck from the surface tension when he blinked and his eyelashes caught in the film. The water had flattened again by the time he saw the surface consciously but his right cheek and the corner of his mouth were under water and were causing a tremble. The other eye was above water and was looking down the trench. The inside of the trench was dirty white, strangely white with more than the glossy reflection from the sky. The corner of his mouth pricked. Sometimes the surface of the water was pitted for a moment or two and faint, interlacing circles spread over it from each pit. His left eye watched them, looking through a kind of arch of darkness where the skull swept round the socket. At the bottom and almost a straight line, was the skin colour of his nose. Filling the arch was the level of shining water.

He began to think slowly.

I have tumbled in a trench. My head is jammed against the farther side and my neck is twisted. My legs must be up in the air over the other wall. My thighs are hurting because the weight of my legs is pushing against the edge of the wall as a fulcrum. My right toes are hurt more than the rest of my leg. My hand is doubled under me and that is why I feel the localized pain in my ribs. My fingers might be made of wood. That whiter white under the water along there is my hand, hidden.

There was a descending scream in the air, a squawk and the beating of wings. A gull was braking wildly over the wall at the end of the trench, legs and claws held out. It yelled angrily at the trench, the wide wings gained a purchase and it hung flapping only a foot or two above the rock. Wind chilled his cheek. The webbed feet came up, the wings steadied and the gull side-slipped away. The commotion of its passage made waves in the white water that beat against his cheek, the shut eye, the corner of his mouth. The stinging increased.

There was no pain sharp enough to compel action. Even the stinging was outside the head. His left eye watched the whiter white of his hand under water. Some of the memory pictures came back. They were new ones of a man climbing up rock and placing limpets.

The pictures stirred him more than the stinging. They made his left hand contract under the surface and the oilskin arm roll in the water. His breathing grew suddenly fierce so that waves rippled away along the trench, crossed and came back. A ripple splashed into his mouth.

Immediately he was convulsed and struggling. His legs kicked and swung sideways. His head ground against rock and turned. He scrabbled in the white water with both hands and heaved himself up. He felt the too-smooth wetness running on his face and the brilliant jab of pain at the corner of his right eye. He spat and snarled. He glimpsed the trenches with their thick layers of dirty white, their trapped inches of solution, a gull slipping away over a green sea. Then he was forcing himself forward. He fell into the next trench, hauled himself over the wall, saw a jumble of broken rock, slid and stumbled. He was going down hill and he fell part of the way. There was moving water round flatfish rocks, a complication of weedy life. The wind went down with him and urged him forward. As long as he went forward the wind was satisfied but if he stopped for a moment's caution it thrust his unbalanced body down so that he scraped and hit. He saw little of the open sea and sky or the whole rock but only flashes of intimate being, a crack or point, a hand's breadth of yellowish surface that was about to strike a blow, unavoidable fists of rock that beat him impersonally, struck bright flashes of light from his body. The pain in the corner of his eye went with him too. This was the most important of all the pains because it thrust a needle now into the dark skull where he lived. The pain could not be avoided. His body revolved round it. Then he was holding brown weed and the sea was washing over his head and shoulders. He pulled himself up and lay on a flat rock with a pool across the top. He rolled the side of his face and his eye backwards and forwards underwater. He moved his hands gently so that the water swished. They left the water and reached round and gathered smears of green weed.

He knelt up and held the smears of green against his eye and the right side of his face. He slumped back against rock among the jellies and scalloped pitches and encampments of limpets and let the encrusted barnacles hurt him as they would. He set his left hand gently on his thigh and squinted sideways at it. The fingers were half-bent. The skin was white with blue showing through and wrinkles cut the surface in regular shapes. The needle reached after him in the skull behind the dark arch. If he moved the eyeball the needle moved too. He opened his eye and it filled immediately with water under the green weed.

He began to snort and make sounds deep in his chest. They were like hard lumps of sound and they jerked him as they came out. More salt

water came out of each eye and joined the traces of the sea and the solution on his cheeks. His whole body began to shiver.

There was a deeper pool on a ledge farther down. He climbed slowly
and heavily down, edged himself across and put his right cheek under
again. He opened and closed his eye so that the water flushed the
needle corner. The memory pictures had gone so far away that they
could be disregarded. He felt round and buried his hands in the pool.
Now and then a hard sound jerked his body.

The sea-gull came back with others and he heard them sounding
their interlacing cries like a trace of their flight over his head. There
were noises from the sea too, wet gurgles below his ear and the running
thump of swells, blanketed by the main of the rock but still able to
sidle round and send offshoots sideways among the rocks and into the
crannies. The idea that he must ignore pain came and sat in the centre
of his darkness where he could not avoid it. He opened his eyes for all
the movement of the needle and looked down at his bleached hands.
He began to mutter.

"Shelter. Must have shelter. Die if I don't."

He turned his head carefully and looked up the way he had come.
The odd patches of rock that had hit him on the way down were visible now as part of each other. His eyes took in yards at a time, sur-
faces that swam as the needle pricked water out of him. He set himself
to crawl back up the rock. The wind was lighter but dropping trails of
rain still fell over him. He hauled himself up a cliff that was no higher
than a man could span with his arms but it was an obstacle that had
to be negotiated with much arrangement and thought for separate
limbs. He lay for a while on the top of the little cliff and looked in
watery snatches up the height of the rock. The sun lay just above the
high part where the white trenches had waited for him. The light was
struggling with clouds and rain-mist and there were birds wheeling
across the rock. The sun was dull but drew more water from his eyes
so that he screwed them up and cried out suddenly against the needle.
He crawled by touch, and then with one eye through trenches and gul-

lies where there was no whiteness. He lifted his legs over the broken walls of trenches as though they belonged to another body. All at once, with the diminishing of the pain in his eye, the cold and exhaustion came back. He fell flat in a gully and let his body look after itself. The deep chill fitted close to him, so close it was inside the clothes, inside the skin.

The chill and the exhaustion spoke to him clearly. Give up, they said, lie still. Give up the thought of return, the thought of living. Break up, leave go. Those white bodies are without attraction or excitement, the faces, the words, happened to another man in another place. An hour on this rock is a lifetime. What have you to lose? There is nothing here but torture. Give up. Leave go.

His body began to crawl again. It was not that there was muscular or nervous strength there that refused to be beaten but rather that the voices of pain were like waves beating against the sides of a ship. There was at the centre of all the pictures and pains and voices a fact like a bar of steel, a thing—that which was so nakedly the centre of everything that it could not even examine itself. In the darkness of the skull, it existed, a darker dark, self-existent and indestructible.

"Shelter. Must have shelter."

The centre began to work. It endured the needle to look sideways, put thoughts together. It concluded that it must crawl this way rather than that. It noted a dozen places and rejected them, searched ahead of the crawling body. It lifted the luminous window under the arch, shifted the arch of skull from side to side like the slow shift of the head of a caterpillar trying to reach a new leaf. When the body drew near to a possible shelter the head still moved from side to side, moving more quickly than the slow thoughts inside.

There was a slab of rock that had slipped and fallen sideways from the wall of a trench. This made a triangular hole between the rock and the side and bottom of the trench. There was no more than a smear of rainwater in this trench and no white stuff. The hole ran away and down at an angle following the line of the trench and inside there was darkness. The hole even looked drier than the rest of the rock. At last his head stopped moving and he lay down before this hole as the sun dipped from view. He began to turn his body in the trench, among a complication of sodden clothing. He said nothing but breathed heavily with open mouth. Slowly he turned until his white seaboot stockings were towards the crevice. He backed to the triangular opening and put his feet in. He lay flat on his stomach and began to wriggle weakly like a snake that cannot cast its skin. His eyes were open and unfocused. He reached back and forced the oilskin and duffle down on either side. The oilskin was hard and he backed with innumerable separate movements like a lobster backing into a deep crevice under water. He was in the crack up to his shoulders and rock held him tightly. He hutched the life belt up till the soft rubber was across the upper part of his chest. The slow thoughts waxed and waned, the eyes were empty except for the water that ran from the needle in the right one. His hand found the tit and he blew again slowly until the rubber was firmed up against his chest. He folded his arms, a white hand on either side. He let the left side of his face fall on an oilskinned sleeve and his eyes were shut—not screwed up but lightly closed. His mouth was still open, the jaw fallen sideways. Now and then a shudder came up out of the crack and set his head and arms shaking. Water ran slowly out of his sleeves, fell from his hair and his nose, dripped from the rucked-up clothing round his neck. His eyes fell open like the mouth because the needle was more controllable that way. Only when he had to blink them against water did the point jab into the place where he lived.

He could see gulls swinging over the rock, circling down. They settled and cried with erect heads and tongues, beaks wide open on the high point of the rock. The sky greyed down and sea-smoke drifted over. The birds talked and shook their wings, folded them one over the other, settled like white pebbles against the rock and tucked in their heads. The greyness thickened into a darkness in which the few birds and the splashes of their dung were visible as the patches of foam were visible on the water. The trenches were full of darkness for down by the shelter for some reason there was no dirty white. The rocks were dim shapes among them. The wind blew softly and chill over the main rock and its unseen, gentle passage made a continual and almost inaudible hiss. Every now and then a swell thumped into the angle by the safety rock. After that there would be a long pause and then the rush and scramble of falling water down the funnel.

The man lay, huddled in his crevice, left cheek pillowed on black oilskin and his hands were glimmering patches on either side. Every now and then there came a faint scratching sound of oilskin as the body shivered.

from N by E
by Rockwell Kent

Rockwell Kent (1882–1971), best known for his work as an illustrator, also was an author, political activist, lobsterman, ship's carpenter and dairy farmer. His travels to him to far-flung places such as Alaska, Newfoundland and Tierra del Fuego. Kent's 1930 book N by E tells of his 1929 attempt to sail the 33-foot cutter Direction *from New York harbor to Greenland. Here Kent and his two companions approach their destination.*

We had been at least two hours on our course for Godthaab when we sighted the first evidence that we were approaching the region of a settlement: there on the summit of a little island stood a cross-shaped beacon.

Two courses, by the chart, now lay before us: the open sea to Godthaab, and an inside passage between successive islands and the mainland. The outside course was longer, and dirty weather was in prospect. That way, however, was my choice; and being then at the tiller I headed seawards.

The skipper and mate were at the charts.

"If we're approaching Godthaab, as you say," spoke the skipper, "can't we take this inside passage?"

"We can—but—"

"Then that's what we'll do," he said.

We headed in.

Putting a cluster of islands with beacons on them to port we entered sheltered waters. Here was less wind; and the surface of the bay, save for the little ripples of the breeze, was as smooth as a fresh-water pond. How sweet it was to sail so evenly, so quietly, and hear again those liquid gurglings on our sides! And see the land again so near! To feel the friendliness of that majestic wilderness, its peacefulness— immense, secure! But a few hours more and we'd go sailing into Godthaab, and drop anchor! And the people would crowd the shores to greet us! How wonderful you are, they'd say! They'd come aboard to see the ship and marvel at it. How small, how strong, how clean and neat and beautiful! How brave you are! And the men—even the hardy Danes—would admire and envy us; and the girls—sweet, gentle, blue-eyed Danish girls—they'd *love* us!

"Clean up!" think I.

"More speed!" says the skipper. And he gets out the spinnaker.

"For God's sake, don't put that on," I protest.

Great headlands frown upon us. Inlets with canyon walls point like the outspread fingers of a hand toward that arctic rookery of storm, the inland ice. Alaska, Cape Horn; brothers to here: I've felt the violence of their sudden squalls, those dreaded "wullys"; how with malignant fury they strike down from mountain heights, lashing the sea to foam; so swift, and terrible!

We set the spinnaker. The wind, as if to shame my fear dropped to a gentle breeze.

"Keep on this course," say I, until you have that hive shaped island fair abeam; then bear off sharp to port." And I go below to cook supper and put everything in order.

It was a splendid supper I prepared that night: corn bread and corned-beef hash and pancakes. And it was with some thought of the scrutiny of Danish housewives that I meanwhile set about that scouring and scrubbing which our long days and nights at sea had put us in such need of. So time passed.

Meanwhile the wind had headed us a bit. This had entailed a change of course and a departure from those simple and, as I now know, correct sailing directions which had been my last word. I was called on deck—only to look upon strange land forms and to share in the general confusion as to where, exactly, we had got to.

But if our course appeared now far from clear it was of no immediate concern; the breeze was failing us. It was nighttime and the sky was so heavily overcast that twilight darkness was around us. A most gentle rain began to fall.

The skipper headed for a small fiord that lay before us. On a faint breeze that scarcely gave us headway, in silence so profound that it became the murmur of the rain, we turned the headland flanking its approach and entered. And all at once, as one—there between mountain walls, sheltered and peaceful, awed by the scale and stillness of that solitude—we knew that rarest and most simple wish: here, for a time so long that it has only a beginning, merely to live!

Just where we anchored I shall never know; we were a long time about it. The sandy bottom of the fiord shoaled rapidly toward the head; and once we gently ran aground. But we poled off to some sufficient depth near to the southern shore. Down in the cabin I took the anchor's splash as signal to serve supper.

How warm and neat and clean they found the cabin! Dressed for port. Port! And tonight we sleep!

"And as late as we want to in the morning," added the skipper.

But, for an hour after the others had gone to bed, I sat in my trim little fo'castle writing those pages of my diary which should have been these; writing through that grateful, midnight calm and stillness while the rain fell gently on the deck.

And of much that being there at last, in port in Greenland, meant to me, the last line that I wrote may speak: "Tomorrow," it read, "I paint!"

The motion woke me. Where was I? I remembered. Daylight came but faintly through the fo'castle ports, shadowed as they were by the dinghy. My clock showed ten-thirty. How I had slept!

We were rolling violently; a sudden roll, a lurch to starboard. I heard steps on deck, voices, the sound of hawser paying out. Oh, well, we're at anchor; and no one has called. I braced my knees against the side board of the bunk; I had need to.

Suddenly we were careened so far that I was almost catapulted onto the floor. I got out, dressed hastily and opened the door into the cabin. It was broad daylight there. The skipper was in bed.

"She's drifting with both anchors," called the mate from deck.

"Give 'em more rope," answered the skipper.

I reached the ladder. At that moment something rolled us over, far, far down, and held us there; and the green sea came pouring in as if to fill the ship.

"Damn it!" I cried, "and I'd made everything so neat!"

On deck a hurricane; I'd never felt such wind before. The sea was beaten flat, with every wave crest shorn and whipped to smoke; cold spray and stinging rain drove over us.

I helped the mate. "We'll need the third anchor," I said, and started aft.

The skipper appeared. "Good, get it out," he said as I passed him. I went below for the last time.

The spare anchor was knocked down and stowed under the coal sacks and provisions in the after hold; it was not easy to come at. Removing the companion ladder I set to work. Hard work it was, cramped in that narrow space on hands and knees. As I dragged the hundred pound sacks out onto the cabin floor—always, strangely, careful not to damage anything—I'd look up and see the gray sky through the opening above my head. Then one time glancing up I saw the brow of the mountain; and always after that more mountain showed and less sky. And at last the mountain side itself seemed to have moved against the ship and to be towering over it.

I had laid a lighted cigarette carefully upon the chart table; this, as I worked, was always in my mind—that it should not be left to burn the wood. And so, from time to time, I'd move it just a bit. We were so careful of our boat, to mar it in no way!

But all the while I had been shifting goods and moving sacks of coal; so that at last I came to the anchor. It was a large anchor and very heavy. I dragged it out into the cabin.

"Come," I called to the mate, "and help me get this thing on deck."
And as I looked up I saw the mate in his yellow oilskins, bright against
the near dark mountain side.

"Not much use now," said the mate; but he came down.

It was hard work to lift that anchor up, and we seemed not to be very
strong. "I lose my strength from excitement," said the mate. I thought
that I did too—but I didn't say so.

We lifted the cumbersome affair head high and tumbled it out into
the cockpit. As I started to follow, a great sea lifted us and rolled us
over; I hung on, half out of the cabin. And I stared straight at an
oncoming wall of rock so near astern it seemed about to crush us. The
sea rose high against it, and broke and became churned water that
seethed around us. It cradled us and lowered us gently; and the dark
land drew quietly away.

Then came another sea that hurled us and the land together. "Now
for the crash!" I thought—and I gripped hard and braced myself
against it, and watched the moment—thrilled by its impending horror.

There was no crash—that time. Ever so gently, just as we seemed to
draw away again, our stern post touched the ledge; so lightly touched
it that it made no sound, only a little tremor. And the tremor ran
through the iron keel and the oak, and through the ribs and planking,
and through every bolt and nail, through every fibre of the boat and us.
Maybe we had not known that the end had come; now, as if God whispered it, we knew.

So for a third time we were floated back.

Then, as if the furies of the sea and wind were freed at last to end
their coquetry, they lifted us—high, high above the ledge—and
dropped us there. And the impact of that shock was only less than
those that followed for that half an hour until *Direction* sank.

That half an hour! We lay, caught in the angle of a giant step of rock,
keel on the tread and starboard side against the riser; held there by

wind and sea; held there to lift and pound; to lift so buoyantly on every wave; to drop—crashing our thirteen iron-shod tons on granite. Lift and pound! There the perfection of our ship revealed itself; only, that having struck just once, she ever lived, a ship, to lift and strike again.

A giant sledge hammer striking a granite mountain; a hollow hammer; and within it a man. Picture yourself the man. I stayed below, and was.

See me as Adam; set full blown into that pandemonium of force, his world—of wind, storm, snow, rain, hail, lightning and thunder, earth-quake and flood, hunger and cold, and the huge terrifying presence of the unknown—using his little wit toward self containedness against the too-much of immensity; and quietly—for Adam lived—doing the little first-at-hands one on another in their natural course, thinking but little and reflecting less. Adam and Man; and me in that compacted miniature of man's universe, the cabin of the yacht *Direction* on the rocks of Greenland.

We live less by imagination than despite it.

Matches: They're in the fo'castle cupboard. I get out a lot. Next: Keep 'em dry. A big tin on the shelf. Lentils! I pour them out on the floor; no, not all; we don't need all that room for matches. Pack in matches, put on the cover. Good. Now something to put the tin into. Sam's little bag lying there; the very thing! Good neckties and white collars! Out with them!

Put in the tin of matches; add odds and ends of food; close it; that's done.

Kerosene: Five-gallon tin too big to get ashore. The one-gallon. Buried under stores.

Over the coal sacks into the after storage space. God what a mess! Dig in the stores; dig—and find it. Good!

Alcohol for priming: Find it—a small bottle.

And the Primus stove? Crushed on the floor.

There's another in my pack-sack with pup tent, nest of pots, etc. Under the starboard fo'castle bunk. Smothered under spare sails, spare rope, spare clothes, painting supplies. Out with everything. Ha! the sack!

Flour, rice, butter, beans, dried soups, coffee, bacon, chocolate, cigarettes: fill up the sack with them. Done.

Chronometers, the beauties! I take them from their boxes and wrap them carefully in layer on layer of clothes. I partly fill a duffle bag with blankets; put in watches; add the sextant, my silver flute, my movie camera, more blankets.

And this and all the rest, plus now and then a garment or a blanket, I pass on deck to the mate.

"Enough!" I think, with pride.

"Come out of there," calls the mate for the fourth time, peering down into the havoc of that hold.

Havoc! It's no-man's land; a mass of wreckage: doors, drawers, shelves, sheathing, stove lids, pots and pans and crockery, springs, mattresses, tools, beans and butter and books,—torn, splintered, crashed and mashed, lifted and churned and hurled again with every shivering impact of the ship.

Over my writing table in the fo'castle, nailed to a timber, was my sweetheart's picture. I had not forgotten it. I will take that picture, I had thought, tuck it for safety next my skin; and carry it, last thing, ashore with me. Then on my return I'll say, "Look, darling, what I have brought home!" And I'll take the picture from over my heart and show it to her. And with not so much modesty as to hide my valor I'll tell how in that hour of confusion and terror I had thought of her. And what a fine fellow I shall be!

So I now clambered, somehow, back to the fo'castle; found her image looking out serenely over the carnage; took her down and tucked her next to me; put an envelope containing my money, my passport and my permit to land in Greenland next to me too; and—wading, climbing, dodging, holding on for dear life—made my way out and to the deck.

• • •

The mate, working like ten stevedores, was getting things to shore. It was not far: a jump from deck to rocks, jump on a rising sea and scramble out of it and up before that step of rock was flooded. Hurling a sack, he'd follow it; clutch it and drag it to the safety of a higher ledge.

The sack containing the chronometers rolled back into the water. It was retrieved intact. Some things, washed from the rocks, were lost. The tide was littered with our gear and goods.

The thrashing of the main boom added confusion to the deck. Only the too stout standing rigging saved the mast.

The skipper was on shore desperately struggling to secure a mast-head line to a great boulder. Finished on board I leaped to help him. The yawing mast-head tore the line away from us each time we'd nearly made it fast. But once as the mast leant far down toward us we got two turns of line around the rock; we braced ourselves and held. The three-inch cable snapped like grocer's twine!

Direction's end was near. Quickly undoing the sack I got out the movie camera. Listen! Even above the noise of sea and wind and rain I hear for a short minute its small whirring like the beating of a heart. And by that sound, what happened there, in Karajak Fiord in Greenland, at eleven in the morning of July 15th, 1929, achieved soundless immortality.

West Greenland, mountainous and wild. A raging storm; cold rain in torrents from low hanging clouds. Streams pouring down the mountain side are turned to vapor by the gale; and the whole face of nature, land and sea, smokes as from internal fires.

Across the rough, grass matted foreland between sea and mountain move three figures, men; the only living things in all that wilderness. Leaning against the wind they labor on.

They climb a rise of land; and from its ridge look down into a sheltered basin. There lies a lake round as the moon. Its pebbly shore shows smooth and clean and bright against the deep green water. They descend to it and, standing there, look over at the mountain wall that bounds it. The dark cliff rises sheer from lake to sky. From its high edge pours a torrent. And the gale, lifting that torrent in mid-air, disperses it in smoke.

The three men stand there looking at it all: at the mountains, at the smoking waterfall, at the dark green lake with wind puffs silvering its plain, at the flowers that fringe the pebbly shore and star the banks. And at last one of them speaks.

"It's right," he says, "that we should pay for beautiful things. And being here in this spot, now, is worth traveling a thousand miles for, and all that that has cost us. Maybe we have lived only to be here now."

from Moby Dick
by Herman Melville

The opening chapters of Melville's (1819–1891) 1851 classic Moby Dick *are familiar to generations of readers. Queequeg still cuts an impressive and hilarious figure, while Ishmael is witty, candid and wise.*

C all me Ishmael. Some years ago—never mind how long precisely—having little or no money in my purse, and nothing particular to interest me on shore, I thought I would sail about a little and see the watery part of the world. It is a way I have of driving off the spleen, and regulating the circulation. Whenever I find myself growing grim about the mouth; whenever it is a damp, drizzly November in my soul; whenever I find myself involuntarily pausing before coffin warehouses, and bringing up the rear of every funeral I meet; and especially whenever my hypos get such an upper hand of me, that it requires a strong moral principle to prevent me from deliberately stepping into the street, and methodically knocking people's hats off—then, I account it high time to get to sea as soon as I can. This is my substitute for pistol and ball. With a philosophical flourish Cato throws himself upon his sword; I quietly take to the ship. There is nothing surprising in this. If they but knew it, almost all men in their degree, some time or other, cherish very nearly the same feelings towards the ocean with me.

There now is your insular city of the Manhattoes, belted round by wharves as Indian isles by coral reefs—commerce surrounds it with her surf. Right and left, the streets take you waterward. Its extreme down-town is the battery, where that noble mole is washed by waves, and cooled by breezes, which a few hours previous were out of sight of land. Look at the crowds of water-gazers there.

Circumambulate the city of a dreamy Sabbath afternoon. Go from Corlears Hook to Coenties Slip, and from thence, by Whitehall, northward. What do you see?—Posted like silent sentinels all around the town, stand thousands upon thousands of mortal men fixed in ocean reveries. Some leaning against the spiles; some seated upon the pier-heads; some looking over the bulwarks of ships from China; some high aloft in the rigging, as if striving to get a still better seaward peep. But these are all landsmen; of week days pent up in lath and plaster—tied to counters, nailed to benches, clinched to desks. How then is this? Are the green fields gone? What do they here?

But look! here come more crowds, pacing straight for the water, and seemingly bound for a dive. Strange! Nothing will content them but the extremest limit of the land; loitering under the shady lee of yonder warehouses will not suffice. No. They must get just as nigh the water as they possibly can without falling in. And there they stand—miles of them—leagues. Inlanders all, they come from lanes and alleys, streets and avenues—north, east, south, and west. Yet here they all unite. Tell me, does the magnetic virtue of the needles of the compasses of all those ships attract them thither?

Once more. Say, you are in the country; in some high land of lakes. Take almost any path you please, and ten to one it carries you down in a dale, and leaves you there by a pool in the stream. There is magic in it. Let the most absent-minded of men be plunged in his deepest reveries—stand that man on his legs, set his feet a-going, and he will infallibly lead you to water, if water there be in all that region. Should you ever be athirst in the great American desert, try this experiment, if your caravan happen to lie supplied with a metaphysical professor. Yes, as every one knows, meditation and water are wedded for ever.

But here is an artist. He desires to paint you the dreamiest, shadiest, quietest, most enchanting bit of romantic landscape in all the valley of the Saco. What is the chief element he employs? There stand his trees, each with a hollow trunk, as if a hermit and a crucifix were within; and here sleeps his meadow, and there sleep his cattle; and up from yonder cottage goes a sleepy smoke. Deep into distant woodlands winds a mazy way, reaching to overlapping spurs of mountains bathed in their hill-side blue. But though the picture lies thus tranced, and though this pine-tree shakes down its sighs like leaves upon this shepherd's head, yet all were vain, unless the shepherd's eye were fixed upon the magic stream before him. Go visit the Prairies in June, when for scores on scores of miles you wade knee-deep among Tiger-lilies—what is the one charm wanting?—Water—there is not a drop of water there! Were Niagara but a cataract of sand, would you travel your thousand miles to see it? Why did the poor poet of Tennessee, upon suddenly receiving two handfuls of silver, deliberate whether to buy him a coat, which he sadly needed, or invest his money in a pedestrian trip to Rockaway Beach? Why is almost every robust healthy boy with a robust healthy soul in him, at some time or other crazy to go to sea? Why upon your first voyage as a passenger, did you yourself feel such a mystical vibration, when first told that you and your ship were now out of sight of land? Why did the old Persians hold the sea holy? Why did the Greeks give it a separate deity, and own brother of Jove? Surely all this is not without meaning. And still deeper the meaning of that story of Narcissus, who because he could not grasp the tormenting, mild image he saw in the fountain, plunged into it and was drowned. But that same image, we ourselves see in all rivers and oceans. It is the image of the ungraspable phantom of life; and this is the key to it all.

Now, when I say that I am in the habit of going to sea whenever I begin to grow hazy about the eyes, and begin to be over conscious of my lungs, I do not mean to have it inferred that I ever go to sea as a passenger. For to go as a passenger you must needs have a purse, and a purse is but a rag unless you have something in it. Besides, passengers get sea-sick—grow quarrelsome—don't sleep of nights—do not enjoy themselves much, as a general thing;—no, I never go as a passenger; nor, though I am something of a salt, do I ever go to sea as a Commodore, or a Captain, or a Cook. I abandon the glory and distinction of such offices to those who like them. For my part, I abominate all honorable respectable toils, trials, and tribulations of every kind whatsoever. It is quite as much as I can do to take care of myself, without taking care of ships, barques, brigs, schooners, and what not. And as for going as cook,—though I confess there is considerable glory in that, a cook being a sort of officer on ship-board—yet, somehow, I never fancied broiling fowls; though once broiled, judiciously buttered, and judgmatically salted and peppered, there is no one who will speak more respectfully, not to say reverentially, of a broiled fowl than I will. It is out of the idolatrous dotings of the old Egyptians upon broiled ibis and roasted river horse, that you see the mummies of those creatures in their huge bake-houses the pyramids.

No, when I go to sea, I go as a simple sailor, right before the mast, plumb down into the forecastle, aloft there to the royal mast-head. True, they rather order me about some, and make me jump from spar to spar, like a grasshopper in a May meadow. And at first, this sort of thing is unpleasant enough. It touches one's sense of honor, particularly if you come of an old established family in the land, the Van Rensselaers, or Randolphs, or Hardicanutes. And more than all, if just previous to putting your hand into the tar-pot, you have been lording it as a country schoolmaster, making the tallest boys stand in awe of you. The transition is a keen one, I assure you, from a schoolmaster to a sailor, and requires a strong decoction of Seneca and the Stoics to enable you to grin and bear it. But even this wears off in time.

What of it, if some old hunks of a sea-captain orders me to get a broom and sweep down the decks? What does that indignity amount to, weighed, I mean, in the scales of the New Testament? Do you think the archangel Gabriel thinks anything the less of me, because I promptly and respectfully obey that old hunks in that particular instance? Who ain't a slave? Tell me that. Well, then, however the old sea-captains may order me about—however they may thump and punch me about, I have the satisfaction of knowing that it is all right; that everybody else is one way or other served in much the same way— either in a physical or metaphysical point of view, that is; and so the universal thump is passed round, and all hands should rub each other's shoulder-blades, and be content.

Again, I always go to sea as a sailor, because they make a point of paying me for my trouble, whereas they never pay passengers a single penny that I ever heard of. On the contrary, passengers themselves must pay. And there is all the difference in the world between paying and being paid. The act of paying is perhaps the most uncomfortable infliction that the two orchard thieves entailed upon us. But *being paid*,—what will compare with it? The urbane activity with which a man receives money is really marvellous, considering that we so earnestly believe money to be the root of all earthly ills, and that on no account can a monied man enter heaven. Ah! how cheerfully we consign ourselves to perdition!

Finally, I always go to sea as a sailor, because of the wholesome exercise and pure air of the forecastle deck. For as in this world, head winds are far more prevalent than winds from astern (that is, if you never violate the Pythagorean maxim), so for the most part the Commodore on the quarter-deck gets his atmosphere at second hand from the sailors on the forecastle. He thinks he breathes it first; but not so. In much the same way do the commonalty lead their leaders in many other things, at the same time that the leaders little suspect it. But wherefore it was that after having repeatedly smelt the sea as a merchant sailor, I should now take it into my head to go on a whaling voyage; this the invisible police officer of the Fates, who has the constant surveillance of me, and secretly dogs me, and influences me in some unaccountable way—he can better answer than any one else. And, doubtless, my going on this whaling voyage, formed part of the grand programme of Providence that was drawn up a long time ago. It came in as a sort of brief interlude and solo between more extensive performances. I take it that this part of the bill must have run something like this:

> *"Grand Contested Election for the Presidency of the*
> *United States"*
> "Whaling Voyage by One Ishmael"
> "Bloody battle in Afghanistan"

Though I cannot tell why it was exactly that those stage managers, the Fates, put me down for this shabby part of a whaling voyage, when others were set down for magnificent parts in high tragedies, and short and easy parts in genteel comedies, and jolly parts in farces—though I cannot tell why this was exactly; yet, now that I recall all the circumstances, I think I can see a little into the springs and motives which being cunningly presented to me under various disguises, induced me to set about performing the part I did, besides cajoling me into the delusion that it was a choice resulting from my own unbiased freewill and discriminating judgment.

Chief among these motives was the overwhelming idea of the great whale himself. Such a portentous and mysterious monster roused all my curiosity. Then the wild and distant seas where he rolled his island bulk; the undeliverable, nameless perils of the whale; these, with all the attending marvels of a thousand Patagonian sights and sounds, helped to sway me to my wish. With other men, perhaps, such things would not have been inducements; but as for me, I am tormented with an everlasting itch for things remote. I love to sail forbidden seas and land on barbarous coasts. Not ignoring what is good, I am quick to perceive a horror, and could still be social with it—would they let me—since it is but well to be on friendly terms with all the inmates of the place one lodges in.

By reason of these things, then, the whaling voyage was welcome; the great flood-gates of the wonder-world swung open, and in the wild conceits that swayed me to my purpose, two and two there floated into my inmost soul, endless processions of the whale, and, mid most of them all, one grand hooded phantom, like a snow hill in the air.

• • •

I stuffed a shirt or two into my old carpet-bag, tucked it under my arm, and started for Cape Horn and the Pacific. Quitting the good city of old Manhatto, I duly arrived in New Bedford. It was on a Saturday night in December. Much was I disappointed upon learning that the little packet for Nantucket had already sailed, and that no way of reaching that place would offer, till the following Monday.

As most young candidates for the pains and penalties of whaling stop at this same New Bedford, thence to embark on their voyage, it may as well be related that I, for one, had no idea of so doing. For my mind was made up to sail in no other than a Nantucket craft, because there was a fine, boisterous something about everything connected with that famous old island, which amazingly pleased me. Besides though New Bedford has of late been gradually monopolizing the business of whaling, and though in this matter poor old Nantucket is now much behind her, yet Nantucket was her great original—the Tyre of this Carthage;—the place where the first dead American whale was stranded. Where else but from Nantucket did those aboriginal whalemen, the Red-Men, first sally out in canoes to give chase to the Leviathan? And where but from Nantucket, too, did that first adventurous little sloop put forth, partly laden with imported cobblestones—so goes the story—to throw at the whales, in order to discover when they were nigh enough to risk a harpoon from the bowsprit?

Now having a night, a day, and still another night following before me in New Bedford, ere I could embark for my destined port, it became a matter of concernment where I was to eat and sleep meanwhile. It was a very dubious-looking, nay, a very dark and dismal night, bitingly cold and cheerless. I knew no one in the place. With anxious grapnels I had sounded my pocket, and only brought up a few pieces of silver,—So, wherever you go, Ishmael, said I to myself, as I stood in the middle of a dreary street shouldering my bag, and comparing the gloom towards the north with the darkness towards the south—wherever in your wisdom you may conclude to lodge for the night, my dear Ishmael, be sure to inquire the price, and don't be too particular.

With halting steps I paced the streets, and passed the sign of "The Crossed Harpoons"—but it looked too expensive and jolly there. Further on, from the bright red windows of the "Sword-Fish Inn," there came such fervent rays, that it seemed to have melted the packed snow and ice from before the house, for everywhere else the congealed frost lay ten inches thick in a hard, asphaltic pavement—rather weary for me, when I struck my foot against the flinty projections, because from hard, remorseless service the soles of my boots were in a most miserable plight. Too expensive and jolly, again thought I, pausing one moment to watch the broad glare in the street, and hear the sounds of the tinkling glasses within. But go on, Ishmael, said I at last; don't you hear? get away from before the door; your patched boots are stopping the way. So on I went. I now by instinct followed the streets that took me waterward, for there, doubtless, were the cheapest, if not the cheeriest inns.

Such dreary streets! blocks of blackness, not houses, on either hand, and here and there a candle, like a candle moving about in a tomb. At this hour of the night, of the last day of the week, that quarter of the town proved all but deserted. But presently I came to a smoky light proceeding from a low, wide building, the door of which stood invitingly open. It had a careless look, as if it were meant for the uses of the public; so, entering, the first thing I did was to stumble over an ash-box in the porch. Ha! thought I, ha, as the flying particles almost choked me, are these ashes from that destroyed city, Gomorrah? But "The Crossed Harpoons," and "The Sword-Fish?"—this, then, must needs be the sign of "The Trap." However, I picked myself up and hearing a loud voice within, pushed on and opened a second, interior door.

It seemed the great Black Parliament sitting in Tophet. A hundred black faces turned round in their rows to peer; and beyond, a black Angel of Doom was beating a book in a pulpit. It was a negro church; and the preacher's text was about the blackness of darkness, and the weeping and wailing and teeth-gnashing there. Ha, Ishmael, muttered I, backing out, Wretched entertainment at the sign of "The Trap!"

Moving on, I at last came to a dim sort of light not far from the docks, and heard a forlorn creaking in the air; and looking up, saw a swinging sign over the door with a white painting upon it, faintly representing a tall straight jet of misty spray, and these words underneath—"The Spouter-Inn:—Peter Coffin."

Coffin?—Spouter?—Rather ominous in that particular connexion, thought I. But it is a common name in Nantucket, they say, and I suppose this Peter here is an emigrant from there. As the light looked so dim, and the place, for the time, looked quiet enough, and the dilapidated little wooden house itself looked as if it might have been carted here from the ruins of some burnt district, and as the swinging sign had a poverty-stricken sort of creak to it, I thought that here was the very spot for cheap lodgings, and the best of pea coffee.

It was a queer sort of place—a gable-ended old house, one side palsied as it were, and leaning over sadly. It stood on a sharp bleak corner, where that tempestuous wind Euroclydon kept up a worst howling than ever it did about poor Paul's tossed craft. Euroclydon, nevertheless, is a mighty pleasant zephyr to any one in-doors, with his feet on the hob quietly toasting for bed. "In judging of that tempestuous wind called Euroclydon," says an old writer—of whose works I possess the only copy extant—"it maketh a marvellous difference, whether thou lookest out at it from a glass window where the frost is all on the outside, or whether thou observest it from that sashless window, where the frost is on both sides, and of which the wight Death is the only glazier." True enough, thought I, as this passage occurred to my mind—old black-letter, thou reasonest well. Yes, these eyes are windows, and this body of mine is the house. What a pity they didn't stop up the chinks and the crannies though, and thrust in a little lint here and there. But it's too late to make any improvements now. The universe is finished; the copestone is on, and the chips were carted off a million years ago. Poor Lazarus there, chattering his teeth against the curbstone for his pillow, and shaking off his tatters with his shiverings, he might plug up both ears with rags, and put a corn-cob into his mouth, and yet that would not keep out the tempestuous Euroclydon. Euroclydon! says old Dives, in his red silken wrapper—(he had a redder one afterwards) pooh, pooh! What a fine frosty night; how Orion glitters; what northern lights! Let them talk of their oriental summer climes of everlasting conservatories; give me the privilege of making my own summer with my own coals.

But what thinks Lazarus? Can he warm his blue hands by holding them up to the grand northern lights? Would not Lazarus rather be in Sumatra than here? Would he not far rather lay him down lengthwise along the line of the equator; yea, ye gods! go down to the fiery pit itself, in order to keep out this frost?

Now, that Lazarus should lie stranded there on the curbstone before the door of Dives, this is more wonderful than that an iceberg should be moored to one of the Moluccas. Yet Dives himself, he too lives like a Czar in an ice palace made of frozen sighs, and being a president of a temperance society, he only drinks the tepid tears of orphans.

But no more of this blubbering now, we are going a-whaling, and there is plenty of that yet to come. Let us scrape the ice from our frosted feet, and see what sort of a place this "Spouter" may be.

Entering that gable-ended Spouter-Inn, you found yourself in a wide, low, straggling entry with old-fashioned wainscots, reminding one of the bulwarks of some condemned old craft. On one side hung a very large oil-painting so thoroughly besmoked, and every way defaced, that in the unequal cross-lights by which you viewed it, it was only by diligent study and a series of systematic visits to it, and careful inquiry of the neighbors, that you could any way arrive at an understanding of its purpose. Such unaccountable masses of shades and shadows, that at first you almost thought some ambitious young artist, in the time of the New England hags, had endeavored to delineate chaos bewitched.

But by dint of much and earnest contemplation, and oft repeated ponderings, and especially by throwing open the little window towards the back of the entry, you at last come to the conclusion that such an idea, however wild, might not be altogether unwarranted.

But what most puzzled and confounded you was a long, limber, portentous, black mass of something hovering in the centre of the picture over three blue, dim, perpendicular lines floating in a nameless yeast. A boggy, soggy, squitchy picture truly, enough to drive a nervous man distracted. Yet was there a sort of indefinite, half-attained, unimaginable sublimity about it that fairly froze you to it, till you involuntarily took an oath with yourself to find out what that marvellous painting meant. Ever and anon a bright, but, alas, deceptive idea would dart you through.—It's the Black Sea in a midnight gale.—It's the unnatural combat of the four primal elements.—It's a blasted heath.—It's a Hyperborean winter scene.—It's the breaking-up of the ice-bound stream of Time. But at last all these fancies yielded to that one portentous something in the picture's midst. *That* once found out, and all the rest were plain. But stop; does it not bear a faint resemblance to a gigantic fish? even the great leviathan himself?

In fact, the artist's design seemed this: a final theory of my own, partly based upon the aggregated opinions of many aged persons with whom I conversed upon the subject. The picture represents a Cape-Horner in a great hurricane; the half-foundered ship weltering there with its three dismantled masts alone visible; and an exasperated whale, purposing to spring clean over the craft, is in the enormous act of impaling himself upon the three mast-heads.

The opposite wall of this entry was hung all over with a heathenish array of monstrous clubs and spears. Some were thickly set with glittering teeth resembling ivory saws; others were tufted with knots of human hair; and one was sickle-shaped, with a vast handle sweeping round like the segment made in the new-mown grass by a long-armed mower. You shuddered as you gazed, and wondered what monstrous cannibal and savage could ever have gone a death-harvesting with such a hacking, horrifying implement. Mixed with these were rusty old whaling lances and harpoons all broken and deformed. Some were sto-ried weapons. With this once long lance, now wildly elbowed, fifty years ago did Nathan Swain kill fifteen whales between a sunrise and a sunset. And that harpoon—so like a corkscrew now—was flung in Javan seas, and run away with by a whale, years afterwards slain off the Cape of Blanco. The original iron entered nigh the tail, and, like a rest-less needle sojourning in the body of a man, travelled full forty feet, and at last was found imbedded in the hump.

Crossing this dusky entry, and on through yon low-arched way—cut through what in old times must have been a great central chimney with fire-places all round—you enter the public room. A still duskier place is this, with such low ponderous beams above, and such old wrinkled planks beneath, that you would almost fancy you trod some old craft's cockpits, especially of such a howling night, when this corner-anchored old ark rocked so furiously. On one side stood a long, low, shelf-like table covered with cracked glass cases, filled with dusty rari-ties gathered from this wide world's remotest nooks. Projecting from the further angle of the room stands a dark-looking den—the bar—a rude attempt at a right whale's head. Be that how it may, there stands the vast arched bone of the whale's jaw, so wide, a coach might almost drive beneath it. Within are shabby shelves, ranged round with old decanters, bottles, flasks; and in those jaws of swift destruction, like another cursed Jonah (by which name indeed they called him), bustles a little withered old man, who, for their money, dearly sells the sailors deliriums and death.

Abominable are the tumblers into which he pours his poison. Though true cylinders without—within, the villanous green goggling glasses deceitfully tapered downwards to a cheating bottom. Parallel meridians rudely pecked into the glass, surround these footpads' gob-lets. Fill to *this* mark, and your charge is but a penny; to *this* a penny more; and so on to the full glass—the Cape Horn measure, which you may gulp down for a shilling.

Upon entering the place I found a number of young seamen gath-ered about a table, examining by a dim light divers specimens of *skrimshander.* I sought the landlord, and telling him I desired to be accommodated with a room, received for answer that his house was full—not a bed unoccupied. "But avast," he added, tapping his forehead, "you hain't no objections to sharing a harpooneer's blanket, have ye? I s'pose you are goin' a whalin', so you'd better get used to that sort of thing."

I told him that I never liked to sleep two in a bed; that if I should ever do so, it would depend upon who the harpooneer might be, and that if he (the landlord) really had no other place for me, and the harpooneer was not decidedly objectionable, why rather than wander further about a strange town on so bitter a night, I would put up with the half of any decent man's blanket.

"I thought so. All right; take a seat. Supper?—you want supper? Supper'll be ready directly."

I sat down on an old wooden settle, carved all over like a bench on the Battery. At one end a ruminating tar was still further adorning it with his jack-knife, stooping over and diligently working away at the space between his legs. He was trying his hand at a ship under full sail, but he didn't make much headway, I thought.

At last some four or five of us were summoned to our meal in an adjoining room. It was cold as Iceland—no fire at all—the landlord said he couldn't afford it. Nothing but two dismal tallow candles, each in a winding sheet. We were fain to button up our monkey jackets, and hold to our lips cups of scalding tea with our half frozen fingers. But the fare was of the most substantial kind—not only meat and potatoes, but dumplings; good heavens! dumplings for supper! One young fellow in a green box coat, addressed himself to these dumplings in a most direful manner.

"My boy," said the landlord, "you'll have the nightmare to a dead sartainty."

"Landlord," I whispered, "that aint the harpooneer, is it?"

"Oh, no," said he, looking a sort of diabolically funny, "the harpooneer is a dark complexioned chap. He never eats dumplings, he don't—he eats nothing but steaks, and likes 'em rare."

"The devil he does," says I. "Where is that harpooneer? Is he here?"

"He'll be here afore long," was the answer.

I could not help it, but I began to feel suspicious of this "dark complexioned" harpooneer. At any rate, I made up my mind that if it so turned out that we should sleep together, he must undress and get into bed before I did.

Supper over, the company went back to the bar-room, when, knowing not what else to do with myself, I resolved to spend the rest of the evening as a looker on.

Presently a rioting noise was heard without. Starting up, the landlord cried, "That's the Grampus's crew. I seed her reported in the offing this morning; a three years' voyage, and a full ship. Hurrah, boys; now we'll have the latest news from the Feegees."

A tramping of sea boots was heard in the entry; the door was flung open, and in rolled a wild set of mariners enough. Enveloped in their shaggy watch coats, and with their heads muffled in woollen comforters, all bedarned and ragged, and their beards stiff with icicles, they seemed an eruption of bears from Labrador. They had just landed from their boat, and this was the first house they entered. No wonder, then, that they made a straight wake for the whale's mouth—the bar—when the wrinkled little old Jonah, there officiating, soon poured them out brimmers all round. One complained of a bad cold in his head, upon which Jonah mixed him a pitch-like potion of gin and molasses, which he swore was a sovereign cure for all colds and catarrhs whatsoever, never mind of how long standing, or whether caught off the coast of Labrador, or on the weather side of an ice-island.

The liquor soon mounted into their heads, as it generally does even with the arrantest topers newly landed from sea, and they began capering about most obstreperously.

I observed, however, that one of them held somewhat aloof, and though he seemed desirous not to spoil the hilarity of his shipmates by his own sober face, yet upon the whole he refrained from making as much noise as the rest. This man interested me at once; and since the sea-gods had ordained that he should soon become my shipmate (though but a sleeping-partner one, so far as this narrative is concerned), I will here venture upon a little description of him. He stood full six feet in height, with noble shoulders, and a chest like a cofferdam. I have seldom seen such brawn in a man. His face was deeply brawn and burnt, making his white teeth dazzling by the contrast; while in the deep shadows of his eyes floated some reminiscences that did not seem to give him much joy. His voice at once announced that he was a Southerner, and from his fine stature, I thought he must be one of those tall mountaineers from the Alleganian Ridge in Virginia. When the revelry of his companions had mounted to its height, this man slipped away unobserved, and I saw no more of him till he became my comrade on the sea. In a few minutes, however, he was missed by his shipmates, and being, it seems, for some reason a huge favorite with them, they raised a cry of "Bulkington! Bulkington! where's Bulkington?" and darted out of the house in pursuit of him.

It was now about nine o'clock, and the room seeming almost supernaturally quiet after these orgies, I began to congratulate myself upon a little plan that had occurred to me just previous to the entrance of the seamen.

No man prefers to sleep two in a bed. In fact, you would a good deal rather not sleep with your own brother. I don't know how it is but people like to be private when they are sleeping. And when it comes to sleeping with an unknown stranger, in a strange inn, in a strange town, and that stranger a harpooneer, then your objections indefinitely multiply. Nor was there any earthly reason why I as a sailor should sleep two in a bed, more than anybody else; for sailors no more sleep two in a bed at sea, than bachelor Kings do ashore. To be sure they all sleep together in one apartment, but you have your own hammock, and cover yourself with your own blanket, and sleep in your own skin.

The more I pondered over this harpooneer, the more I abominated the thought of sleeping with him. It was fair to presume that being a harpooneer, his linen or woollen, as the case might be, would not be of the tidiest, certainly none of the finest. I began to twitch all over. Besides, it was getting late, and my decent harpooneer ought to be home and going

bedwards. Suppose now, he should tumble in upon me at midnight—
how could I tell from what vile hole he had been coming?

"Landlord! I've changed my mind about that harpooneer.—I shan't
sleep with him. I'll try the bench here."

"Just as you please; I'm sorry I can't spare ye a tablecloth for a mattress,
and it's a plaguy rough board here"—feeling of the knots and notches.
"But wait a bit, Skrimshander; I've got a carpenter's plane there in the
bar—wait, I say, and I'll make ye snug enough." So saying he procured the
plane; and with his old silk handkerchief first dusting the bench,
vigorously set to planing away at my bed, the while grinning like an ape.
The shavings flew right and left; till at last the plane-iron came bump
against an indestructible knot. The landlord was near spraining his
wrist, and I told him for heaven's sake to quit—the bed was soft enough
to suit me, and I did not know how all the planing in the world could
make eider down of a pine plank. So gathering up the shavings with
another grin, and throwing them into the great stove in the middle of the
room, he went about his business, and left me in a brown study.

I now took the measure of the bench, and found that it was a foot
too short; but that could be mended with a chair. But it was a foot too
narrow, and the other bench in the room was about four inches higher
than the planed one—so there was no yoking them. I then placed the
first bench lengthwise along the only clear space against the wall,
leaving a little interval between, for my bark to settle down in. But I
soon found that there came such a draught of cold air over me from
under the sill of the window, that this plan would never do at all, especially as another current from the rickety door met the one from the
window, and both together formed a series of small whirlwinds in the
immediate vicinity of the spot where I had thought to spend the night.

The devil fetch that harpooneer, thought I, but stop, couldn't I steal
a march on him—bolt his door inside, and jump into his bed, not to
be wakened by the most violent knockings? It seemed no bad idea; but
upon second thoughts I dismissed it. For who could tell but what the
next morning, so soon as I popped out of the room, the harpooneer
might be standing in the entry, all ready to knock me down!

Still, looking round me again, and seeing no possible chance of spending a sufferable night unless in some other person's bed, I began to think that after all I might be cherishing unwarrantable prejudices against this unknown harpooneer. Thinks I, I'll wait awhile; he must be dropping in before long. I'll have a good look at him then, and perhaps we may become jolly good bedfellows after all—there's no telling.

But though the other boarders kept coming in by ones, twos, and threes, and going to bed, yet no sign of my harpooneer.

"Landlord!" said I, "what sort of a chap is he—does he always keep such late hours?" It was now hard upon twelve o'clock.

The landlord chuckled again with his lean chuckle, and seemed to be mightily tickled at something beyond my comprehension. "No," he answered, "generally he's an early bird—airley to bed and early to rise—yes, he's the bird what catches the worm. But to-night he went out a peddling, you see, and I don't see what on airth keeps him so late, unless, may be, he can't sell his head."

"Can't sell his head?—What sort of a bamboozingly story is this you are telling me?" getting into a towering rage. "Do you pretend to say, landlord, that this harpooneer is actually engaged this blessed Saturday night, or rather Sunday morning, in peddling his head around this town?"

"That's precisely it," said the landlord, "and I told him he couldn't sell it here, the market's overstocked."

"With what?" shouted I.

"With heads to be sure; ain't there too many heads in the world?"

"I tell you what it is, landlord," said I, quite calmly, "you'd better stop spinning that yarn to me—I'm not green."

"May be not," taking out a stick and whittling a toothpick, "but I rayther guess you'll be done *brown* if that ere harpooneer hears you a slanderin' his head."

"I'll break it for him," said I, now flying into a passion again at this unaccountable farrago of the landlord's.

"It's broke a'ready," said he.

"Broke," said I—"*broke*, do you mean?"

"Sartain, and that's the very reason he can't sell it, I guess."

"Landlord," said I, going up to him as cool as Mt. Hecla in a snow storm,—'landlord, stop whittling. You and I must understand one another, and that too without delay. I come to your house and want a bed; you tell me you can only give me half a one; that the other half belongs to a certain harpooneer. And about this harpooneer, whom I have not yet seen, you persist in telling me the most mystifying and exasperating stories, tending to beget in me an uncomfortable feeling towards the man whom you design for my bedfellow—a sort of con-nexion, landlord, which is an intimate and confidential one in the highest degree. I now demand of you to speak out and tell me who and what this harpooneer is, and whether I shall be in all respects safe to spend the night with him. And in the first place, you will be so good as to unsay that story about selling his head, which if true I take to be good evidence that this harpooneer is stark mad, and I've no idea of sleeping with a madman; and you, sir, *you* I mean, landlord, *you*, sir, by trying to induce me to do so knowingly, would thereby render yourself liable to a criminal prosecution."

"Wall," said the landlord, fetching a long breath, "that's a purty long sarmon for a chap that rips a little now and then. But be easy, be easy, this here harpooneer I have been tellin' you of has just arrived from the south seas, where he bought up a lot of 'balmed New Zealand heads (great curios, you know), and he's sold all on 'em but one, and that one he's trying to sell to-night, cause to-morrow's Sunday, and it would not do to be sellin' human heads about the streets when folks is goin' to churches. He wanted to, last Sunday, but I stopped him just as he was goin' out of the door with four heads strung on a string; for all the airth like a string of onions."

This account cleared up the otherwise unaccountable mystery, and showed that the landlord, after all, had had no idea of fooling me— but at the same time what could I think of a harpooneer who stayed out of a Saturday night clean into the holy Sabbath, engaged in such a cannibal business as selling the heads of dead idolators?

"Depend upon it, landlord, that harpooneer is a dangerous man."

"He pays reg'lar," was the rejoinder. "But come, it's getting dreadful late, you had better be turning flukes—it's a nice bed: Sal and me slept in that ere bed the night we were spliced. There's plenty room for two to kick about in that bed; it's an almighty big bed that. Why, afore we give it up, Sal used to put our Sam and little Johnny in the foot of it. But I got a dreaming and sprawling about one night, and somehow, Sam got pitched on the floor, and came near breaking his arm. Arter that, Sal said it wouldn't do. Come along here, I'll give ye a glim in a jiffy;" and so saying he lighted a candle and held it towards me, offering to lead the way. But I stood irresolute; when looking at a clock in the corner, he exclaimed "I vum it's Sunday—you won't see that harpooneer to-night; he's come to anchor somewhere—come along then; *do* come; *won't* ye come?"

I considered the matter a moment, and then up stairs we went, and I was ushered into a small room, cold as a clam, and furnished, sure enough, with a prodigious bed, almost big enough indeed for any four harpooneers to sleep abreast.

"There," said the landlord, placing the candle on a crazy old sea chest that did double duty as a wash-stand and centre table; "there, make yourself comfortable now, and good night to ye." I turned round from eyeing the bed, but he had disappeared.

Folding back the counterpane, I stooped over the bed. Though none of the most elegant, it yet stood the scrutiny tolerably well. I then glanced round the room; and besides the bedstead and centre table, could see no other furniture belonging to the place, but a rude shelf, the four walls, and a papered fireboard representing a man striking a whale. Of things not properly belonging to the room, there was a hammock lashed up, and thrown upon the floor in one corner; also a large seaman's bag, containing the harpooneer's wardrobe, no doubt in lieu of a land trunk. Likewise, there was a parcel of outlandish bone fish hooks on the shelf over the fire-place, and a tall harpoon standing at the head of the bed.

But what is this on the chest? I took it up, and held it close to the light, and felt it, and smelt it, and tried every way possible to arrive at some satisfactory conclusion concerning it. I can compare it to nothing but a large door mat, ornamented at the edges with little tinkling tags something like the stained porcupine quills round an Indian moccasin. There was a hole or slit in the middle of this mat, as you see the same in South American ponchos. But could it be possible that any sober harpooneer would get into a door mat, and parade the streets of any Christian town in that sort of guise? I put it on, to try it, and it weighed me down like a hamper, being uncommonly shaggy and thick, and I thought a little damp, as though this mysterious harpooneer had been wearing it of a rainy day. I went up in it to a bit of glass stuck against the wall, and I never saw such a sight in my life. I tore myself out of it in such a hurry that I gave myself a kink in the neck.

I sat down on the side of the bed, and commenced thinking about this head-peddling harpooneer, and his door mat. After thinking some time on the bed-side, I got up and took off my monkey jacket, and then stood in the middle of the room thinking. I then took off my coat, and thought a little more in my shirt sleeves. But beginning to feel very cold now, half undressed as I was, and remembering what the landlord said about the harpooneer's not coming home at all that night, it being so very late, I made no more ado, but jumped out of my pantaloons and boots, and then blowing out the light tumbled into bed, and commended myself to the care of heaven.

Whether that mattress was stuffed with corn-cobs or broken crockery, there is no telling, but I rolled about a good deal, and could not sleep for a long time. At last I slid off into a light doze, and had pretty nearly made a good offing towards the land of Nod, when I heard a heavy footfall in the passage, and saw a glimmer of light come into the room from under the door.

Lord save me, thinks I, that must be the harpooneer, the infernal head-peddler. But I lay perfectly still, and resolved not to say a word till spoken to. Holding a light in one hand, and that identical New

Zealand head in the other, the stranger entered the room, and without looking towards the bed, placed his candle a good way off from me on the floor in one corner, and then began working away at the knotted cords of the large bag I before spoke of as being in the room. I was all eagerness to see his face, but he kept it averted for some time while employed in unlacing the bag's mouth. This accomplished, however, he turned round—when, good heavens! what a sight! Such a face! It was of a dark, purplish, yellow color, here and there stuck over with large, blackish looking squares. Yes, it's just as I thought, he's a terrible bedfellow; he's been in a fight, got dreadfully cut, and here he is, just from the surgeon. But at that moment he chanced to turn his face so towards the light, that I plainly saw they could not be sticking-plasters at all, those black squares on his cheeks. They were stains of some sort or other. At first I knew not what to make of this; but soon an inkling of the truth occurred to me. I remembered a story of a white man—a whaleman too—who, falling among the cannibals, had been tattooed by them. I concluded that this harpooneer, in the course of his distant voyages, must have met with a similar adventure. And what is it, thought I, after all! It's only his outside; a man can be honest in any sort of skin. But then, what to make of his unearthly complexion, that part of it, I mean, lying round about, and completely independent of the squares of tattooing. To be sure, it might be nothing but a good coat of tropical tanning; but I never heard of a hot sun's tanning a white man into a purplish yellow one. However, I had never been in the South Seas; and perhaps the sun there produced these extraordinary effects upon the skin. Now, while all these ideas were passing through me like lightning, this harpooneer never noticed me at all. But, after some difficulty having opened his bag, he commenced fumbling in it, and presently pulled out a sort of tomahawk, and a seal-skin wallet with the hair on. Placing these on the old chest in the middle of the room, he then took the New Zealand head—a ghastly thing enough—and crammed it down into the bag. He now took off his hat—a new beaver hat—when I came nigh singing out with fresh sur-

prise. There was no hair on his head—none to speak of at least—
nothing but a small scalpknot twisted up on his forehead. His bald purplish head now looked for all the world like a mildewed skull. Had not
the stranger stood between me and the door, I would have bolted out of
it quicker than ever I bolted a dinner.

Even as it was, I thought something of slipping out of the window,
but it was the second floor back. I am no coward, but what to make of
this head-peddling purple rascal altogether passed my comprehension.
Ignorance is the parent of fear, and being completely nonplussed and
confounded about the stranger, I confess I was, now, as afraid of him
as if it was the devil himself who had thus broken into my room at the
dead of night. In fact; I was so afraid of him that I was not game
enough just then to address him, and demand a satisfactory answer
concerning what seemed inexplicable in him.

Meanwhile, he continued the business of undressing, and at last
showed his chest and arms. As I live, these covered parts of him were
checkered with the same squares as his face; his back, too, was all over
the same dark squares; he seemed to have been in a Thirty Years' War,
and just escaped from it with a sticking-plaster shirt. Still more, his very
legs were marked, as if a parcel of dark green frogs were running up the
trunks of young palms. It was now quite plain that he must be some
abominable savage or other shipped aboard of a whaleman in the South
Seas, and so landed in this Christian country. I quaked to think of it. A
peddler of heads too—perhaps the heads of his own brothers. He might
take a fancy to mine—heavens! look at that tomahawk!

But there was no time for shuddering, for now the savage went
about something that completely fascinated my attention, and convinced me that he must indeed be a heathen. Going to his heavy grego,
or wrapall, or dreadnaught, which he had previously hung on a chair,
he fumbled in the pockets, and produced at length a curious little
deformed image with a hunch on its back, and exactly the color of a
three days' old Congo baby. Remembering the embalmed head, at first
I almost thought that this black manikin was a real baby preserved in

some similar manner. But seeing that it was not at all limber, and that it glistened a good deal like polished ebony, I concluded that it must be nothing but a wooden idol, which indeed it proved to be.

For now the savage goes up to the empty fire-place, and removing the papered fire-board, sets up this little hunchbacked image, like a tenpin, between the andirons. The chimney jambs and all the bricks inside were very sooty, so that I thought this fire-place made a very appropriate little shrine or chapel for his Congo idol.

I now screwed my eyes hard towards the half hidden image, feeling but ill at ease meantime—to see what was next to follow. First he takes about a double handful of shavings out of his grego pocket, and places them carefully before the idol; then laying a bit of ship biscuit on top and applying the flame from the lamp, he kindled the shavings into a sacrificial blaze. Presently, after many hasty snatches into the fire, and still hastier withdrawals of his fingers (whereby he seemed to be scorching them badly), he at last succeeded in drawing out the biscuit; then blowing off the heat and ashes a little, he made a polite offer of it to the little negro. But the little devil did not seem to fancy such dry sort of fare at all; he never moved his lips. All these strange antics were accompanied by still stranger guttural-noises from the devotee, who seemed to be praying in a sing-song or else singing some pagan psalmody or other, during which his face twitched about in the most unnatural manner. At last extinguishing the fire, he took the idol up very unceremoniously, and bagged it again in his grego pocket as carelessly as if he were a sportsman bagging a dead woodcock.

All these queer proceedings increased my uncomfortableness, and seeing him now exhibiting strong symptoms of concluding his business operations, and jumping into bed with me, I thought it was high time, now or never, before the light was put out, to break the spell in which I had so long been bound.

But the interval I spent in deliberating what to say, was a fatal one. Taking up his tomahawk from the table, he examined the head of it for an instant, and then holding it to the light, with his mouth at the handle, he puffed out great clouds of tobacco smoke. The next moment the light was extinguished, and this wild cannibal, tomahawk between his teeth, sprang into bed with me. I sang out, I could not help it now; and giving a sudden grunt of astonishment he began feeling me.

Stammering out something, I knew not what, I rolled away from him against the wall, and then conjured him, whoever or whatever he might be, to keep quiet, and let me get up and light the lamp again. But his guttural responses satisfied me at once that he but ill comprehended my meaning.

"Who-e debel you?"—he at last said—"you no speak-e, dam-me, I kill-e." And so saying the lighted tomahawk began flourishing about me in the dark.

"Landlord, for God's sake, Peter Coffin!" shouted I. "Landlord! Watch! Coffin! Angels! save me!"

"Speak-e! tell-ee me who-ee be, or dam-me, I kill-e!" again growled the cannibal, while his horrid flourishings of the tomahawk scattered the hot tobacco ashes about me till I thought my linen would get on fire. But thank heaven, at that moment the landlord came into the room light in hand, and leaping from the bed I ran up to him.

"Don't be afraid now," said he, grinning again. "Queequeg here wouldn't harm a hair of your head."

"Stop your grinning," shouted I, "and why didn't you tell me that that infernal harpooneer was a cannibal?"

"I thought ye know'd it;—didn't I tell ye, he was a peddlin' heads around town?—but turn flukes again and go to sleep. Queequeg, look here—you sabbee me, I sabbee you—this man sleepe you—you sabbee?"

"Me sabbee plenty"—grunted Queequeg, puffing away at his pipe and sitting up in bed.

"You gettee in," he added, motioning to me with his tomahawk, and throwing the clothes to one side. He really did this in not only a civil but a really kind and charitable way. I stood looking at him a moment.

For all his tattooings he was on the whole a clean, comely looking cannibal. What's all this fuss I have been making about, thought I to myself—the man's a human being just as I am: he has just as much reason to fear me, as I have to be afraid of him. Better sleep with a sober cannibal than a drunken Christian.

"Landlord," said I, "tell him to stash his tomahawk there, or pipe, or whatever you call it; tell him to stop smoking, in short, and I will turn in with him. But I don't fancy having a man smoking in bed with me. It's dangerous. Besides, I ain't insured."

This being told to Queequeg, he at once complied, and again politely motioned me to get into bed—rolling over to one side as much as to say—I won't touch a leg of ye.

"Good night, landlord," said I, "you may go."

I turned in, and never slept better in my life.

from In the Heart of the Sea
by Nathaniel Philbrick

The whaleship Essex *left its home port of Nantucket in August, 1819. Fifteen months later, Captain George Pollard and first mate Owen Chase steered the ship west from the Galapagos Islands into the Pacific Ocean. The bizarre events that followed inspired the climactic scene in Moby Dick. Nathaniel Philbrick (born 1956) reconstructed the story using historical accounts and cabin-boy Thomas Nickerson's recently-discovered journal.*

E ven today, in an age of instantaneous communication and high-speed transportation, the scale of the Pacific is difficult to grasp. Sailing due west from Panama, it is 11,000 miles to the Malay Peninsula—almost four times the distance Columbus sailed to the New World—and it is 9,600 miles from the Bering Strait to Antarctica. The Pacific is also deep. Hidden beneath its blue surface are some of the planet's most spectacular mountain ranges, with canyons that plunge more than six miles into the watery blackness. Geologically, the volcano-rimmed Pacific is the most active part of the world. Islands rise up; islands disappear. Herman Melville called this sixty-four-million-square-mile ocean the "tide-beating heart of the earth."

By November 16, 1820, the *Essex* had sailed more than a thousand miles west of the Galapagos, following the equator as if it were an invisible lifeline leading the ship ever farther into the largest ocean in the world. Nantucket whalemen were familiar with at least part of the Pacific. Over the last three decades the coast of South America had become their own backyard. They also knew the western edge of the Pacific quite well. By the early part of the century, English whalers, most of them captained by Nantucketers, were regularly rounding the Cape of Good Hope and taking whales in the vicinity of Australia and New Zealand. In 1815, Hezekiah Coffin, the father of Pollard's young cousin Owen, had died during a provisioning stop in the fever-plagued islands off Timor, between Java and New Guinea.

Lying between the island of Timor and the west coast of South America is the Central Pacific, what Owen Chase called "an almost untraversed ocean." The longitudes and latitudes of islands with names such as Ohevahoa, Marokinee, Owyhee, and Mowee might be listed in Captain Pollard's navigational guide, but beyond that they were—save for blood-chilling rumors of native butchery and cannibalism—a virtual blank.

All this was about to change. Unknown to Pollard, only a few weeks earlier, on September 29, the Nantucket whaleships *Equator* and *Balaena* stopped at the Hawaiian island of Oahu for the first time. In 1823, Richard Macy would be the first Nantucketer to provision his ship at the Society Islands, now known as French Polynesia. But as far as Pollard and his men knew in November of 1820, they were at the edge of an unknown world filled with unimaginable dangers. And if they were to avoid the fate of the ship they'd encountered at Atacames, whose men had almost died of scurvy before they could reach the South American coast for provisions, there was no time for far-flung exploration. It had taken them more than a month to venture out this far, and it would take at least that to return. They had, at most, only a few months of whaling left before they must think about returning to South America and eventually to Nantucket.

So far, the whales they had sighted in this remote expanse of ocean had proved frustratingly elusive. "Nothing occurred worthy of note during this passage," Nickerson remembered, "with the exception of occasionally chasing a wild shoal of whales to no purpose." Tensions mounted among the *Essex*'s officers. The situation prompted Owen Chase to make an adjustment aboard his whaleboat. When he and his boat-crew did finally approach a whale, on November 16, it was he, Chase reported, not his boatsteerer, Benjamin Lawrence, who held the harpoon.

This was a radical and, for Lawrence, humiliating turn of events. A mate took over the harpoon only after he had lost all confidence in his boatsteerer's ability to fasten to a whale. William Comstock told of two instances when mates became so disgusted with their boat-steerers' unsuccessful attempts to harpoon whales that they ordered them aft and took the iron themselves. One mate, Comstock wrote, screamed, "Who are you? What are you? Miserable trash, scum of Nantucket, a whimpering boy from the chimney corner. By Neptune I think you are afraid of a whale." When the boatsteerer finally burst into tears, the mate ripped the harpoon from his hands and ordered him to take the steering oar.

With Chase at the bow and Lawrence relegated to the steering oar, the first mate's boat approached a patch of water where, Chase predicted, a whale would surface. Chase was, in his own words, "standing in the fore part, with the harpoon in my hand, well braced, expecting every instant to catch sight of one of the shoal which we were in, that I might strike." Unfortunately, a whale surfaced directly under their boat, hurling Chase and his crew into the air. Just as had occurred after their first attempt at killing a whale, off the Falkland Islands, Chase and his men found themselves clinging to a wrecked whaleboat.

Given the shortage of spare boats aboard the *Essex*, caution on the part of the officers might have been expected, but caution, at least when it came to pursuing whales, was not part of the first mate's makeup. Taking to heart the old adage "A dead whale or a stove boat," Chase reveled in the risk and danger of whaling. "The profession is one of great ambition," he would boast in his narrative, "and full of honorable excitement: a tame man is never known amongst them."

Four days later, on November 20, more than 1,500 nautical miles west of the Galapagos and just 40 miles south of the equator, the lookout saw spouts. It was about eight in the morning of a bright clear day. Only a slight breeze was blowing. It was a perfect day for killing whales.

Once they had sailed to within a half mile of the shoal, the two shipkeepers headed the *Essex* into the wind with the maintopsail aback, and the three boats were lowered. The whales, unaware that they were being pursued, sounded.

Chase directed his men to row to a specific spot, where they waited "in anxious expectation," scanning the water for the dark shape of a surfacing sperm whale. Once again, Chase tells us, he was the one with the harpoon, and sure enough, a small whale emerged just ahead of them and spouted. The first mate readied to hurl the harpoon and, for the second time in as many days of whaling, ran into trouble.

Chase had ordered Lawrence, the ex-harpooner, to steer the boat in close to the whale. Lawrence did so, so close that as soon as the harpoon sliced into it, the panicked animal whacked the already battered craft with its tail, opening up a hole in the boat's side. As water poured in, Chase cut the harpoon line with a hatchet and ordered the men to stuff their coats and shirts into the jagged opening. While one man bailed, they rowed back to the ship. Then they pulled the boat up onto the *Essex*'s deck.

By this time, both Pollard's and Joy's crews had fastened to whales. Angered that he had once again been knocked out of the hunt, Chase began working on his damaged boat with a fury, hoping to get the craft operable while whales were still to be taken. Although he could have outfitted and lowered the extra boat (the one they had bargained for in the Cape Verde Islands, now lashed to the rack over the quarterdeck), Chase felt it would be faster to repair the damaged boat temporarily by stretching some canvas across the hole. As he nailed the edges of the canvas to the boat, his after oarsman, Thomas Nickerson—all of fifteen years old—took over the helm of the *Essex* and steered the ship toward Pollard and Joy, whose whales had dragged them several miles to leeward. It was then that Nickerson saw something off the port bow.

It was a whale—a huge sperm whale, the largest they'd seen so far— a male about eighty-five feet long, they estimated, and approximately eighty tons. It was less than a hundred yards away, so close that they could see that its giant blunt head was etched with scars, and that it was pointed toward the ship. But this whale wasn't just large. It was acting strangely. Instead of fleeing in panic, it was floating quietly on the surface of the water, puffing occasionally through its blowhole, as if it were watching them. After spouting two or three times, the whale dove, then surfaced less than thirty-five yards from the ship.

Even with the whale just a stone's throw from the *Essex*, Chase did not see it as a threat. "His appearance and attitude gave us at first no alarm," he wrote. But suddenly the whale began to move. Its twenty-foot-wide tail pumped up and down. Slowly at first, with a slight side-to-side waggle, it picked up speed until the water crested around its massive barrel-shaped head. It was aimed at the *Essex*'s port side. In an instant, the whale was only a few yards away—"coming down for us," Chase remembered, "with great celerity."

In desperate hopes of avoiding a direct hit, Chase shouted to Nickerson, "Put the helm hard up!" Several other crew members cried out warnings. "Scarcely had the sound of the voices reached my ears," Nickerson remembered, "when it was followed by a tremendous crash." The whale rammed the ship just forward of the forechains.

The *Essex* shook as if she had struck a rock. Every man was knocked off his feet. Galapagos tortoises went skittering across the deck. "We looked at each other with perfect amazement," Chase recalled, "deprived almost of the power of speech."

As they pulled themselves up off the deck, Chase and his men had good reason to be amazed. Never before, in the entire history of the Nantucket whale fishery, had a whale been known to attack a ship. In 1807 the whaleship *Union* had accidentally plowed into a sperm whale at night and sunk, but something very different was happening here.

After the impact, the whale passed underneath the ship, bumping the bottom so hard that it knocked off the false keel—a formidable six-by-twelve-inch timber. The whale surfaced at the *Essex*'s starboard quarter. The creature appeared, Chase remembered, "stunned with the violence of the blow" and floated beside the ship, its tail only a few feet from the stern.

Instinctively, Chase grabbed a lance. All it would take was one perfectly aimed throw and the first mate might slay the whale that had dared to attack a ship. This giant creature would yield more oil than two, maybe even three, normal-sized whales. If Pollard and Joy also proved successful that day, they would be boiling down at least 150 barrels of oil in the next week—more than 10 percent of the *Essex*'s total capacity. They might be heading back to Nantucket in a matter of weeks instead of months.

Chase motioned to stab the bull—still lying hull-to-hull with the *Essex*. Then he hesitated. The whale's flukes, he noticed, were perilously close to the ship's rudder. If provoked, the whale might smash the delicate steering device with its tail. They were too far from land, Chase decided, to risk damaging the rudder.

For the first mate, it was a highly uncharacteristic display of caution. "But could [Chase] have foreseen all that so soon followed," Nickerson wrote, "he would probably have chosen the lesser evil and have saved the ship by killing the whale even at the expense of losing the rudder."

A sperm whale is uniquely equipped to survive a head-on collision with a ship. Stretching for a third of its length between the front of the whale's battering ram–shaped head and its vital organs is an oil-filled cavity perfectly adapted to cushioning the impact of a collision. In less than a minute, this eighty-ton bull was once again showing signs of life.

Shaking off its woozy lethargy, the whale veered off to leeward, swimming approximately six hundred yards away. There it began snapping its jaws and thrashing the water with its tail, "as if distracted," Chase wrote, "with rage and fury." The whale then swam to windward, crossing the *Essex*'s bow at a high rate of speed. Several hundred yards ahead of the ship, the whale stopped and turned in the *Essex*'s direction. Fearful that the ship might be taking on water, Chase had, by this point, ordered the men to rig the pumps. "[W]hile my attention was thus engaged," the first mate remembered, "I was aroused with the cry

of a man at the hatchway, 'Here he is—he is making for us again.' "
Chase turned and saw a vision of "fury and vengeance" that would
haunt him in the long days ahead.

With its huge scarred head halfway out of the water and its tail
beating the ocean into a white-water wake more than forty feet across,
the whale approached the ship at twice its original speed—at least six
knots. Chase, hoping "to cross the line of his approach before he could
get up to us, and thus avoid what I knew, if he should strike us again,
would prove our inevitable destruction," cried out to Nickerson, "Hard
up!" But it was too late for a change of course. With a tremendous
cracking and splintering of oak, the whale struck the ship just beneath
the anchor secured at the cathead on the port bow. This time the men
were prepared for the hit. Still, the force of the collision caused the
whalemen's heads to jounce on their muscled necks as the ship lurched
to a halt on the slablike forehead of the whale. The creature's tail continued to work up and down, pushing the 238-ton ship backward
until—as had happened after the knockdown in the Gulf Stream—
water surged up over the transom.

One of the men who had been belowdecks ran up onto the deck
shouting, "The ship is filling with water!" A quick glance down the
hatchway revealed that the water was already above the lower deck,
where the oil and provisions were stored.

No longer going backward, the *Essex* was now going down. The
whale, having humbled its strange adversary, disengaged itself from the
shattered timbers of the copper-sheathed hull and swam off to leeward,
never to be seen again.

The ship was sinking bow-first. The forecastle, where the black sailors
slept, was the first of the living quarters to flood, the men's sea chests and
mattresses floating on the rising tide. Next the water surged aft into the
blubber room, then into steerage, where Nickerson and the other Nantucketers slept. Soon even the mates' and captain's cabins were awash.

As the belowdecks creaked and gurgled, the black steward, William
Bond, on his own initiative, returned several times to the rapidly filling

aft cabins to retrieve Pollard's and Chase's trunks and—with great foresight—the navigational equipment. Meanwhile Chase and the rest of the crew cut the lashing off the spare whaleboat and carried it to the waist of the ship.

The *Essex* began to list dangerously to port. Bond made one last plunge below. Chase and the others carried the whaleboat to the edge of the deck, now only a few inches above the ocean's surface. When the trunks and other equipment had been loaded aboard, everyone, including Bond, scrambled into the boat, the tottering masts and yards looming above them. They were no more than two boat lengths away when the *Essex*, with an appalling slosh and groan, capsized behind them.

Just at that moment, two miles to leeward, Obed Hendricks, Pollard's boatsteerer, casually glanced over his shoulder. He couldn't believe what he saw. From that distance it looked as if the *Essex* had been hit by a sudden squall, the sails flying in all directions as the ship fell onto her beam-ends.

"Look, look," he cried, "what ails the ship? She is upsetting!"

But when the men turned to look, there was nothing to see. "[A] general cry of horror and despair burst from the lips of every man," Chase wrote, "as their looks were directed for [the ship], in vain, over every part of the ocean." The *Essex* had vanished below the horizon.

The two boat-crews immediately released their whales and began rowing back toward the place the *Essex* should have been—all the time speculating frantically about what had happened to the ship. It never occurred to any of them that, in Nickerson's words, "a whale [had] done the work." Soon enough, they could see the ship's hull "floating upon her side and presenting the appearance of a rock."

As Pollard and Joy approached, the eight men crowded into Chase's boat continued to stare silently at the ship. "[E]very countenance was marked with the paleness of despair," Chase recalled. "Not a word was spoken for several minutes by any of us; all appeared to be bound in a spell of stupid consternation."

From the point at which the whale first attacked, to the escape from the capsizing ship, no more than ten minutes had elapsed. In only a portion of that time, spurred by panic, eight of the crew had launched an unrigged whaleboat from the rack above the quarterdeck, a process that would have normally taken at least ten minutes and required the effort of the entire ship's crew. Now, here they were, with only the clothes on their backs, huddled in the whaleboat. It was not yet ten in the morning.

It was then that Chase fully appreciated the service that William Bond had rendered them. He had salvaged two compasses, two copies of Nathaniel Bowditch's *New American Practical Navigator,* and two quadrants. Chase later called this equipment "the probable instruments of our salvation. . . . [W]ithout them," he added, "all would have been dark and hopeless."

For his part, Thomas Nickerson was swept by a sense of grief, not for himself, but for the ship. The giant black craft that he had come to know so intimately had been dealt a deathblow. "Here lay our beautiful ship, a floating and dismal wreck," Nickerson lamented, "which but a few minutes before appeared in all her glory, the pride and boast of her captain and officers, and almost idolized by her crew."

Soon the other two whaleboats came within hailing distance. But no one said a word. Pollard's boat was the first to reach them. The men stopped rowing about thirty feet away. Pollard stood at the steering oar, staring at the capsized hulk that had once been his formidable command, unable to speak. He dropped down onto the seat of his whaleboat, so overcome with astonishment, dread, and confusion that Chase "could scarcely recognize his countenance." Finally Pollard asked, "My God, Mr. Chase, what is the matter?"

Chase's reply: "We have been stove by a whale."

Even by the colossal standards of a sperm whale, an eighty-five-foot bull is huge. Today, male sperm whales, which are on average three to four times bulkier than females, never grow past sixty-five feet. Sperm whale expert Hal Whitehead has his doubts that the *Essex* whale could have been as large as Chase and Nickerson claimed it was. However, the logs of Nantucket whalemen are filled with references to bulls that, given the amount of oil they yielded, must have been on the order of the *Essex* whale. It is an established fact that whalemen in both the nineteenth and twentieth centuries killed male sperm whales in disproportionate numbers: not only were they longer than the females but the males' oil-rich spermaceti organs accounted for a larger portion of that length. In 1820, before a century and a half of selective killing had rid the world of large bulls, it may have indeed been possible to encounter an eighty-five-foot sperm whale. Perhaps the most convincing evidence resides in the hallowed halls of the Nantucket Whaling Museum. There, leaning against the wall, is an eighteen-foot jaw taken from a bull that was esti-mated to have been at least eighty feet long.

The sperm whale has the largest brain of any animal that has ever lived on earth, dwarfing even that of the mighty blue whale. The large size of the sperm whale's brain may be related to its highly sophisticated ability to generate and process sound. Just beneath its blowhole, a sperm whale has what the whalemen referred to as a monkey's muzzle, a cartilaginous clapper system that scientists believe to be the source of the clicking sounds it uses to "see" the world through echolocation. Whales also use clicking signals to communicate over distances of up to five miles. Females tend to employ a Morse code–like series of clicks, known as a coda, and male sperm whales make slower, louder clicks called clangs. It has been speculated that males use clangs to announce themselves to eligible females and to warn off competing males.

Whalemen often heard sperm whales through the hulls of their ships. The sound—steady clicks at roughly half-second intervals—bore such a startling similarity to the tapping of a hammer that the whalemen dubbed the sperm whale "the carpenter fish." On the morning of November 20, 1820, sperm whales were not the only creatures filling the ocean with clicking sounds; there was also Owen Chase, busily nailing a piece of canvas to the bottom of an upturned whaleboat. With every blow of his hammer against the side of the damaged boat, Chase was unwittingly transmitting sounds down through the wooden skin of the whaleship out into the ocean. Whether or not the bull perceived these sounds as coming from another whale, Chase's hammering appears to have attracted the creature's attention.

Chase maintained that when the whale first struck the ship, it was going about three knots, the velocity of a whale at normal cruising speed. Whitehead, whose research vessel was once bumped into by a pregnant whale, speculates that the bull might have even initially run into the *Essex* by mistake.

Whatever prompted the encounter, the whale was clearly not pre-pared for something as solid and heavy as a whaleship, which at 238 tons weighed approximately three times more than it did. The *Essex* might have been an old, work-worn whaleship, but she had been built to take her share of abuse. She was constructed almost entirely of white oak, one of the toughest and strongest of woods. Her ribs had been hewn from immense timbers, at least a foot square. Over that, laid fore and aft, were oak planks four inches thick. On top of the planks was a sheathing of yellow pine, more than half an inch thick. Extending down from the waterline (the point of impact, according to Nickerson) was a layer of copper. The bull had slammed into a solid wooden wall.

What had begun as an experimental, perhaps unintentional jab with its head soon escalated into an all-out attack.

Like male elephants, bull sperm whales tend to be loners, moving from group to group of females and juveniles and challenging what-ever males they meet along the way. The violence of these encounters is legendary. One whaleman described what happened when a bull sperm whale tried to move in on another bull's group:

> When the approaching bull attempted to join the herd, he was attacked by one of the established bulls, which rolled over on its back and attacked with its jaw. . . . Large pieces of blubber and flesh were taken out. Both bulls then with-drew and again charged at full tilt. They locked jaws and wrestled, each seemingly to try to break the other's jaw. Great pieces of flesh again were torn from the animals' heads. Next they either withdrew or broke their holds, and

then charged each other again. The fight was even more strenuous this time, and little could be seen because of the boiling spray. The charge and withdrawal were repeated two or three times before the water quieted, and then for a few seconds the two could be seen lying head to head. The smaller bull then swam slowly away and did not attempt to rejoin the cows. . . . A whaleboat was dispatched, and the larger bull was captured. The jaw had been broken and was hanging by the flesh. Many teeth were broken and there were extensive head wounds.

Instead of fighting with its jaws and tail—the way whales commonly dispatched whaleboats—the *Essex* whale rammed the ship with its head, something that, Chase insisted, "has never been heard of amongst the oldest and most experienced whalers." But what most impressed the first mate was the remarkably astute way in which the bull employed its God-given battering ram. Both times the whale had approached the vessel from a direction "calculated to do us the most injury, by being made ahead, and thereby combining the speed of the two objects for the shock." Yet, even though it had come at the *Essex* from ahead, the whale had avoided striking the ship directly head-on, where the ship's heavily reinforced stem, the vertical timber at the leading edge of the bow, might have delivered a mortal gash.

Chase estimated that the whale was traveling at six knots when it struck the *Essex* the second time and that the ship was traveling at three knots. To bring the *Essex* to a complete standstill, the whale, whose mass was roughly a third of the ship's, would have to be moving at more than three times the speed of the ship, at least nine knots. One naval architect's calculations project that if the *Essex* had been a new ship, her oak planking would have withstood even this tremendous blow. Since the whale did punch a hole in the bow, the *Essex*'s twenty-one-year-old planking must have been significantly weakened by rot or marine growth.

Chase was convinced that the *Essex* and her crew had been the victims of "decided, calculating mischief" on the part of the whale. For a Nantucketer, it was a shocking thought. If other sperm whales should start ramming ships, it would be only a matter of time before the island's whaling fleet was reduced to so much flotsam and jetsam.

Chase began to wonder what "unaccountable destiny or design" had been at work. It almost seemed as if something—could it have been God?—had possessed the beast for its own strange, unfathomable purpose. Whatever or whoever might be behind it, Chase was convinced that "anything but chance" had sunk the *Essex*.

After listening to the first mate's account of the sinking, Pollard attempted to take command of the dire situation. Their first priority, he announced, was to get as much food and water out of the wreck as possible. To do that, they needed to cut away the masts so that the still partially floating hull could right. The men climbed onto the ship and began to hack away at the spars and rigging with hatchets from the whaleboats. As noon approached, Captain Pollard shoved off in his boat to take an observation with his quadrant. They were at latitude 0°40° south, longitude 119°0° west, just about as far from land as it was possible to be anywhere on earth.

Forty-five minutes later, the masts had been reduced to twenty-foot stumps and the *Essex* was floating partly upright again, at a forty-five-degree angle. Although most of the provisions were unreachable in the lower hold, there were two large casks of bread between decks in the waist of the ship. And since the casks were on the *Essex*'s upper side, the men could hope that they were still dry.

Through the holes they chopped into the deck they were able to extract six hundred pounds of hardtack. Elsewhere they broke through the planks to find casks of freshwater—more, in fact, than they could safely hold in their whaleboats. They also scavenged tools and equipment, including two pounds of boat nails, a musket, two pistols, and a small canister of powder. Several Galapagos tortoises swam to the whaleboats from the wreck, as did two skinny hogs. Then it began to blow.

In need of shelter from the mounting wind and waves, yet fearful the *Essex* might at any moment break up and sink like a stone, Pollard ordered that they tie up to the ship but leave at least a hundred yards of line between it and themselves. Like a string of ducklings trailing their mother, they spent the night in the lee of the ship.

The ship shuddered with each wave. Chase lay sleepless in his boat, staring at the wreck and reliving the catastrophe over and over again in his mind. Some of the men slept and others "wasted the night in unavailing murmurs," Chase wrote. Once, he admitted, he found himself breaking into tears.

Part of him was guilt-wracked, knowing that if he had only hurled the lance, it might have all turned out differently. (When it came time to write his own account of the attack, Chase would neglect to mention that he had the chance to lance the whale—an omission Nickerson made sure to correct in his narrative.) But the more Chase thought about it, the more he realized that no one could have expected a whale to attack a ship, and not just once but twice. Instead of acting as a whale was supposed to—as a creature "never before suspected of premeditated violence, and proverbial for its inoffensiveness"—this big bull had been possessed by what Chase finally took to be a very human concern for the other whales. "He came directly from the shoal which we had just before entered," the first mate wrote, "and in which we had struck three of his companions, as if fired with revenge for their sufferings."

The Open Boat
by Stephen Crane

Looking for story ideas, Stephen Crane (1871–1900) in 1897 signed on to work as an able seaman on the steamer Commodore *out of Florida. The ship, which was smuggling weapons to Cubans fighting for independence from Spain, sank in heavy seas 20 miles off the Florida coast. Crane and three companions escaped in a tiny dinghy. Subsequent events inspired this short story.*

None of them knew the colour of the sky. Their eyes glanced level, and were fastened upon the waves that swept toward them. These waves were of the hue of slate, save for the tops, which were of foaming white, and all of the men knew the colours of the sea. The horizon narrowed and widened, and dipped and rose, and at all times its edge was jagged with waves that seemed thrust up in points like rocks.

Many a man ought to have a bathtub larger than the boat which here rode upon the sea. These waves were most wrongfully and barbarously abrupt and tall, and each froth-top was a problem in small-boat navigation.

The cook squatted in the bottom, and looked with both eyes at the six inches of gunwale which separated him from the ocean. His sleeves were rolled over his fat forearms, and the two flaps of his unbuttoned vest dangled as he bent to bail out the boat. Often he said, "Gawd! that was a narrow clip." As he remarked it he invariably gazed eastward over the broken sea.

The oiler, steering with one of the two oars in the boat, sometimes raised himself suddenly to keep clear of water that swirled in over the stern. It was a thin little oar, and it seemed often ready to snap.

The correspondent, pulling at the other oar, watched the waves and wondered why he was there.

The injured captain, lying in the bow, was at this time buried in that profound dejection and indifference which comes, temporarily at least, to even the bravest and most enduring when, willy-nilly, the firm fails, the army loses, the ship goes down. The mind of the master of a vessel is rooted deep in the timbers of her, though he command for a day or a decade; and this captain had on him the stern impression of a scene in the greys of dawn of seven turned faces, and later a stump of a topmast with a white ball on it, that slashed to and fro at the waves, went low and lower, and down. Thereafter there was something strange in his voice. Although steady, it was deep with mourning, and of a quality beyond oration or tears.

"Keep 'er a little more south, Billie," said he.

"A little more south, sir," said the oiler in the stern.

A seat in his boat was not unlike a seat upon a bucking broncho, and by the same token a broncho is not much smaller. The craft pranced and reared and plunged like an animal. As each wave came, and she rose for it, she seemed like a horse making at a fence outrageously high. The manner of her scramble over these walls of water is a mystic thing, and, moreover, at the top of them were ordinarily these problems in white water, the foam racing down from the summit of each wave requiring a new leap, and a leap from the air. Then, after scornfully bumping a crest, she would slide and race and splash down a long incline, and arrive bobbing and nodding in front of the next menace.

A singular disadvantage of the sea lies in the fact that after successfully surmounting one wave you discover that there is another behind it just as important and just as nervously anxious to do something effective in the way of swamping boats. In a ten-foot dinghy one can get an idea of the resources of the sea in the line of waves that is not probable to the average experience which is never at sea in a dinghy. As each slaty wall of water approached, it shut all else from the view of the men in the boat, and it was not difficult to imagine that this particular wave was the final outburst of the ocean, the last effort of the grim water. There was a terrible grace in the move of the waves, and they came in silence, save for the snarling of the crests.

In the wan light the faces of the men must have been grey. Their eyes must have glinted in strange ways as they gazed steadily astern. Viewed from a balcony, the whole thing would doubtless have been weirdly picturesque. But the men in the boat had no time to see it, and if they had had leisure, there were other things to occupy their minds. The sun swung steadily up the sky, and they knew it was broad day because the colour of the sea changed from slate to emerald green streaked with amber lights, and the foam was like tumbling snow. The process of the breaking day was unknown to them. They were aware only of this effect upon the colour of the waves that rolled toward them.

In disjointed sentences the cook and the correspondent argued as to the difference between a life-saving station and a house of refuge. The cook had said: "There's a house of refuge just north of the Mosquito Inlet Light, and as soon as they see us they'll come off in their boat and pick us up."

"As soon as who see us?" said the correspondent.

"The crew," said the cook.

"Houses of refuge don't have crews," said the correspondent. "As I understand them, they are only places where clothes and grub are stored for the benefit of shipwrecked people. They don't carry crews."

"Oh, yes, they do," said the cook.

"No, they don't," said the correspondent.

"Well, we're not there yet, anyhow," said the oiler, in the stern.

"Well," said the cook, "perhaps it's not a house of refuge that I'm thinking of as being near Mosquito Inlet Light; perhaps it's a life-saving station."

"We're not there yet," said the oiler in the stern.

• • •

As the boat bounced from the top of each wave the wind tore through the hair of the hatless men, and as the craft plopped her stern down again the spray slashed past them. The crest of each of these waves was a hill, from the top of which the men surveyed for a moment a broad tumultuous expanse, shining and wind-riven. It was probably splendid, it was probably glorious, this play of the free sea, wild with lights of emerald and white and amber.

"Bully good thing it's an on-shore wind," said the cook. "If not, where would we be? Wouldn't have a show."

"That's right," said the correspondent.

The busy oiler nodded his assent.

Then the captain, in the bow, chuckled in a way that expressed humour, contempt, tragedy, all in one. "Do you think we've got much of a show now, boys?" said he.

Whereupon the three were silent, save for a trifle of hemming and hawing. To express any particular optimism at this time they felt to be childish and stupid, but they all doubtless possessed this sense of the situation in their minds. A young man thinks doggedly at such times. On the other hand, the ethics of their condition was decidedly against any open suggestion of hopelessness. So they were silent.

"Oh, well," said the captain, soothing his children, "we'll get ashore all right."

But there was that in his tone which made them think; so the oiler quoth, "Yes! if this wind holds."

The cook was bailing. "Yes! if we don't catch hell in the surf."

Canton-flannel gulls flew near and far. Sometimes they sat down on the sea, near patches of brown seaweed that rolled over the waves with a movement like carpets on a line in a gale. The birds sat comfortably in groups, and they were envied by some in the dinghy, for the wrath of the sea was no more to them than it was to a covey of prairie chickens a thousand miles inland. Often they came very close and stared at the men with black bead-like eyes. At these times they were uncanny and sinister in their unblinking scrutiny, and the men hooted angrily at them, telling them to be gone. One came, and evidently decided to alight on the top of the captain's head. The bird flew parallel to the boat and did not circle, but made short sidelong jumps in the air in chicken-fashion. His black eyes were wistfully fixed upon the captain's head. "Ugly brute," said the oiler to the bird. "You look as if you were made with a jackknife." The cook and the correspondent swore darkly at the creature. The captain naturally wished to knock it away with the end of the heavy painter, but he did not dare do it, because anything resembling an emphatic gesture would have capsized this freighted boat; and so, with his open hand, the captain gently and carefully waved the gull away. After it had been discouraged from the pursuit the captain breathed easier on account of his hair, and others breathed easier because the bird struck their minds at this time as being somehow gruesome and ominous.

In the meantime the oiler and the correspondent rowed. And also they rowed. They sat together in the same seat, and each rowed an oar. Then the oiler took both oars; then the correspondent took both oars; then the oiler; then the correspondent. They rowed and they rowed. The very ticklish part of the business was when the time came for the reclining one in the stern to take his turn at the oars. By the very last star of truth, it is easier to steal eggs from under a hen than it was to change seats in the dinghy. First the man in the stern slid his hand along the thwart and moved with care, as if he were of Sèvres. Then the man in the rowing-seat slid his hand along the other thwart. It was all done with the most extraordinary care. As the two sidled past each other, the whole party kept watchful eyes on the coming wave, and the captain cried: "Look out, now! Steady, there!"

The brown mats of seaweed that appeared from time to time were like islands, bits of earth. They were travelling, apparently, neither one way nor the other. They were, to all intents, stationary. They informed the men in the boat that it was making progress slowly toward the land.

The captain, rearing cautiously in the bow after the dinghy soared on a great swell, said that he had seen the lighthouse at Mosquito Inlet. Presently the cook remarked that he had seen it. The correspondent was at the oars then, and for some reason he too wished to look at the lighthouse; but his back was toward the far shore, and the waves were important, and for some time he could not seize an opportunity to turn his head. But at last there came a wave more gentle than the others, and when at the crest of it he swiftly scoured the western horizon.

"See it?" said the captain.

"No," said the correspondent, slowly; "I didn't see anything."

"Look again," said the captain. He pointed. "It's exactly in that direction."

At the top of another wave the correspondent did as he was bid, and this time his eyes chanced on a small, still thing on the edge of the swaying horizon. It was precisely like the point of a pin. It took an anxious eye to find a lighthouse so tiny.

"Think we'll make it, Captain?"

"If this wind holds and the boat don't swamp, we can't do much else," said the captain.

The little boat, lifted by each towering sea and splashed viciously by the crests, made progress that in the absence of seaweed was not apparent to those in her. She seemed just a wee thing wallowing, miraculously top up, at the mercy of five oceans. Occasionally a great spread of water, like white flames, swarmed into her.

"Bail her, cook," said the captain, serenely.

"All right, Captain," said the cheerful cook.

It would be difficult to describe the subtle brotherhood of men that was here established on the seas. No one said that it was so. No one mentioned it. But it dwelt in the boat, and each man felt it warm him. They were a captain, an oiler, a cook, and a correspondent, and they were friends—friends in a more curiously iron-bound degree than may be common. The hurt captain, lying against the water-jar in the bow, spoke always in a low voice and calmly; but he could never command a more ready and swiftly obedient crew than the motley three of the dinghy. It was more than a mere recognition of what was best for the common safety. There was surely in it a quality that was personal and heart-felt. And after this devotion to the commander of the boat, there was this comradeship, that the correspondent, for instance, who had been taught to be cynical of men, knew even at the time was the best experience of his life. But no one said that it was so. No one mentioned it.

"I wish we had a sail," remarked the captain. "We might try my overcoat on the end of an oar, and give you two boys a chance to rest." So the cook and the correspondent held the mast and spread wide the overcoat; the oiler steered; and the little boat made good way with her new rig. Sometimes the oiler had to scull sharply to keep a sea from breaking into the boat, but otherwise sailing was a success.

Meanwhile the lighthouse had been growing slowly larger. It had now almost assumed colour, and appeared like a little grey shadow on the sky. The man at the oars could not be prevented from turning his head rather often to try for a glimpse of this little grey shadow.

At last, from the top of each wave, the men in the tossing boat could see land. Even as the lighthouse was an upright shadow on the sky, this land seemed but a long black shadow on the sea. It certainly was thinner than paper. "We must be about opposite New Smyrna," said the cook, who had coasted this shore often in schooners. "Captain, by the way, I believe they abandoned that life-saving station there about a year ago."

"Did they?" said the captain.

The wind slowly died away. The cook and the correspondent were not now obliged to slave in order to hold high the oar. But the waves continued their old impetuous swooping at the dinghy, and the little craft, no longer under way, struggled woundily over them. The oiler or the correspondent took the oars again.

Shipwrecks are apropos of nothing. If men could only train for them and have them occur when the men had reached pink condition, there would be less drowning at sea. Of the four in the dinghy none had slept any time worth mentioning for two days and two nights previous to embarking in the dinghy, and in the excitement of clambering about the deck of a foundering ship they had also forgotten to eat heartily.

For these reasons, and for others, neither the oiler nor the correspondent was fond of rowing at this time. The correspondent wondered ingenuously how in the name of all that was sane could there be people who thought it amusing to row a boat. It was not an amusement; it was a diabolical punishment, and even a genius of mental aberrations could never conclude that it was anything but a horror to the muscles and a crime against the back. He mentioned to the boat in general how the amusement of rowing struck him, and the weary-faced oiler smiled in full sympathy. Previously to the foundering, by the way, the oiler had worked a double watch in the engine-room of the ship.

"Take her easy now, boys," said the captain. "Don't spend yourselves. If we have to run a surf you'll need all your strength, because we'll sure have to swim for it. Take your time."

Slowly the land arose from the sea. From a black line it became a line of black and a line of white—trees and sand. Finally the captain said that he could make out a house on the shore. "That's the house of refuge, sure," said the cook. "They'll see us before long, and come out after us."

The distant lighthouse reared high. "The keeper ought to be able to make us out now, if he's looking through a glass," said the captain. "He'll notify the life-saving people."

"None of those other boats could have got ashore to give word of this wreck," said the oiler, in a low voice, "else the life-boat would be out hunting us."

Slowly and beautifully the land loomed out of the sea. The wind came again. It had veered from the north-east to the south-east. Finally a new sound struck the ears of the men in the boat. It was the low thunder of the surf on the shore. "We'll never be able to make the lighthouse now," said the captain. "Swing her head a little more north, Billie."

"A little more north, sir," said the oiler.

Whereupon the little boat turned her nose once more down the wind, and all but the oarsman watched the shore grow. Under the influence of this expansion doubt and direful apprehension were leaving the minds of the men. The management of the boat was still most absorbing, but it could not prevent a quiet cheerfulness. In an hour, perhaps, they would be ashore.

Their backbones had become thoroughly used to balancing in the boat, and they now rode this wild colt of a dinghy like circus men. The correspondent thought that he had been drenched to the skin, but happening to feel in the top pocket of his coat, he found therein eight cigars. Four of them were soaked with sea-water; four were perfectly scatheless. After a search, somebody produced three dry matches; and thereupon the four waifs rode impudently in their little boat and, with an assurance of an impending rescue shining in their eyes, puffed at the big cigars, and judged well and ill of all men. Everybody took a drink of water.

"Cook," remarked the captain, "there don't seem to be any signs of life about your house of refuge."

"No," replied the cook. "Funny they don't see us!"

A broad stretch of lowly coast lay before the eyes of the men. It was of low dunes topped with dark vegetation. The roar of the surf was plain, and sometimes they could see the white lip of a wave as it spun up the beach. A tiny house was blocked out black upon the sky. Southward, the slim lighthouse lifted its little grey length.

Tide, wind, and waves were swinging the dinghy northward. "Funny they don't see us," said the men.

The surf's roar was here dulled, but its tone was nevertheless thunderous and mighty. As the boat swam over the great rollers the men sat listening to this roar. "We'll swamp sure," said everybody.

It is fair to say here that there was not a life-saving station within twenty miles in either direction; but the men did not know this fact, and in consequence they made dark and opprobrious remarks concerning the eyesight of the nation's life-savers. Four scowling men sat in the dinghy and surpassed records in the invention of epithets.

"Funny they don't see us."

The light-heartedness of a former time had completely faded. To their sharpened minds it was easy to conjure pictures of all kinds of incompetency and blindness and, indeed, cowardice. There was the shore of the populous land, and it was bitter and bitter to them that from it came no sign.

"Well," said the captain, ultimately, "I suppose we'll have to make a try for ourselves. If we stay out here too long, we'll none of us have strength left to swim after the boat swamps."

And so the oiler, who was at the oars, turned the boat straight for the shore. There was a sudden tightening of muscles. There was some thinking.

"If we don't all get ashore," said the captain—"I suppose you fellows know where to send news of my finish?"

They then briefly exchanged some addresses and admonitions. As for the reflections of the men, there was a great deal of rage in them. Perchance they might be formulated thus: "If I am going to be drowned—if I am going to be drowned—if I am going to be drowned, why, in the name of the seven mad gods who rule the sea, was I allowed to come thus far and contemplate sand and trees? Was I brought here merely to have my nose dragged away as I was about to nibble the sacred cheese of life? It is preposterous. If this old ninny-woman, Fate, cannot do better than this, she should be deprived of the management of men's fortunes. She is an old hen who knows not her intention. If she has decided to drown me, why did she not do it in the beginning and save me all this trouble? The whole affair is absurd.— But no; she cannot mean to drown me. She dare not drown me. She cannot drown me. Not after all this work." Afterward the man might have had an impulse to shake his fist at the clouds. "Just you drown me, now, and then hear what I call you!"

The billows that came at this time were more formidable. They seemed always just about to break and roll over the little boat in a turmoil of foam. There was a preparatory and long growl in the speech of them. No mind unused to the sea would have concluded that the dinghy could ascend these sheer heights in time. The shore was still afar. The oiler was a wily surfman. "Boys," he said swiftly, "she won't live three minutes more, and we're too far out to swim. Shall I take her to sea again, Captain?"

"Yes; go ahead!" said the captain.

This oiler, by a series of quick miracles and fast and steady oarsmanship, turned the boat in the middle of the surf and took her safely to sea again.

There was a considerable silence as the boat bumped over the furrowed sea to deeper water. Then somebody in gloom spoke: "Well, anyhow, they must have seen us from the shore by now."

The gulls went in slanting flight up the wind toward the grey, desolate east. A squall, marked by dingy clouds and clouds brick-red like smoke from a burning building, appeared from the south-east.

"What do you think of those life-saving people? Ain't they peaches?"

"Funny they haven't seen us."

"Maybe they think we're out here for sport! Maybe they think we're fishin'. Maybe they think we're damned fools."

It was a long afternoon. A changed tide tried to force them southward, but wind and wave said northward. Far ahead, where coast-line, sea, and sky formed their mighty angle, there were little dots which seemed to indicate a city on the shore.

"St. Augustine?"

The captain shook his head. "Too near Mosquito Inlet."

And the oiler rowed, and then the correspondent rowed; then the oiler rowed. It was a weary business. The human back can become the seat of more aches and pains than are registered in books for the composite anatomy of a regiment. It is a limited area, but it can become the theatre of innumerable muscular conflicts, tangles, wrenches, knots, and other comforts.

"Did you ever like to row, Billie?" asked the correspondent.

"No," said the oiler; "hang it!"

When one exchanged the rowing-seat for a place in the bottom of the boat, he suffered a bodily depression that caused him to be careless of everything save an obligation to wiggle one finger. There was cold sea-water swashing to and fro in the boat, and he lay in it. His head, pillowed on a thwart, was within an inch of the swirl of a wave-crest, and sometimes a particularly obstreperous sea came inboard and drenched him once more. But these matters did not annoy him. It is almost certain that if the boat had capsized he would have tumbled comfortably out upon the ocean as if he felt sure that it was a great soft mattress.

"Look! There's a man on the shore!"

"Where?"

"There! See 'im? See 'im?"

"Yes, sure! He's walking along."

"Now he's stopped. Look! He's facing us!"

"He's waving at us!"

"So he is! By thunder!"

"Ah, now we're all right! Now we're all right! There'll be a boat out here for us in half an hour."

"He's going on. He's running. He's going up to that house there."

The remote beach seemed lower than the sea, and it required a searching glance to discern the little black figure. The captain saw a floating stick, and they rowed to it. A bath towel was by some weird chance in the boat, and, tying this on the stick, the captain waved it. The oarsman did not dare turn his head, so he was obliged to ask questions.

"What's he doing now?"

"He's standing still again. He's looking, I think.—There he goes again—toward the house.—Now he's stopped again."

"Is he waving at us?"

"No, not now; he was, though."

"Look! There comes another man!"

"He's running."

"Look at him go, would you!"

"Why, he's on a bicycle. Now he's met the other man. They're both waving at us. Look!"

"There comes something up the beach."

"What the devil is that thing?"

"Why, it looks like a boat."

"Why, certainly, it's a boat."

"No; it's on wheels."

"Yes, so it is. Well, that must be the life-boat. They drag them along shore on a wagon."

"That's the life-boat, sure."

"No, by God, it's—it's an omnibus."

"I tell you it's a life-boat."

"It is not! It's an omnibus. I can see it plain. See? One of these big hotel omnibuses."

"By thunder, you're right. It's an omnibus, sure as fate. What do you suppose they are doing with an omnibus? Maybe they are going around collecting the life-crew, hey?"

"That's it, likely. Look! There's a fellow waving a little black flag. He's standing on the steps of the omnibus. There come those other two fellows. Now they're all talking together. Look at the fellow with the flag. Maybe he ain't waving it!"

"That ain't a flag, is it? That's his coat. Why, certainly, that's his coat."

"So it is; it's his coat. He's taken it off and is waving it around his head. But would you look at him swing it!"

"Oh, say, there isn't any life-saving station there. That's just a winter-resort hotel omnibus that has brought over some of the boarders to see us drown."

"What's that idiot with the coat mean? What's he signalling, anyhow?"

"It looks as if he were trying to tell us to go north. There must be a life-saving station up there."

"No; he thinks we're fishing. Just giving us a merry hand. See? Ah, there, Willie!"

"Well, I wish I could make something out of those signals. What do you suppose he means?"

"He don't mean anything; he's just playing."

"Well, if he'd just signal us to try the surf again, or to go to sea and wait, or go north, or go south, or go to hell, there would be some reason in it. But look at him! He just stands there and keeps his coat revolving like a wheel. The ass!"

"There come more people."

"Now there's quite a mob. Look! Isn't that a boat?"

"Where? Oh, I see where you mean. No, that's no boat."

"That fellow is still waving his coat."

"He must think we like to see him do that. Why don't he quit it? It don't mean anything."

"I don't know. I think he is trying to make us go north. It must be that there's a life-saving station there somewhere."

"Say, he ain't tired yet. Look at 'im wave!"

"Wonder how long he can keep that up. He's been revolving his coat ever since he caught sight of us. He's an idiot. Why aren't they getting men to bring a boat out? A fishing-boat—one of those big yawls—could come out here all right. Why don't he do something?"

"Oh, it's all right now."

"They'll have a boat out here for us in less than no time, now that they've seen us."

A faint yellow tone came into the sky over the low land. The shadows on the sea slowly deepened. The wind bore coldness with it, and the men began to shiver.

"Holy smoke!" said one, allowing his voice to express his impious mood, "if we keep on monkeying out here! If we've got to flounder out here all night!"

"Oh, we'll never have to stay here all night! Don't you worry. They've seen us now, and it won't be long before they'll come chasing out after us."

The shore grew dusky. The man waving a coat blended gradually into this gloom, and it swallowed in the same manner the omnibus and the group of people. The spray, when it dashed uproariously over the side, made the voyagers shrink and swear like men who were being branded.

"I'd like to catch the chump who waved the coat. I feel like socking him one, just for luck."

"Why? What did he do?"

"Oh, nothing, but then he seemed so damned cheerful."

In the meantime the oiler rowed, and then the correspondent rowed, and then the oiler rowed. Grey-faced and bowed forward, they mechanically, turn by turn, plied the leaden oars. The form of the light-house had vanished from the southern horizon, but finally a pale star appeared, just lifting from the sea. The streaked saffron in the west passed before the all-merging darkness, and the sea to the east was black. The land had vanished, and was expressed only by the low and drear thunder of the surf.

"If I am going to be drowned—if I am going to be drowned—if I am going to be drowned, why, in the name of the seven mad gods who rule the sea, was I allowed to come thus far and contemplate sand and trees? Was I brought here merely to have my nose dragged away as I was about to nibble the sacred cheese of life?"

The patient captain, drooped over the water-jar, was sometimes obliged to speak to the oarsman.

"Keep her head up! Keep her head up!"

"Keep her head up, sir." The voices were weary and low.

This was surely a quiet evening. All save the oarsman lay heavily and listlessly in the boat's bottom. As for him, his eyes were just capable of noting the tall black waves that swept forward in a most sinister silence, save for an occasional subdued growl of a crest.

The cook's head was on a thwart, and he looked without interest at the water under his nose. He was deep in other scenes. Finally he spoke. "Billie," he murmured, dreamfully, "what kind of pie do you like best?"

"Pie!" said the oiler and the correspondent, agitatedly. "Don't talk about those things, blast you!"

"Well," said the cook, "I was just thinking about ham sandwiches and—"

A night on the sea in an open boat is a long night. As darkness settled finally, the shine of the light, lifting from the sea in the south, changed to full gold. On the northern horizon a new light appeared, a small bluish gleam on the edge of the waters. These two lights were the furniture of the world. Otherwise there was nothing but waves.

Two men huddled in the stern, and distances were so magnificent in the dinghy that the rower was enabled to keep his feet partly warm by thrusting them under his companions. Their legs indeed extended far under the rowing-seat until they touched the feet of the captain forward. Sometimes, despite the efforts of the tired oarsman, a wave came piling into the boat, an icy wave of the night, and the chilling water soaked them anew. They would twist their bodies for a moment and groan, and sleep the dead sleep once more, while the water in the boat gurgled about them as the craft rocked.

The plan of the oiler and the correspondent was for one to row until he lost the ability, and then arouse the other from his sea-water couch in the bottom of the boat.

The oiler plied the oars until his head drooped forward and the overpowering sleep blinded him; and he rowed yet afterward. Then he touched a man in the bottom of the boat, and called his name. "Will you spell me for a little while?" he said, meekly.

"Sure, Billie," said the correspondent, awaking and dragging himself to a sitting position. They exchanged places carefully, and the oiler, cuddling down in the seawater at the cook's side, seemed to go to sleep instantly.

The particular violence of the sea had ceased. The waves came without snarling. The obligation of the man at the oars was to keep the boat headed so that the tilt of the rollers would not capsize her, and to preserve her from filling when the crests rushed past. The black waves were silent and hard to be seen in the darkness. Often one was almost upon the boat before the oarsman was aware.

In a low voice the correspondent addressed the captain. He was not sure that the captain was awake, although this iron man seemed to be always awake. "Captain, shall I keep her making for that light north, sir?"

The same steady voice answered him. "Yes. Keep it about two points off the port bow."

The cook had tied a life-belt around himself in order to get even the warmth which this clumsy cork contrivance could donate, and he seemed almost stove-like when a rower, whose teeth invariably chattered wildly as soon as he ceased his labour, dropped down to sleep.

The correspondent, as he rowed, looked down at the two men sleeping underfoot. The cook's arm was around the oiler's shoulders, and, with their fragmentary clothing and haggard faces, they were the babes of the sea—a grotesque rendering of the old babes in the wood.

Later he must have grown stupid at his work, for suddenly there was a growling of water, and a crest came with a roar and a swash into the boat, and it was a wonder that it did not set the cook afloat in his life-belt. The cook continued to sleep, but the oiler sat up, blinking his eyes and shaking with the new cold.

"Oh, I'm awful sorry, Billie," said the correspondent, contritely.

"That's all right, old boy," said the oiler, and lay down again and was asleep.

Presently it seemed that even the captain dozed, and the correspondent thought that he was the one man afloat on all the oceans. The wind had a voice as it came over the waves, and it was sadder than the end.

There was a long, loud swishing astern of the boat, and a gleaming trail of phosphorescence, like blue flame, was furrowed on the black waters. It might have been made by a monstrous knife.

Then there came a stillness, while the correspondent breathed with open mouth and looked at the sea.

Suddenly there was another swish and another long flash of bluish light, and this time it was alongside the boat, and might almost have been reached with an oar. The correspondent saw an enormous fin speed like a shadow through the water, hurling the crystalline spray and leaving the long glowing trail.

The correspondent looked over his shoulder at the captain. His face was hidden, and he seemed to be asleep. He looked at the babes of the sea. They certainly were asleep. So, being bereft of sympathy, he leaned a little way to one side and swore softly into the sea.

But the thing did not then leave the vicinity of the boat. Ahead or astern, on one side or the other, at intervals long or short, fled the long sparkling streak, and there was to be heard the *whirroo* of the dark fin. The speed and power of the thing was greatly to be admired. It cut the water like a gigantic and keen projectile.

The presence of this biding thing did not affect the man with the same horror that it would if he had been a picnicker. He simply looked at the sea dully and swore in an undertone.

Nevertheless, it is true that he did not wish to be alone with the thing. He wished one of his companions to awake by chance and keep him company with it. But the captain hung motionless over the water-jar, and the oiler and the cook in the bottom of the boat were plunged in slumber.

"If I am going to be drowned—if I am going to be drowned—if I am going to be drowned, why, in the name of the seven mad gods who rule the sea, was I allowed to come thus far and contemplate sand and trees?"

During this dismal night, it may be remarked that a man would conclude that it was really the intention of the seven mad gods to drown him, despite the abominable injustice of it. For it was certainly an abominable injustice to drown a man who had worked so hard, so hard. The man felt it would be a crime most unnatural. Other people had drowned at sea since galleys swarmed with painted sails, but still—

When it occurs to a man that nature does not regard him as important, and that she feels she would not maim the universe by disposing of him, he at first wishes to throw bricks at the temple, and he hates deeply the fact that there are no bricks and no temples. Any visible expression of nature would surely be pelleted with his jeers.

Then, if there be no tangible thing to hoot, he feels, perhaps, the desire to confront a personification and indulge in pleas, bowed to one knee, and with hands supplicant, saying, "Yes, but I love myself."

A high cold star on a winter's night is the word he feels that she says to him. Thereafter he knows the pathos of his situation.

The men in the dinghy had not discussed these matters, but each had, no doubt, reflected upon them in silence and according to his mind. There was seldom any expression upon their faces save the general one of complete weariness. Speech was devoted to the business of the boat.

To chime the notes of his emotion, a verse mysteriously entered the correspondent's head. He had even forgotten that he had forgotten this verse, but it suddenly was in his mind.

> *A soldier of the Legion lay dying in Algiers;*
> *There was lack of woman's nursing, there was dearth of woman's*
> *   tears;*
> *But a comrade stood beside him, and he took that comrade's*
> *   hand,*
> *And he said, "I never more shall see my own, my native land."*

In his childhood the correspondent had been made acquainted with the fact that a soldier of the Legion lay dying in Algiers, but he had never regarded the fact as important. Myriads of his school-fellows had informed him of the soldier's plight, but the dinning had naturally ended by making him perfectly indifferent. He had never considered it his affair that a soldier of the Legion lay dying in Algiers, nor had it appeared to him as a matter for sorrow. It was less to him than the breaking of a pencil's point.

Now, however, it quaintly came to him as a human, living thing. It was no longer merely a picture of a few throes in the breast of a poet, meanwhile drinking tea and warming his feet at the grate; it was an actuality—stern, mournful, and fine.

The correspondent plainly saw the soldier. He lay on the sand with his feet out straight and still. While his pale left hand was upon his chest in an attempt to thwart the going of his life, the blood came between his fingers. In the far Algerian distance, a city of low square forms was set against a sky that was faint with the last sunset hues. The correspondent, plying the oars and dreaming of the slow and slower movements of the lips of the soldier, was moved by a profound and perfectly impersonal comprehension. He was sorry for the soldier of the Legion who lay dying in Algiers.

The thing which had followed the boat and waited had evidently grown bored at the delay. There was no longer to be heard the slash of the cutwater, and there was no longer the flame of the long trail. The light in the north still glimmered, but it was apparently no nearer to the boat. Sometimes the boom of the surf rang in the correspondent's ears, and he turned the craft seaward then and rowed harder. Southward, someone had evidently built a watch-fire on the beach. It was too low and too far to be seen, but it made a shimmering, roseate reflection upon the bluff in back of it, and this could be discerned from the boat. The wind came stronger, and sometimes a wave suddenly raged out like a mountain cot, and there was to be seen the sheen and sparkle of a broken crest.

The captain, in the bow, moved on his water-jar and sat erect. "Pretty long night," he observed to the correspondent. He looked at the shore. "Those life-saving people take their time."

"Did you see that shark playing around?"

"Yes, I saw him. He was a big fellow, all right."

"Wish I had known you were awake."

Later the correspondent spoke into the bottom of the boat. "Billie!" There was a slow and gradual disentanglement. "Billie, will you spell me?"

"Sure," said the oiler.

As soon as the correspondent touched the cold, comfortable sea-water in the bottom of the boat and had huddled close to the cook's life-belt he was deep in sleep, despite the fact that his teeth played all the popular airs. This sleep was so good to him that it was but a moment before he heard a voice call his name in a tone that demonstrated the last stages of exhaustion. "Will you spell me?"

"Sure, Billie."

The light in the north had mysteriously vanished, but the correspondent took his course from the wide-awake captain.

Later in the night they took the boat farther out to sea, and the captain directed the cook to take one oar at the stern and keep the boat facing the seas. He was to call out if he should hear the thunder of the surf. This plan enabled the oiler and the correspondent to get respite together. "We'll give those boys a chance to get into shape again," said the captain. They curled down and, after a few preliminary chatterings and trembles, slept once more the dead sleep. Neither knew they had bequeathed to the cook the company of another shark, or perhaps the same shark.

As the boat caroused on the waves, spray occasionally humped over the side and gave them a fresh soaking, but this had no power to break their repose. The ominous slash of the wind and the water affected them as it would have affected mummies.

"Boys," said the cook, with the notes of every reluctance in his voice, "she's drifted in pretty close. I guess one of you had better take her to sea again." The correspondent, aroused, heard the crash of the toppled crests.

As he was rowing, the captain gave him some whisky-and-water, and this steadied the chills out of him. "If I ever get ashore and anybody shows me even a photograph of an oar—"

At last there was a short conversation.

"Billie!—Billie, will you spell me?"

"Sure," said the oiler.

When the correspondent again opened his eyes, the sea and the sky were each of the grey hue of the dawning. Later, carmine and gold was painted upon the waters. The morning appeared finally, in its splendour, with a sky of pure blue, and the sunlight flamed on the tips of the waves.

On the distant dunes were set many little black cottages, and a tall white windmill reared above them. No man, nor dog, nor bicycle appeared on the beach. The cottages might have formed a deserted village.

The voyagers scanned the shore. A conference was held in the boat. "Well," said the captain, "if no help is coming, we might better try a run through the surf right away. If we stay out here much longer we will be too weak to do anything for ourselves at all." The others silently acquiesced in this reasoning. The boat was headed for the beach. The correspondent wondered if none ever ascended the tall wind-tower, and if then they never looked seaward. This tower was a giant, standing with its back to the plight of the ants. It represented in a degree, to the correspondent, the serenity of nature amid the struggles of the individual—nature in the wind, and nature in the vision of men. She did not seem cruel to him then, nor beneficent, nor treacherous, nor wise. But she was indifferent, flatly indifferent. It is, perhaps, plausible that a man in this situation, impressed with the unconcern of the universe, should see the innumerable flaws of his life, and have them taste wickedly in his mind, and wish for another chance. A distinction between right and wrong seems absurdly clear to him, then, in this new ignorance of the grave-edge, and he understands that if he were given another opportunity he would mend his conduct and his words, and be better and brighter during an introduction or at a tea.

"Now, boys," said the captain, "she is going to swamp sure. All we can do is to work her in as far as possible, and then when she swamps, pile out and scramble for the beach. Keep cool now, and don't jump until she swamps sure."

The oiler took the oars. Over his shoulders he scanned the surf. "Captain," he said, "I think I'd better bring her about and keep her head-on to the seas and back her in."

"All right, Billie," said the captain. "Back her in." The oiler swung the boat then, and, seated in the stern, the cook and the correspondent were obliged to look over their shoulders to contemplate the lonely and indifferent shore.

The monstrous inshore rollers heaved the boat high until the men were again enabled to see the white sheets of water scudding up the slanted beach. "We won't get in very close," said the captain. Each time a man could wrest his attention from the rollers, he turned his glance toward the shore, and in the expression of the eyes during this contemplation there was a singular quality. The correspondent, observing the others, knew that they were not afraid, but the full meaning of their glances was shrouded.

As for himself, he was too tired to grapple fundamentally with the fact. He tried to coerce his mind into thinking of it, but the mind was dominated at this time by the muscles, and the muscles said they did not care. It merely occurred to him that if he should drown it would be a shame.

There were no hurried words, no pallor, no plain agitation. The men simply looked at the shore. "Now, remember to get well clear of the boat when you jump," said the captain.

Seaward the crest of a roller suddenly fell with a thunderous crash, and the long white comber came roaring down upon the boat.

"Steady now," said the captain. The men were silent. They turned their eyes from the shore to the comber and waited. The boat slid up the incline, leaped at the furious top, bounced over it, and swung down the long back of the wave. Some water had been shipped, and the cook bailed it out.

But the next crest crashed also. The tumbling, boiling flood of white water caught the boat and whirled it almost perpendicular. Water swarmed in from all sides. The correspondent had his hands on the gunwale at this time, and when the water entered at that place he swiftly withdrew his fingers, as if he objected to wetting them.

The little boat, drunken with this weight of water, reeled and snuggled deeper into the sea.

"Bail her out, cook! Bail her out!" said the captain.

"All right, Captain," said the cook.

"Now, boys, the next one will do for us sure," said the oiler. "Mind to jump clear of the boat."

The third wave moved forward, huge, furious, implacable. It fairly swallowed the dinghy, and almost simultaneously the men tumbled into the sea. A piece of life-belt had lain in the bottom of the boat, and as the correspondent went overboard he held this to his chest with his left hand.

The January water was icy, and he reflected immediately that it was colder than he had expected to find it off the coast of Florida. This appeared to his dazed mind as a fact important enough to be noted at the time. The coldness of the water was sad; it was tragic. This fact was somehow mixed and confused with his opinion of his own situation, so that it seemed almost a proper reason for tears. The water was cold.

When he came to the surface he was conscious of little but the noisy water. Afterward he saw his companions in the sea. The oiler was ahead in the race. He was swimming strongly and rapidly. Off to the correspondent's left, the cook's great white and corked back bulged out of the water; and in the rear the captain was hanging with his one good hand to the keel of the overturned dinghy.

There is a certain immovable quality to a shore, and the correspondent wondered at it amid the confusion of the sea.

It seemed also very attractive; but the correspondent knew that it was a long journey, and he paddled leisurely. The piece of life-preserver lay under him, and sometimes he whirled down the incline of a wave as if he were on a hand-sled.

But finally he arrived at a place in the sea where travel was beset with difficulty. He did not pause swimming to inquire what manner of current had caught him, but there his progress ceased. The shore was set before him like a bit of scenery on a stage, and he looked at it and understood with his eyes each detail of it.

As the cook passed, much farther to the left, the captain was calling to him, "Turn over on your back, cook! Turn over on your back and use the oar."

"All right, sir." The cook turned on his back, and, paddling with an oar, went ahead as if he were a canoe.

Presently the boat also passed to the left of the correspondent, with the captain clinging with one hand to the keel. He would have appeared like a man raising himself to look over a board fence if it were not for the extraordinary gymnastics of the boat. The correspondent marvelled that the captain could still hold to it.

They passed on nearer to shore—the oiler, the cook, the captain—and following them went the water-jar, bouncing gaily over the seas.

The correspondent remained in the grip of this strange new enemy—a current. The shore, with its white slope of sand and its green bluff topped with little silent cottages, was spread like a picture before him. It was very near to him then, but he was impressed as one who, in a gallery, looks at a scene from Brittany or Algiers.

He thought: "I am going to drown? Can it be possible? Can it be possible? Can it be possible?" Perhaps an individual must consider his own death to be the final phenomenon of nature.

But later a wave perhaps whirled him out of this small deadly current, for he found suddenly that he could again make progress toward the shore. Later still he was aware that the captain, clinging with one hand to the keel of the dinghy, had his face turned away from the shore and toward him, and was calling his name. "Come to the boat! Come to the boat!"

In his struggle to reach the captain and the boat, he reflected that when one gets properly wearied drowning must really be a comfortable arrangement—a cessation of hostilities accompanied by a large degree of relief; and he was glad of it, for the main thing in his mind for some moments had been horror of the temporary agony. He did not wish to be hurt.

Presently he saw a man running along the shore. He was undressing with most remarkable speed. Coat, trousers, shirt, everything flew magically off him.

"Come to the boat!" called the captain.

"All right, Captain." As the correspondent paddled, he saw the captain let himself down to bottom and leave the boat. Then the correspondent performed his one little marvel of the voyage. A large wave caught him and flung him with ease and supreme speed completely over the boat and far beyond it. It struck him even then as an event in gymnastics and a true miracle of the sea. An overturned boat in the surf is not a plaything to a swimming man.

The correspondent arrived in water that reached only to his waist, but his condition did not enable him to stand for more than a moment. Each wave knocked him into a heap, and the undertow pulled at him.

Then he saw the man who had been running and undressing, and undressing and running, come bounding into the water. He dragged ashore the cook, and then waded toward the captain; but the captain waved him away and sent him to the correspondent. He was naked—naked as a tree in winter; but a halo was about his head, and he shone like a saint. He gave a strong pull, and a long drag, and a bully heave at the correspondent's hand. The correspondent, schooled in the minor formulae, said, "Thanks, old man." But suddenly the man cried, "What's that?" He pointed a swift finger. The correspondent said, "Go."

In the shallows, face downward, lay the oiler. His forehead touched sand that was periodically, between each wave, clear of the sea.

The correspondent did not know all that transpired afterward. When he achieved safe ground he fell, striking the sand with each particular part of his body. It was as if he had dropped from a roof, but the thud was grateful to him.

It seemed that instantly the beach was populated with men with blankets, clothes, and flasks, and women with coffee-pots and all the remedies sacred to their minds. The welcome of the land to the men from the sea was warm and generous; but a still and dripping shape was carried slowly up the beach, and the land's welcome for it could only be the different and sinister hospitality of the grave.

When it came night, the white waves paced to and fro in the moonlight, and the wind brought the sound of the great sea's voice to the men on the shore, and they felt that they could then be interpreters.

from Every Man for Himself
by Beryl Bainbridge

Beryl Bainbridge's (born 1933) 1996 novel Every Man for Himself juxtaposes the frantic last moments aboard the Titanic with the self-absorption of the book's characters, from the pompous Scurra to the narcissistic Wallis Ellery to the overbearing Archie Ginsberg. The narrator, Morgan (fictitious nephew of J. P. Morgan) watches the sinking of the "unsinkable" ship destroy illusions by which his society has defined itself: myths of courage, nobility and power.

T here is no way of knowing how one will react to danger until faced with it. Nor can we know what capacity we have for nobility and self-sacrifice unless something happens to rouse such conceits into activity. In the nature of things, simply because I had survived without lasting hurt, I remembered little of those other occasions on which I'd been in considerable peril, once half-way up Mount Solaro when I'd been foolish enough to climb on to a wall and lost my footing, the other when tumbling from the side of a boat negotiating the Suez canal. Besides, I had been a boy then and it had been my own lack of sense that had landed me in trouble. As I trailed Thomas Andrews to his suite I confess I fairly glowed with exhilaration and can only suppose I'd failed to grasp the full import of that exchange in the wheelhouse. Andrews hadn't uttered a word to me since leaving the bridge; now, coming within a few paces of his door, he turned and said, 'They'll be lowering the life-boats shortly and will need extra hands. Take nothing with you save what can be put in your pockets. Avoid alarming people. Tell the truth only to those among your friends who can be relied upon to keep a cool head. Have you a pocket knife?'

'I have,' I said.

'Keep it with you,' and with that he went inside.

The crowd had dispersed when I crossed back through the foyer. Most of the men had returned to the smoke-room bar; judging by the noise they were in boisterous mood. Ginsberg and Melchett were at our old table, Ginsberg occupied in building a house out of the pack of bridge cards. This surprised me. I had thought he'd be in the thick of it, spouting his opinions about a lost propeller to all and sundry. I sat down feeling important.

'Look here,' I began, 'I think it would be best if we went out to give a hand with the life-boats. Most of the crew will be needed for other things.'

'You've experience of davits and such like, have you?' asked Ginsberg. 'I mean you've been through the drill?'

'Well, no . . . but—'

'Then you'll be a lot of use, won't you?'

'We won't actually be getting into the boats,' scoffed Hopper. 'It won't come to that. Why, the women would never stand for it. It's too cold.'

I said, 'I happen to know that it's more serious than you think. I have it on the best authority that things are looking pretty bad. There isn't a great deal of time.'

'Time for what?' Hopper asked.

'For us to get into the boats,' I said. 'It's essential we put on more clothes.'

'I think not,' Ginsberg said. 'I doubt we'll be getting into any boats, not unless the clothing you have in mind includes petticoats.' He was still playing with his house of cards, his tongue caught between his teeth with the effort of laying on the roof. Hopper looked mystified. There'd been a time, years ago, when I too had gone out of my way to baffle him.

'Look here,' I shouted, 'this isn't a game, you know.' I tugged at Ginsberg's elbow to make him listen and sent his cards in a heap.

'How many boats did you say there were?' he asked.

'I didn't,' I retorted. 'But as a matter of fact there are sixteen, plus four collapsibles.'

'Capable of carrying how many? Fifty at the most?'

'More like sixty,' I snapped.

'And how many of us would you estimate are on board?' He was watching me through half-closed eyes, waiting. A burst of laughter came from the direction of the bar. A voice began to bellow the 'Eton Boating Song'. What a fool I am, I thought, and the elation which had buoyed me up drained away and I was left swirling the cards round and round on the table-top in imitation of a whirlpool to stop my hands from shaking.

Just then Rosenfelder rushed in, his expression deeply gloomy. As always, he was looking for Scurra. A steward had come into the Palm Court, where he and Adele had been drinking high-balls with the Duff Cordons, and ordered them to their quarters to put on life-preservers before going up on deck. They had asked what luggage they'd be required to take with them and been told they couldn't take anything, nothing but the clothes they stood up in. What was he going to do about his dress? He wasn't allowed to carry it in its box and it was unthinkable that Adele should wear it in a life-boat. 'There is the oil,' he wailed, 'the dirt, the salt-spray . . . it will be ruined. Where is Scurra? He will use his influence. Where are his rooms?'

None of us could tell him. Hopper had seen him in the passageways of both A and C decks. Ginsberg had bumped into him along the main corridor of B deck, but he could have been coming from anywhere. Rosenfelder looked at me. 'I've not been to his room,' I told him. 'My steward hasn't even heard of him.'

'Then he's one in a million,' said Hopper.

'Why not ask Wallis Ellery,' Ginsberg said. I noticed his voice was unsteady. He seemed to be having difficulty with his breathing. I fancied he was more alarmed than he let on.

'She is not to be found either,' Rosenfelder moaned. 'Adele's clothes are in her room. I have knocked at her door but there is no reply.'

At that moment the bar steward came over and politely asked us to leave. We must all go as quickly as possible to fetch our life-preservers and assemble on deck. There was no cause for panic. It was simply a precaution. I arranged with Hopper that we meet in the gymnasium in ten minutes. 'We'll stick together, won't we,' he insisted. 'It'll be like the old days.' 'Yes,' I assured him. Ginsberg strolled into the foyer and low-ered himself into a leather armchair. Rosenfelder panted up the Grand Staircase in search of Scurra. Before we parted, Hopper touched my arm, 'You're my oldest friend,' he murmured, 'and my best.' His eyes were scared. Ginsberg looked up and waved sardonically as the doors of the elevator clanged shut; he was holding a handkerchief to his nostrils.

I rode below in the company of two ladies in wrappers and a man wearing pyjamas beneath a golfing jacket. I swear the stouter of the women was the one who had expressed disappointment at there not being more of a show when we left Southampton. She was going to the purser's office to withdraw her valuables from the safe. Not that they amounted to much. She had a watch left to her by a grandmother born in Kent, England, a diamond pin that had belonged to her dead mother and an album of family photographs. If it came to the pinch, she said, she'd choose the album every time. The steward had told her to fetch what small items she had because everyone might have to get into the boats. The man in the golfing jacket laughed and said this was highly unlikely. 'I'm not entirely sure,' he said, 'this isn't some elabo-rate hoax. After all, the ship is unsinkable.'

When I entered the passage McKinlay and the night steward were knocking on doors, urging people to go up on deck. I felt curiously detached and had the notion I swaggered rather than walked; I'd never been so conscious of how good it was be young, for I knew it was my youthful resolution as well as my strong arms that would enable me to survive the next two hours. I thought of old man Seefax and his feeble grasp on life and reckoned he might perish from nothing more than lack of hope. By now, wireless messages would have been dispatched to every vessel in the area, and even if there wasn't enough room for all in the boats, there would still be time for those left behind to switch from one ship to another. Somewhere in my mind I pored over an illustration, in a child's book of heroic deeds, of a rescue at sea, ropes slung between two heaving decks and men swinging like gibbons above the foaming waves. How Sissy would gasp when I recounted my story! How my aunt would throw up her hands when I shouted the details of my midnight adventure! Why, as long as I wrapped up well it would be the greatest fun in the world.

Accordingly, having reached my stateroom, I put my cricket pullover on under my jacket and taking off my dancing pumps struggled into three pairs of thick stockings. I had to pull one pair off again because I couldn't fit into my boots. Then I went into the corridor and got McKinlay to help tie the strings of my life-preserver. He jokingly remarked that I'd put on weight since we last met and asked if I had with me everything I wanted to take. He'd been instructed to lock all the doors until the emergency was over—in case things went missing. They were having a spot of trouble keeping the steerage class from surging up from below.

'I'm working for Mr Andrews,' I told him. 'I may need my room as a base . . . to write reports . . . that sort of rigmarole.'

'It's orders, sir,' he said.

'Well, in my case, just forget them, there's a good chap.' He hesitated, but the 'good chap' did the trick and he left my door alone. On an impulse I went back inside and took up the painting of my mother. Taking out my knife I levered the picture from its frame, tore out the stretchers and rolling up the canvas stuck it in my pocket.

There were now a dozen or more people filing in procession towards the elevator. They were mostly pretty cheerful, engaging in banter to do with each other's quaint attire. A gentleman carrying a top hat and wearing tennis shoes beneath a coat with an astrakhan collar was much admired. He said he thought his hat would come in useful if baling-out was required. One woman cradled a Pekinese dog with the snuffles, another a pink china pig.

I decided to go below to see for myself what was happening. Descending the stairs I was aware of there being something not quite right about the slope of them. They looked perfectly level but my step was slightly off balance; my feet didn't seem to know where to land, and I was tilting forward. I put it down to imagination, that and the bulky clothing which encumbered me, and marvelled that Rosenfelder must feel this propulsion all the time.

I didn't get very far. There were too many people streaming in an opposite direction. On F deck an officer barred my way. He was holding on to the arm of a steerage woman who was carrying a baby against her cheek. The officer tried to restrain her and turn me back at the same time. 'Why have we stopped?' she kept asking. 'What for have we stopped?' Behind the officer's shoulders I saw a line of postal clerks at the bend of the companionway, heaving mail sacks, one to the other, up from the lower level. The sacks were stained to the seals with damp.

Retracing my steps I made my way upwards again. On the staircase landing of C deck I passed White, the racquets professional. He didn't acknowledge me though I raised my hand in greeting. From somewhere along the corridor a voice called out, 'Hadn't we better cancel that appointment for tomorrow morning?' I didn't hear White's reply.

Colonel Astor was in the foyer talking to Bruce Ismay. Ismay had the appearance of a man on his death bed; his face had become as old as time. Owing to the numbers thronging the stairs I was prevented from going immediately up top and heard Astor say, 'Is it essential I bring my wife on deck? Her condition is delicate,' and Ismay's response, 'You must fetch her at once. The ship is torn to pieces below but she won't sink if her bulkheads hold.'

There was a fearful crush in the gymnasium, spilling out on deck and flowing in again as the cold stabbed to the bone. Hopper was nowhere to be seen. Mrs Brown jogged my sleeve and asked if it would be a good idea to start community singing, but before I could answer the far door was thrust open and the ship's band struck up something jolly. Kitty Webb sat astride one of the mechanical bicycles. She wore silk pyjamas under a man's leather automobile coat and was accompanied by Guggenheim's valet. I went out in search of Hopper. Save for a solitary man gripping the rail there was no one about under that glorious panoply of stars. I imagined the crew must be all assembled at the stern; before quitting the wheelhouse I had heard Captain Smith's call for all hands on deck.

I was walking towards the port side when suddenly the night was rendered hideous by a tremendous blast of steam escaping from the safety valves of the pipes fore and aft of the funnels. I clapped my palms over my ears under the onslaught and turned giddy, for the noise was like a thousand locomotives thundering through a culvert. Even the stars seemed to shake. Recovering, I spied Hopper watching an officer attempting to parley with the bridge above. The officer was pointing at the life-boats and soundlessly roaring for instructions. Hopper and I, bent double under the din, ran back inside.

The crowd in the gymnasium had mostly retreated to the landing of the Grand Staircase and the foyer beneath. The band was now playing rag-time. Kitty Webb, head lolling like a doll, danced with Mrs Brown. Mrs Carter asked if Captain Smith was on the boat deck and whether I knew the whereabouts of Mr Ismay. I said I expected they were both on the bridge seeing to things. There was such a dearth of information, of confirmation or denial of rumours—the racquets court was under water but not the Turkish baths; a spur of the iceberg had ripped the ship from one end to the other but the crew was fully equipped to make good the damage and were even now putting it to rights—and such an absence of persons in authority to whom one might turn that it was possible to imagine the man in the golfing jacket had spoken no more than the truth when presupposing we were victims of a hoax. In part, this lack of communication was due to the awesome size of the wounded ship. It was simply not possible to keep everyone abreast of events. An accident at the summit of a mountain is hardly observable from the slopes. For the rest, what was Smith expected to do? Should he appear on the landing of the Grand Staircase beneath that rococo clock whose hands now stood at twenty-five to one in the morning and announce that in spite of the watertight compartments, the indestructible bulkheads, the unimaginable technology, the unthinkable was in process and his unsinkable vessel, now doomed, unfortunately carried insufficient life-boats to accommodate all on board?

Ginsberg was still in his armchair opposite the elevator, still clutching a handkerchief to his nose. An unknown girl was chatting to him; he introduced her but the loudness of the band blotted out her name. She had an enormous expanse of brow, beneath which her features sat truncated like those of an infant's; it was possibly on account of her hair being dragged back in a fearsome bun. She said, without preamble, that she had known for several years past, from dreams and such like, that it was her destiny to drown. She spoke of it quite calmly and without resorting to melodrama. Her doctor had dismissed her condition as no more than nerves; her mother had enrolled her in the local tennis club, in the hopes that strenuous exercise in the fresh air would banish such fancies. She had become quite exceptionally adroit on the courts, but the dreams persisted.

'There is nothing to worry about,' I said. 'I myself have been plagued by nightmares. I'm convinced they consist of memories of the past rather than portents of the future.'

Ginsberg was leaning back in his chair, breathing like a man recovering from a record-breaking run round the tracks. Hopper asked what was wrong and he explained he was afflicted with asthma. It came on sometimes without reason. His handkerchief was smeared with a concoction of honey obtained from a bee-keeper in a Shaker community in Massachusetts and would do the trick shortly. I thought it was an inspired excuse and fancied he was in a blue funk.

It was then that I realised I hadn't seen Charlie Melchett since the interruption to our game of bridge. In Hopper's opinion it was probable he'd galloped off to play knight errant to the Ellery sisters and Molly Dodge. I made my excuses to the girl with the forehead and went looking for him. Lady Melchett, but six weeks before, had drawn me to one side and entreated me to keep an eye on her boy. 'He is so very fond of you,' she'd said. 'He looks up to you.' 'You may rely on me,' I'd told her, fighting off those damn dogs threatening to lick my face away.

I ran him to earth quite quickly, standing in the deserted gymnasium gazing out at the shadowy deck. The funnels continued intermittently to release those deafening blasts of steam and though the sound
was muted by the glass I had to shout to draw his attention. He didn't
turn round. 'Why does it keep on with that ghastly noise?' he asked.

'It's a bit like a train,' I said.

'I thought I saw a ship out there a few minutes ago.'

'I expect it's coming to assist us.'

'No,' he said. 'It's stopped moving. Perhaps it's just starlight.'

'You ought to fetch your life-preserver,' I said. 'I've got mine on.'

'I will . . . soon. I needed to mull things over. I should have liked—'
The gush of steam started up again; when it had died away he was still
rabbiting on and I reckoned he was speaking of his father—'. . . I know
he's fond of me but it worries him how I'll face up to things when he's
gone. I'm not brainy and I don't often think of anything downright
important. My mother dotes on me, and that's rather held me back. I've
never had to go it alone, not like some chaps. Not that I'd want to. I'm
no good on my own . . . I lack common-sense.'

'Charlie,' I protested, 'you have more common-sense than any man
I know . . . and kindness and a generous heart—'

'I would have so liked to make him proud.'

'Hopper and I are in the foyer,' I told him. 'We rather wanted you
with us.'

'I'll come and join you in a bit,' he said. I hesitated, but felt it my
duty to ask, 'You're not frightened are you, Charlie? There's no need
to be.'

'There's nothing on this earth that frightens me,' he said. 'It's what
comes after that concerns one. I've not always behaved decently.' His
voice wobbled. I couldn't help smiling. If the worst happens, I thought,
God will surely send all his angels to bring Charlie to heaven. 'You'll
have plenty of time to atone,' I said, 'a life-time, in fact,' and at that he
faced me and, sheepishly grinning, followed me down the stairs.

Ida and Rosenfelder hurried to meet us. Neither of them could find
Wallis. Ida had looked for her everywhere, asked everyone if they

recalled seeing her, but nobody had. 'She was in the dining room when I got back after your faint,' she babbled, 'but then I went off to a concert in the second class lounge and later I had coffee with Molly in the Café Parisien . . . then that dreadful bump came and Molly said it was safer to remain where we were. Mr Rosenfelder's been awfully kind. He went to our room but it's locked, in case of looting or something, and the steward shooed him away.'

'I knock and knock,' Rosenfelder said. 'And I think I hear voices, but there is no one opening and the steward tells me I have no business in that passage.'

I offered to go there again, just to set Ida's mind at rest, and walked away in a deceptively leisurely manner. Once out of sight I fairly sprinted. The corridors of A deck were deserted, as though this was an ordinary night and all good folk were abed. I didn't attempt to knock on Wallis's door; instead I sought out the steward and demanded he hand over the key. He refused, saying it was more than his job was worth. I told him I would break the door down, if necessary, to which he retorted he would report me to the chief steward. I shouted he could report me to Captain Smith for all I cared, and we glowered at one another for some moments. 'Listen,' I said. 'I have reason to believe that Miss Ellery is in there with a gentleman friend. This sort of thing can't be new to you. Naturally, when you first knocked she thought it would compromise her to respond. She possibly waited until she believed you'd gone away, only to find the door locked. You take my meaning?'

'Perfectly, sir,' he said. ' Why didn't you tell me that in the first place?' Taking the key off its ring he planted it in my hand. I told him to make himself scarce, which he did, beetling off down the passageway no doubt eager to inform the second steward of the salacious goings-on. I turned the lock, slipped the key under the door and ran for the companionway. I had no wish to confront Scurra.

In the short space of time I'd been absent, the atmosphere in the foyer had undergone a change. Some course of action had at last been resolved upon; there was a sense of relief rather than urgency as the stewards moved discreetly from one group to another, urging the women to proceed to the top deck. Ida refused to budge an inch without her sister until I said I'd go with her, mark where she was and bring Wallis to her side the moment she was found. I assured her it wouldn't be long.

The chief saloon steward led us by way of the crew's narrow companionway up to the forward boat deck. Colonel Astor and his bride, the Garters, the Theyers and Mrs Hogeboom went ahead, slowed down by the stately progress of Mr and Mrs Straus, linked as always. Hedged by Hopper and Charlie I held tight to Ida's hand. Mrs Brown's grandchild, riding his father's shoulders, bobbed above our heads blowing on a tin whistle. There was even some laughter as we squeezed upwards. Behind, abreast with Lady Duff Gordon, nudged Rosenfelder, clad in a fur coat the colour of beeswax.

Captain Smith appeared at the top, waiting agitatedly to descend. Astor asked him a question, something to do with how the situation now stood, and he answered stoutly enough that all was under control, but we must hurry. We emerged on to the bridge, a little below the officers' house, and were told to wait. Thankfully, the steam pipes remained silent. A stir was caused by Mr Theyer excitedly pointing to what he took to be the lights of a ship to the right of our stern. We watched intently but the lights receded and we came to the conclusion we were confused by starlight.

Some of the men, myself included, climbed down the companionway, starboard side, to be closer to the boats in case we were needed. There were very few seamen about and only two officers, both grappling with the complicated machinery of the davits. We called out that we were willing to assist but they waved us away. The night was perfectly still, save for our footfalls, the low murmur of voices and the crackle of canvas as the boat covers were trampled over. Astor paced alone, the tiny glow of his cigarette arching through the air as he flung it overboard. I remember Charlie talked to me about cricket. Above, a million stars sprinkled the heavens.

Some fifteen minutes later, nothing having been accomplished on our part of the deck, Hopper and I went round to the port side. Here, we saw one boat, free of its tackle, being lowered towards the rail. Suddenly there was a flash of light from the forward deck, a hissing whoosh sufficient to turn the stomach over as a rocket soared to meet the stars. Up, up it went, and we craned our heads to watch it go, until, exploding with a report that tore the night in two, illuminating for one stark instant the fretwork of wires upon the tapering mast, it sent its own stars sailing down. The women and children on the bridge clapped their hands in wonder at the pretty sight; we men could scarce look at one another, recognising it for a desperate measure.

Mrs Brown's voice floated down from the bridge. 'I wish you would make up your minds. We were told to come up here,' and at that the crowd began to move inside again. Hopper and I hurried through the gymnasium doors and made our way below to meet them.

Jerkily, the boats were being lowered alongside the windows of the enclosed promenade of A deck. Someone had to fetch a chisel to crank up the glass. Mr Carter said the list of the ship had meant the boats hung too far out from the top rail for the women to enter safely. An officer thrust steamer chairs through the windows; when the nearest boat was level, he climbed out, one foot on the chair, one foot on the gunwale. There was no panic or undue excitement until he ordered the men to stand back from the women and children. Then, several of the women began to blub. Mr Carter challenged him, at which he bellowed, 'Women and children first.'

To a man we obeyed him. Ida clung to my arm, whimpering Wallis's name, but I shook her off and gave her into the charge of Mrs Brown. A young woman carrying a baby refused to leave her husband, but he said she ought because of the child. 'There's nothing to worry about,' he told her. 'I'll be on the next boat, sure thing.' Mrs Straus was being led to the window when she stopped and said, 'I'm not going without Mr Straus.' Someone, Theyer I think, asked the officer if an exception couldn't be made for such a revered and elderly man? Whereupon, Straus turned away, remarking he would not take advantage of his age. Mrs Straus, dragged a further few steps, broke free and stumbled to his side. 'We shall stay together, old dear,' she said. 'As we have lived, so will we die.' This remark, though noble in sentiment, convinced the woman with the baby that she was parting from her own husband for ever. Shrieking, she attempted to clamber out of the boat and was pushed back by the officer. The infant set up a thin howl. Mr and Mrs Straus strolled a little way off and sat in steamer chairs, watching the proceedings as though from the stalls of a theatre.

Remembering my promise, I went inside to look for Wallis. I passed through the swing doors, propped open to the night, to that landing from which an eternity ago Madame Butterfly had glimpsed a ship on the far horizon. The orchestra stood there now, playing for the benefit of those outside. They had assembled in a hurry; I could see the score in the carpet where the cellist had dragged up his instrument.

Scurra sat below in the Palm Court, sprawled at a table with his legs stretched out. He was discussing the Peloponnesian War with Stead, the journalist. Neither of them took any notice of me. Mr Stead was neatly dressed for a windy morning on Wall Street. His life-preserver lay draped across his knee. Scurra wore a long black overcoat beneath which dangled the hem of my purple dressing-gown.

I was forced to interrupt their conversation. 'Look here,' I said, 'it's important I find Wallis. Ida won't get into the boats without her.'

'She's somewhere around,' Scurra said. 'She was rather tied up when the call came.'

I couldn't fight him. I slumped into a chair and fought my own demons, calculating in my head how long I might survive in that icy water, should it come to it, while Scurra debated whether Thucydides' account of the destruction of the Athenian fleet was truthful or not. He dwelt particularly on the drowning incidents, arguing that as the Greeks were half fish by nature and as the temperature of the sea off the harbour was generally high, it was surprising so many had perished. My mind drifted, until I swam with Hopper in that lazy lake at Warm Springs.

Presently, the journalist stood and shook us both by the hand. 'It's been an interesting trip,' he observed. 'I doubt we'll see another one like it.'

'Quite,' said Scurra.

When Stead had gone, the room became deathly quiet. Save for a man at a table in the far corner, a full bottle of Gordon's gin at his elbow, we were alone. The orchestra had decamped to the deck outside. Scurra appeared lost in thought; one finger tapped at his gouged lip. The silence lay like a weight. Clearing my throat, I considered asking how he had really come by his scarred mouth, then changed my mind. For all it mattered, God himself could have taken a bite out of him.

At last, Scurra said, 'I was in the Turkish baths earlier. How very exhausting it is lying on an Egyptian couch with the perspiration collecting in the folds of one's belly. The only thing missing was a plate of grapes.' I didn't reply, knowing him for a liar; the baths were closed on a Sunday. He looked at me quizzically. 'You appear angry,' he said. 'Or is it your way of preparing for the ordeal to come?'

'Something like that,' I muttered.

'Apparently the liner *Carpathia* is on its way to us.'

'Is it?' My heart leapt in my breast.

'So Ismay tells me. Unfortunately she won't reach us in time.'

'I don't intend to throw in the towel,' I told him.

'I should think not. Still, it's curious, don't you think, how we cling to life when everything profound exhorts us to let go?'

'I'm not aware of it,' I said. I was tired of his philosophising. All I wanted was for Sissy to come through the swing doors and take me by the hand.

'Think of music,' he said. 'Why is it that we are most moved by those works composed in a minor key? Or disturbed to tears by the phrase . . . "half in love with easeful death"?'

'I'm not,' I replied brusquely, and got to my feet.

'You mustn't worry about Wallis,' he called after me. 'She and Molly Dodge are in the care of Ginsberg. He took them up top ten minutes ago.'

On the promenade of A deck a handful of passengers strolled sedately back and forth. I was astonished to see Mrs Brown and Mrs Carter among them, having imagined they had got away sometime before. Mrs Brown said it was over seventy feet down to the water and that the language used by one of the crew members was too foul to repeat. He had insisted on smoking, she said, and threw spent matches among them. She and Mrs Carter and young Mrs Astor had all got out again, though Ida had stayed. She'd attempted to clamber out, but her foot had caught in a rope. Mrs Carter had torn her coat prising herself through the window. It wasn't her best coat but she intended to sue the company when all this was over. The boat had been lowered only a quarter full. Mr Carter explained they were waiting for instructions to go further down into the ship. The second officer had ordered the gangway hatches to be opened so that they could enter the boats nearer the water. As yet, nobody had returned to fetch them. I asked why there were so few people about and was told that most preferred to hold on a little longer, seeing that the *Carpathia* was now steaming towards us.

I was making for the companionway to the upper deck when Rosenfelder approached. He urged me to come with him to find Adele who had gone to her cabin determined to rescue her Madame Butterfly costume. For some extraordinary reason he twice addressed me as lamb chop, once when we were rounding the landing on C deck and again when I made a wrong turning on level F. 'You are going backwards, lamb chop,' he scolded. 'Please concentrate.' I guess he was being affectionate.

There was terrible confusion below, the passageways jammed with people, their possessions stowed in pillow-cases slung across their shoulders. We saw not a single officer or steward as we forced our way through. A boy riding a home-made hobby horse with a skein of red yarn for a mane scraped my ankle; his mother scurried behind carrying an infant, a shawl over her breast, the tiny fingers of the child caught like a brooch in the wool. In the public lounge an untidy circle of men and women surrounded a priest reciting the rosary. Some knelt, others rocked backwards and forwards as though the ship rolled beneath them. The priest was a bear of a man with a great splodge of a nose and he gabbled rather than spoke, the responses swirling about him like the hectic buzzing of disturbed bees. Coming to a bend in the passage near the dormitories, we had to flatten ourselves against the tiled wall as a dozen or more stokers, faces black with grease and some carrying shovels, swept headlong past. The fans in the ceiling had stopped spinning and it was uncomfortably warm. I couldn't help contrasting this subterranean hell with the Eden above, where, under the twinkling stars, they paced to the swoon of violins.

Moments later we spotted Adele coming from the direction of the kitchens. One hand balanced aloft a cheap suitcase, a loaf of bread teetering on top, the other hitched up the skirt of Rosenfelder's dress, exposing her handsome legs to the knee. She wore a black cloak lent by Lady Duff Gordon; even so, we could clearly see the edges of that waterfall train had become trimmed with dirt.

'My God,' cried Rosenfelder. He pulled a handkerchief from the pocket of his honey-coloured fur and, sinking to the floor, frantically dabbed at the material. He was knocked sideways by the blundering run of a middle-aged man carrying a dinner plate rattling with spoons. I was ashamed on Rosenfelder's behalf—so much more was at stake than a ruined gown—and dragged him to his feet. Adele said, 'There's sea water trickling across the floor of the kitchen. My shoes have turned crusty,' and sure enough, her ivory slippers were stained yellow at the toes.

We escorted her to the boat deck, starboard. A boat was being prepared for lowering. Either the ropes were too new and too stiff or the cleats weren't oiled sufficiently, but the handlers were having a devil of a job getting her down from the davits. There was no sign of Ginsberg and the girls. Ascot and his wife were standing nearby, not touching, he looking out into the night, she drooping beneath the studded sky. He had brought up his dog; yawning, its breath curled like smoke. Mrs Brown was there too with the Carters and Mrs Hogeboom. Mrs Carter said she was worn out traipsing the stairs from one deck to another and would be glad to sit down. While we were waiting I strolled towards the stern. Ahead of me an officer hurried towards two women coming from the port side in the direction of the gate separating the first and second class. He held up his arm. 'May we pass?' one of the women asked, and he replied, 'No, madam, your boats are down on your own deck,' and they trailed away.

When our boat was at last ready and Mrs Carter had boarded, Mr Carter cried out, 'If anything should prevent me from following, everything you need to know is in the third drawer down in the bureau.'

'Yes, dear,' replied Mrs Carter.

The Astors stepped forward. Helping his wife over the gunwale Astor asked, 'I can go with her, can't I? She needs me.' His foot was raised, ready to climb. The officer replied, 'I'm afraid you can't, sir. We have to see to the women first.' 'I understand,' Astor said, and dropped back instantly. His wife looked at him; she gave a plucky little smile as he waved his farewell. I turned to Adele and seized her elbow. She was tearing chunks out of the loaf with her teeth, as though famished. She shook me away and crumbs flew in all directions. 'I'm not getting in that thing,' she said. 'I'll go when the Duff Gordons tell me it's time.' I think Rosenfelder was relieved at her refusal. Mrs Carter had shown him her torn coat.

The boat descended with creaks and groans. It was half full, no more. We peered down, waiting to hear it hit the water. 'We need a man,' bellowed the spunky Mrs Brown, her hat in the light of the portholes assuming the shape of a swooping vulture. 'There's no one at the tiller.' The officer shouted for a seaman and a wine steward from the à la carte restaurant darted forward and shimmied down the rope before anyone could stop him. Someone screamed out he was a damned scoundrel. We watched the boat row away.

There were no lanterns on board and once it had moved out of the shimmer of the porthole lights we heard only the ghostly splashings of the oars. 'Garfield has the key,' called Mr Carter. There was no reply.

The second boat was almost in place when it jammed some three feet above the rail. A complicated procedure required it to jerk upwards before coming down; I supposed this was to make sure the ropes were running free. The officer in charge turned—I was fortunate to be standing nearest to him—and called for assistance. I leapt at the chance, glad to be active at last, and put my whole heart into the task, tugging and pushing as though it was my own life that depended on it. And when we had got it straight, or fairly so, and the officer shouted for the women to come forward, I was able to help them up and tumble them aboard. Again the boat was cranked away half full, and I couldn't but do arithmetic in my head and subtract the saved from those left behind, particularly those bewildered souls I had seen below in the steerage class.

I was now ordered to the port side where there were more men than women gathered on deck. I learnt later that a rumour had gone round to the effect that men were to be taken off from here and women from the starboard side. Whatever the truth of it, when boat Number 5 was ready to be filled there were so few women that a dozen or more men were allowed to clamber in. I asked the officer if we shouldn't wait but he said there wasn't time and he daren't fill it to capacity, not at this height, because the boat might break in two under the strain. 'There are women and children waiting below at the gangway hatches,' he said. 'They can enter more easily from there.' As the boat dropped in fits and starts, the women clinging to each other, a commotion broke out to my right and a man shouted, 'Faster . . . faster . . . lower away faster, I tell you.' It was Bruce Ismay, whirling his arms round like a windmill. He had lost one of his slippers and his bare foot stamped the deck as he cried out again in a fever of impatience, 'Faster, damn you . . . faster.' Then the officer supervising got angry, and shouted back, 'If you'll get the hell out of the way, I'll be able to do my job. You want me to lower away faster? You fool, you'll have me drown the lot of them.' At this Ismay limped off, his arms still swinging. I craned over the rail, expecting to see the boat halt on a level with the hatches, but it met the water and rowed away.

Shortly after, they started sending up more rockets, this time at five-minute intervals. As each glare flashed the deck with light the upturned faces froze in shock. In one such instant I glimpsed Adele, curved like a mermaid with that glimmering train swished aside. I made my way along the now crowded deck and reaching her, urged her to follow me. She told me she had arranged to meet up with Rosenfelder and the Duff Gordons on the forward area, but had lost them in a sudden stampede to starboard. I asked if she had seen Wallis and she said she had, in the foyer with Ginsberg and another girl, but that was a while ago. Wallis had been smoking a cigarette.

I was escorting her forward when an officer marched up and demanded I fetch blankets from the store room. Just then the Strauses passed by with their maid. The girl was crying, protesting that she didn't want to leave them, and they were assuring her that it was for the best and that she must think of her widowed mother. I pressed Mr Straus to look after Adele and he replied it would give him pleasure.

I hadn't the faintest idea where the store room might be, but remembering the rugs flung to the floor as they utilised the steamer chairs on the enclosed promenade, I hurried below. Securing a hefty pile I was about to return when I glanced through the windows into the smoke-room. It appeared empty save for a circle of men playing cards in front of the fire—but then, one of the players shifted and to my amazement, behind him in the alcove, I saw Wallis sitting with Ginsberg. Dreadfully concerned, I dashed inside.

When she saw me she waved her hand excitedly and cried out, 'Now we'll know what's happening.'

I could tell by their flushed faces that they'd both been drinking. Knowing what I knew about her, I suppose I shouldn't have been so shocked, but I was. Absurdly, I felt I was to blame in some way. Furiously I turned on Ginsberg and called him a blazing idiot for not taking her up on deck.

'Steady on,' he protested. 'I did try. She wouldn't have it.'

'I almost went,' she said. 'Earlier, with Molly. I feel rather guilty about it. She was clutching my arm and at the last moment I just twisted away. I couldn't stand the idea of being cooped up with all those bawling children.'

'Ida, at least, is safe,' I said.

'Safe?'

'Yes, safe,' I ground out. 'The ship is sinking, or hadn't you heard? She looked all over for you. The door to your room was locked.'

'I was with Ginsberg,' she insisted. 'I can't think why the door was locked.'

There was the slightest pause, in which she and Ginsberg exchanged glances. Defiantly, she took one of his cigarettes and waited for him to light it. 'Stay and have a drink,' she urged. 'The stewards have all vanished but Ginsberg keeps leaping over the bar.'

'You needn't look at me like that, Morgan,' Ginsberg said. 'I've been scrupulous in leaving money behind. It's as well to be honest, don't you think, even if no one will ever know.'

Tearing the cigarette from Wallis's fingers I crushed it flat in the spittoon.

'Dear me,' she cried, 'you're as touchy as Ida.'

'She didn't want to get into the boat,' I shouted, 'not without you. She would have stayed if the officer in charge hadn't shoved her aboard.'

'Poor dear Ida,' Wallis murmured, 'she's always responded to shoving,' at which, exasperated beyond endurance, I left them.

Guggenheim was blocking the gymnasium doorway, peering through the window to watch Kitty Webb walk away. He stepped aside to let me pass and Kitty looked back and called out, 'Be seeing you, Benny.' He said, 'Goodbye, little girl,' but I doubt if she heard because the door was already closing and the orchestra stood near by. In spite of the cold the cellist wore no gloves and I marvelled that he managed to hold his bow so steady on the strings.

Captain Smith had come down from the bridge and was standing with the quartermaster at the foot of the companionway. They were both staring into the night. I wanted Smith to notice I was being useful, so I approached and handed the rugs to the quartermaster. He took them without comment; Smith's gaze never wavered from the horizon. It was possible to believe a whole fleet of ships lay anchored there, for the stars shone so brightly that where the heavens dipped to meet the sea it swam with points of diamond light. I walked further off, stamping my feet to stop my toes from freezing, until I heard the creaking of the davits on the forward area. They were releasing Number 1 boat and I raced to assist.

This time my help wasn't welcome; there were at least six or seven members of the crew manoeuvring it into position. Ready to shift, they all climbed in, and at that moment a man and three women crossed out of the shadows and I heard Duff Gordon's voice say, 'May we get into the boat?' and the rough reply, 'if you must.' I supposed two of the women to be Adele and the Strauses' maid, but as I got closer I saw both were elderly. I called out to Lady Duff Gordon, asking what had happened to Adele, but already the boat was swinging away and she couldn't have heard me. I shouted up to the officer to wait, for I had clearly seen there was room for thirty or more aboard, but he continued to work the ropes, bellowing at me to stand back; I guess he was under the impression that I was trying to save myself.

As the last life-boat on the starboard side dropped from sight, a great swoosh of smoke belched from the funnels and rubbed out the sky. When it had drifted on and the milky stars came back I heard the first gun-shot.

I was running in the direction of the report when Charlie came haring up.

'Wallis wants you,' he panted. 'You must come and talk to her. She refuses to move unless you speak to her. Hopper tried to carry her off bodily but she kicked him. She's frightfully squiffy.'

'The shot,' I said. 'I heard a shot.'

'There was a bit of a rumpus on the port side. Some of the men tried to rush the boats and the second officer fired over their heads. They were steerage passengers, of course.'

The men in the smoke-room were still playing cards. Ginsberg had gone. Hopper stood with his leg raised on a chair, scowling and rubbing at his shins. 'You talk sense into her,' he muttered. 'She's gone crazy.'

Wallis looked at me with glittering eyes. Such a look! Not crazy at all but ugly with suffering. I knew what was wrong with her without being told, as though her soul had flashed on mine. Pity welled up in me, and envy too, for I might never know the sort of love that gripped her by the throat.

'Please,' she croaked. 'I must speak to him. You will find him, won't you?'

'I'll try,' I said. 'But you must come on deck to be near the boats.'

'I can't move,' she said.

'I know,' I soothed. 'Charlie will carry you.'

I didn't look for Scurra. Not right away. There were more urgent matters to attend to, for when I came out on to the promenade there were
at least a hundred people milling about the deck, shouting and
shoving at each other in their attempts to get to a life-boat swaying at
the rail. There were steerage passengers among them now; I caught
sight of the priest with the nose and the boy with the hobby-horse. The
officers were striking out with their feet at the men and hauling the
women up like so many sacks. There was no thought in my mind of
going back for Wallis; it would have been well-nigh impossible for
Charlie to get her through such a crush. Hopper and I fought our way
to the front and once there stood shoulder to shoulder, heaving the
men aside and passing the women and children into the arms of the
officer who knelt on the gunwale. Fists punched my face but I scarcely
felt the blows.

This time there was no question of the boat going away half filled;
seventy or more, mostly women, and some of those standing, made that
lurching descent. They had almost reached the sea when something
went wrong with the tackle and the ropes jammed—then she was nearly
swamped by a jet of water propelled from the ship's waste pipe. A wail
of terror gushed up. I had a good view of the whole desperate scene, for
the moment the boat had begun to drop the crowd had fled further
along the deck to where the next one swung. Below, no sooner was the
danger over than another dilemma arose, in that they couldn't detach
the falls; the water was so calm there was no lift. The boat drifted aft,
still caught, and again the women wailed. The second boat was falling
now, directly above the first. A voice called out, 'For God's sake, she'll
scuttle us,' and then the helmsman must have used his knife for the next
instant the boat swerved and slid free.

I wasn't cold any more, that's for sure; the sweat ran into my eyes.
Hopper had a split lip. We went up top to see what more could be done
and found a collapsible had been hitched to the empty davits where

the Duff Gordons' boat had hung. Mr Carter and Bruce Ismay stood beside it. They had their hands cupped to their mouths and were bellowing for women to come forward, but there didn't seem to be any in sight. I shouted that there were plenty on the decks below and with that the officer helped Mr Carter and Mr Ismay on board. Mr Carter called out for Hopper and me to join them, but we shook our heads. I can't know for certain what Hopper was thinking, yet I guess we both felt it would be an unmanly thing to do with so many women still stranded. Mr Carter wasn't a bad old stick and I didn't want him to feel we'd shown him up, so I ran to the rail and wished him God Speed and said I hoped to see him and Mrs Carter before long. Such was the list of the ship that as the collapsible dropped it banged against the hull and they had to lever it away with the oars for fear the rivet-heads tore the canvas. We could hear Ismay yelling for Mr Carter to put his back into it.

We were hurrying aft when Hopper spied Charlie sitting on a bench at the base of the second funnel. He was cradling Wallis in his arms. 'She won't stop shaking,' he said. 'Rosenfelder's given her his coat but it hasn't made any difference.' Guiltily, I remembered my promise. I told him not to move from the spot, not unless he could manage to get Wallis into a life-boat. He pursed his mouth and said that was unlikely. He had tried to do just that ten minutes before and she'd bitten his hand.

Scurra was still in the Palm Court. The man with the bottle of Gordon's gin had joined him; he was middle-aged and had mild, if somewhat inflamed, blue eyes. The bottle was almost empty but Scurra hadn't been drinking.

'Wallis needs you,' I said. 'She has to talk to you.' There didn't seem any point in beating about the bush.

'About anything in particular?'

'Come now,' I cried. 'You know damn well what I mean.'

'Is this a private conversation?' asked the gin drinker.

'What would you like me to say to her?' Scurra said. 'What would you advise?' His expression was grave, which took the steam out of me.

'I don't know,' I said. 'Perhaps you could pretend to—'

'If it is,' our table companion interrupted, 'I can always go away. I'm used to going away. I can tip-toe away like a fairy.'

'Pretend what?' Scurra asked.

'To care,' I said.

'It's dangerous to pretend—'

'But if it gets her into the boats—'

'And what if she should survive?' he said. 'No doubt I would then be faced with a breach of promise case.' Now he shook with laughter, but I reckoned it wasn't genuine.

'Perhaps all she wants is for you to say goodbye.'

'Just say the word,' muttered the drinker, his head sinking to the table.

'There's not much time,' I said. 'She's sitting up there, refusing to enter the boats. Do you want her on your conscience?' He said slowly, 'I'm not entirely sure I have one.' He looked away, trying to find an argument. I couldn't force him to go with me, I knew that. The drunk was dreaming, snorting. Scurra patted his head like a mother.

I was prepared to give up when he said, 'I'm not as cruel as you think, you know. I do have my feelings, though they appear to be different from those generally considered suitable. There are many women on this ship who would have granted me their favours, just as there are many men who stepped into the breach once it became obvious I was not available. I say this without vanity, hard as it is for someone of your age and disposition to believe. I am simply stating a fact. I chose Wallis because I recognised a creature similar to myself, that is, in matters of the heart. I use the phrase loosely, you understand, for in a liaison such as I describe the heart is usually absent.'

'Then you chose wrong,' I said hotly. 'She's fearfully upset.'

'That is because of unfortunate circumstances,' he reasoned. 'I didn't expect to couple with death so soon after engaging in what passes for love.'

'I don't want to hear it,' I shouted, and I meant death, not the other thing, of which I knew nothing.

'Supposing I come with you,' he argued, 'and do as you say. Ten to one she'll rebuff me. Women are like that, don't you agree? And if I say those comforting words, which have no basis in truth, she may spend the rest of her life deceived into believing that the best has gone for ever, simply because this night is like no other.'

I could stand it no longer and jumped to my feet. 'Goodbye,' I said. 'There is nothing more to say.'

'Goodbye,' echoed the drunk, struggling upright. 'Delighted to have met you.'

All the same, Scurra came with me. I led him to Charlie who had remained at his post with Wallis in his arms. He and I stood a little way off to give them privacy. Poor old Charlie was blue with cold, and mystified, but he held his tongue. We could hear a hubbub of angry voices coming from the port side and women screaming.

I don't know what Scurra said to her. At one point she lifted her hand as though to slap his face and he caught her wrist to stop her. After no more than a few minutes she rose and came over to Charlie. She had recovered her poise and even something of her vivacity. She said matter-of-factly, 'I'm ready to go now,' and tugged the collar of Rosenfelder's fur coat more snugly about her ears.

'Ships that pass in the night,' murmured Scurra, as he sauntered back inside. It was then that I heard the second gun-shot, followed by several more, and a scream louder than all the rest.

I didn't recognise Rosenfelder right away because Adele knelt over him, holding his head against her breast and shielding his face with her hand. We prised her away from him, fearful he might be trampled underfoot by the mob who raged about the collapsible now being lowered towards the deck. Between us Charlie and I got him to the nearest bench and laid him down. He wasn't badly hurt but he squealed like a stuck pig when I handled his shoulder too roughly. He said he'd been endeavouring to get Adele closer to the boat when an officer had begun firing wildly into the crowd. Another officer had tried to take the gun off him because of the women, but by then it was too late. He thought he had been hit in the upper part of the arm.

I left Charlie in charge of him and, ordering Adele and Wallis to hold on tight to the tails of my coat, thrust my way into the centre of that frenzied throng. Groans and curses accompanied my every strug- gling inch. The list was so bad now that people fell over and were stepped upon and we didn't care. In an attempt to stop all but the women from boarding the officers had linked arms in a circle about the boat. Fortunately, one of them recognised me from my labours on the enclosed promenade and gestured me on. When I reached him I swung the girls round, Wallis first, and he pulled her through. I was in the process of thrusting Adele to safety when that damn gun went off again and in the surge backwards lost my place and was swept to the perimeter. Adele trembled like a leaf and appeared quite incapable of going forward again and, indeed, I too felt I didn't have it in me, for I was exhausted. I had to half carry her back to the bench. Her cloak had been torn off and the front of her gown was smeared with blood, though it was Rosenfelder's not hers. She sat shivering beside the wounded tailor; wincing, he eased himself out of his jacket and draped it about her shoulders. 'You go on,' he said to me. 'I expect you have things to do.'

'If I find there's another boat,' I told him, 'I'll come back for you and Adele.' He nodded. I didn't say goodbye to him, not until later, and I was sorry for it, for when I did he couldn't hear me.

We walked towards the stern. Midships, another collapsible was edging its way down to the water. It appeared fairly full. As we watched it go a figure climbed on to the rail beneath, stepped out, and sliding rather than leaping landed half over the gunwale. His head was in the water and when they jerked him upright and he fell on his back we saw it was Ginsberg, insensible and still clutching his sticky handkerchief. I guess his fall had knocked the breath out of him. For a moment it crossed my mind that I too might make a jump for it, but already the boat was moving out of the lights. 'Rats always leave a sinking ship,' remarked Charlie, and I thought that damned unfair, and stupidly told him so. His eyes filled up with tears. Hopper went over to the officer who had just come down from the davits and asked him what we should do. 'Pray,' was the reply.

Now that all the boats had gone, the waiting began. We went inside to search for something that we might cling to in the water. This was Hopper's idea. It was ten minutes to two by the clock on the Grand Staircase and we marvelled that time had crept so slowly, for it seemed we had lived a life-time in the space of an hour.

The card players had remained stoically at their table in the smoke-room. Hopper asked one of them for a cigarette and was told there were hundreds in the bar and all free. He came back with the orna-mental lifebuoy that had hung on the wall above the spirits shelf. He tried to put it on but it wouldn't go further than his shoulders, which pinned his arms to his sides so that he couldn't get it off again. In spite of everything, this made me laugh out loud, at which the card players had the cheek to tick me off for being rowdy.

Then I remembered Rosenfelder telling me that they sold souvenirs of the voyage in the barber's shop on C deck. He'd bought a shaving brush with the White Star flag enamelled on the handle. I'd asked him, thinking of Sissy's baby, if they had anything suitable for small chil-dren, and he'd said he'd seen teddy bears and inflatable rings for sea-side excursions. I suggested to Charlie that he come with me but he turned pale at the idea of going so far below. 'I'm sorry,' he said, 'I can't help being a coward.' I didn't show it, but I lost patience with him. After all, most of us are cowards, but it's simply not on to shout it from the roof-tops.

It was eerie passing down through the ship. There was no one about, and still all the lights blazed. I didn't use the elevator for fear there was a sudden stagger and I got trapped. The tilt was pronounced now and I walked along the corridors with my hands braced on either side of the walls. When I came to the barber's shop the door was swinging inwards on its hinges. Riley sat in one of the swivel chairs, combing his hair in the mirror. He grinned when he saw me, and spun himself round and round. 'Try it,' he said. 'It's a good lark.' I took the chair next to him and we both whirled. Truly, I felt very much at ease.

'What are you after down here?' he said. 'Did you think you needed a shave?'

'I was looking for something to hold on to . . . when we hit the water.'

'Get away with you,' he scoffed. 'You'll have her whole bloody innards to choose from once she starts to plunge.' My eyes must have held a shadow of alarm, for he added, 'She won't go just yet, take it from me. Maybe half an hour, longer if we're lucky.'

'Had it anything to do with the fire?' I asked. 'The one in the bunker.'

'Doubt it,' he said. 'We was just going too fast and not heeding the ice warnings.'

'Is the *Carpathia* really on its way?'

'So the Marconi fellow has it. But she won't get to us till the morning.'

'It is the morning.'

'Proper morning,' he said. 'Brekky time.' He stopped spinning and began to unscrew the stoppers of the bottles above the basin, sniffing the contents in turn. When the smell didn't meet with his approval he emptied the liquid down the plug hole. An aroma of scented soap hung in the air. Reflected in the mirror a row of teddy bears sat stiff on the shelf behind me. They wore while sailor hats but the band about each crown bore the letters, backwards, RMS *Olympic*.

'I suppose it's best to jump,' I said. 'And from the stern.'

'Wrong, bloody wrong. Best place is the roof of the officers' house. Where the collapsible is. Her bows will go down and the sea will wash you off. Mind you, the first funnel will likely keep you company.'

'There's another boat?'

'The officers is keeping it for themselves. Leastways, we weren't told to get it down.' He was watching me in the mirror, studying my build. 'You might make it,' he said. 'You'd think the fat ones would do best, having more flesh on them, but mostly their tickers give up under the shock. Now me, I'm on the scrawny side, but that only means the cold will freeze my blood quicker.' I reckoned he was trying to frighten me and stared him out. I asked, 'What did I do to make you so angry . . . before?'

'It's water under the bridge now,' he said.

'All the same, I'd like to know.'

'That bleeding half-crown you tossed me.' I stared at him. I thought he meant that in tipping him I'd treated him as an inferior. 'I'm sorry,' I stammered. 'I didn't think.'

'No, you bloody well didn't. Still, it don't matter now . . . you with your millions and me with me half-crown, we're both in the same boat.' And with that he took a silver coin out of his pocket and dropped it in the sink. Then he went out of the door. I sat there a moment, feeling sick. I think it was the smell of lavender, not his treatment of me that turned my stomach. I left the coin where it lay, in case he came back, but when I went out into the passage there was no sign of him.

All the way up to A deck I argued with him in my head, protesting that I wasn't stingy and that on his wages I wouldn't have turned my nose up at two shillings and sixpence—but then, I thought of the money Charlie had said I'd thrown away at cards the night before and fairly burned with shame.

Hopper and Charlie had gone from the smoke-room. So had the card players. Thomas Andrews was standing with his back to me at the fire, balancing up on his toes, positioning a picture in place above the mantelpiece. It was the Plymouth Harbour painting, the one I'd last seen hanging in the library. He stepped back to see if it hung straight, and I called out his name. He didn't turn round. His life-preserver lay across the table. I went closer and said, 'Will you not come up on deck, sir? There isn't much time.' Still with his back to me he fluttered his hand in the air, either waving me away or waving goodbye.

I did as Riley had told me and once on the boat deck climbed the companionway up to the officers' house which was forward of the first funnel. There were seamen on the roof, struggling to release the collapsible. I peered down and saw Guggenheim and his valet both dressed as though off to a swell party. They were listening to the orchestra which was playing rag-time to raise our spirits, Guggenheim tap-tapping his cane on the rail. Hopper stood not a yard from them, looking first one way then the other. I guessed he was trying to find me and shouted to him. By good luck he heard and sprinted towards the stairs. He told me Charlie was further along the deck. They had both gone aft to where a priest was giving conditional absolution to a demented congregation. When Charlie had fallen to his knees and started to blub out the most damn fool confessions, like how he'd tormented a cat when he was a child and how he'd stolen a dollar from his mother's purse, he had to leave him. 'Honest to God, Morgan, he's turned yellow.'

At that moment the orchestra changed tune and struck up a hymn, one I knew well because it was a favourite of my aunt's and sometimes she used to sing it when she was in one of her brighter moods . . . *E'en though it be a cross that raiseth me, Still all my song shall be, Nearer my God to Thee, Nearer to Thee.* Hearing it, I knew I had to go in search of Charlie, for Lady Melchett's sake if not my own, and would have gone on searching for him if Scurra hadn't been waiting for me at the bottom of the steps. He said, 'A man bears the weight of his own body without knowing it, but he soon feels the weight of any other object. There is nothing, absolutely nothing, that a man cannot forget—but not himself.' Then, before walking away, he said those other things, about it being the drop, not the height, that was terrible, and I left Charlie to God and went back up to the officers' house.

And now, the moment was almost upon us. The stern began to lift from the water. Guggenheim and his valet played mountaineers, going hand over hand up the rail. The hymn turned ragged; ceased altogether. The musicians scrambled upwards, the spike of the cello scraping the deck. Clinging to the rung of the ladder I tried to climb to the roof but there was such a sideways slant that I waved like a flag on a pole. I thought I must make a leap for it and turned to look for Hopper. Something, some inner voice urged me to glance below and I saw Scurra again, one arm hooked through the rail to steady himself. I raised my hand in greeting—then the water, first slithering, then tumbling, gushed us apart.

As the ship staggered and tipped, a great volume of water flowed in over the submerged bows and tossed me like a cork to the roof. Hopper was there too. My fingers touched some kind of bolt near the ventilation grille and I grabbed it tight. I filled my lungs with air and fixed my eyes on the blurred horizon, determined to hang on until I was sure I could float free rather than be swilled back and forth in a maelstrom. I wouldn't waste my strength in swimming, not yet, for I knew the ship was now my enemy and if I wasn't vigilant would drag me with her to the grave. I waited for the next slithering dip and when it came and the waves rushed in and swept me higher, I released my grip and let myself be carried away, over the tangle of ropes and wires and davits, clear of the rails and out into the darkness. I heard the angry roaring of the dying ship, the deafening cacophony as she stood on end and all her guts tore loose. I choked on soot and cringed beneath the sparks dancing like fire-flies as the forward funnel broke and smashed the sea in two. I thought I saw Hopper's face but one eye was ripped away and he gobbled like a fish on the hook. I was sucked under, as I knew I would be, down, down, and still I waited, waited until the pull slackened—then I struck out with all my strength.

I don't know how long I swam under that lidded sea—time had stopped with my breath—and just as it seemed as if my lungs would burst the blackness paled and I kicked to the surface. I had thought I was entering paradise, for I was alive and about to breathe again, and then I heard the cries of souls in torment and believed myself in hell. Dear God! Those voices! *Father . . . Father . . . For the love of Christ . . . Help me, for pity's sake! . . . Where is my son.* Some called for their mothers, some on the Lord, some to die quickly, a few to be saved. The lamentations rang through the frosty air and touched the stars; my own mouth opened in a silent howl of grief. The cries went on and on, trembling, lingering—and God forgive me, but I wanted them to end. In all that ghastly night it was the din of the dying that chilled the most. Presently, the voices grew fainter, ceased—yet still I heard them, as though the drowned called to one another in a ghostly place where none could follow. Then silence fell, and that was the worst sound of all. There was no trace of the *Titanic*. All that remained was a grey veil of vapour drifting above the water.

Gradually I grew accustomed to the darkness and made out a boat some distance away. Summoning up all my strength I swam closer; it was a collapsible, wrong side up and sagging in the sea. I tried to climb on to the gunwale but the occupants gazed through me and offered no assistance; they might have been dead men for all the life in their eyes. Swimming round to the far side, I commandeered a bobbing barrel, and, mounting it like a horse, hand-paddled to the stern and flung myself aboard.

We slushed there, twenty or more of us, lying like sponges in the icy pond within that canvas bag, looking up at the stars, students of the universe, each man lost in separate thoughts and dreams. I saw the library and that figure now clinging to the tilted mantelpiece, and old man Seefax, arms raised in terror as his chair skidded the room and the water leapt to douse the coals. Then I was in London again standing outside the Café Royal, the wet pavement shining in the lamp-light, a bunch of violets in my hand. And as I waited the revolving doors began to spin and out they came—Hopper, smiling, asking where the devil I'd been; Ginsberg, slapping me on the back in greeting; Charlie, cheeks pink with pleasure at the sight of me; Ben Guggenheim with his top hat jaunty on his head; Riley, hands in pockets, jingling coins; lastly, Scurra, staying within the doors, now facing me, now showing me his back, then facing me again, eyes sadly fixed on mine. Each time he passed he made an upward gesture with his hand and I stepped to join him, but the doors spun round and round and when they slowed he'd gone. Then Charlie pointed to the sky and we all looked up to watch a shooting star.

Now it was very cold in the boat and we were sinking deeper as we floated. I sat up and rubbed my frozen limbs, shouting at the others to stir themselves unless they wished to die. Some grumbled and resisted but most saw the sense in it and we worked together, baling out as much water as we could, though we still sat in that icy pool and sloped alarmingly. Fearing we might be swamped I organised them to stand up, not all at once, but in twos and separated by the length of an arm to maintain a balance. When this was accomplished and we all faced the horizon someone declared there was a ship out there and that she was moving. We stared as hard as we could, but there was such a display of shooting stars that night it was difficult to distinguish one light from another. An hour crept by, and to our delight we heard voices. Pretty soon, by means of shouting back and forth, two life-boats loomed. There was space in one of them for three of us, but we daren't disturb our balance and they rowed off.

It must have been thirty minutes or so later when that second lot of shooting stars went arching to the sea. We gazed in disbelief because they burst asunder before they fell. A solitary cheer came from somewhere to our right and a woman's voice shouted, 'It's the *Carpathia* for sure.' For one instant I wanted to cheer too, the next that momentary leap of relief was replaced by unease which deepened into guilt, for in that moment I had already begun to forget the dead. Now that I knew I was going to live there was something dishonourable in survival.

Dawn came and as far as the eye could see the ocean was dotted with islands and fields of ice. Some floated with tapering mast-heads, some sailed with monstrous bows rising sheer to the pink-flushed sky, some glided the water in the shapes of ancient vessels. Between this pale fleet the little life-boats rocked. There were other things caught upon the water—chairs and tables, crates, an empty gin bottle, a set of bagpipes, a cup without a handle, a creased square of canvas with a girl's face painted on it; and two bodies, she in a gown of ice with a mermaid's tail, he in shirt sleeves, the curls stiff as wood shavings on his head, his two hands frozen to the curve of a metal rail. Beyond, where the sun was beginning to show its burning rim, smoke blew from a funnel.

acknowledgments

Many people made this anthology.

Clint Willis gave me the opportunity to edit this book. I'm grateful for his guidance, patience, enthusiasm and skill.

At Thunder's Mouth Press and Avalon Publishing Group:
Neil Ortenberg and Susan Reich offered vital support and expertise. Dan O'Connor and Ghadah Alrawi also were indispensable.

At Balliett & Fitzgerald Inc.:
Will Balliett made this book possible. Tom Dyja and f-stop Fitzgerald lent intellectual and moral support. Sue Canavan created the book's look. Maria Fernandez oversaw production, and kept us on track with help from Paul Paddock.

At the Writing Company:
Nat May helped find and choose the selections for this book. It was a pleasure to work with him. Lee Rader cheerfully took on various tasks. Kate Fletcher was a determined researcher. Taylor Smith and Mark Klimek made me laugh, and took up slack on other projects.

At Shawneric.com:
Shawneric Hachey doggedly pursued permissions and photographs.

At the Portland Public Library in Portland, Maine:
The librarians cheerfully worked to locate and borrow books from across the country.

Finally, I am grateful to the writers whose work appears in this book.

We gratefully acknowledge all those who gave permission for material to appear in this book. We have made every effort to trace and contact copyright holders, but if errors or omissions are brought to our attention we shall be pleased to publish corrections in future editions of this book. For further information, please contact the publisher.

From *The Nutmeg of Consolation* by Patrick O'Brian. Copyright © 1991 by Patrick O'Brian. Used by permission of W.W. Norton & Company, Inc. ❖ "Everest at the Bottom of the Sea" by Bucky MacMahon. First published in *Esquire Magazine*, July 2000. Reprinted courtesy of *Esquire* and the Hearst Corporation. ❖ From *North to the Night* by Alvah Simon. Copyright © 1998 by Alvah Simon. Reprinted by permission of International Marine and the McGraw-Hill Companies. ❖ From *The Boat Who Wouldn't Float* by Farley Mowat. Copyright © 1969, 1970 by Farley Mowat, Ltd. Used by permission of Little, Brown and Company, Inc. ❖ From *Run Silent, Run Deep* by Edward L. Beach. Copyright © 1955 by Edward Latimer Beach. Reprinted with permission of Henry Holt & Company. ❖ From *Pincher Martin, The Two Deaths of Christopher Martin*. Copyright © 1956 by William Gerald Golding and renewed 1984 by William Gerald Golding, reprinted by permission of Harcourt, Inc. ❖ From *N by E* by Rockwell Kent. Copyright © 1930 and renewed 1958 by Rockwell Kent. Reprinted by permission of Wesleyan University Press. ❖ From *In the Heart of the Sea* by Nathaniel Philbrick. Copyright © 2000 by Nathaniel Philbrick. Reprinted by permission of Penguin Putnam, Inc. ❖ From *Every Man For Himself* by Beryl Bainbridge. Copyright © 1997 by Beryl Bainbridge. Reprinted by arrangement with Carroll & Graf Publishing.

b i b l i o g r a p h y

The selections used in this anthology were taken from the editions listed below. In some cases, other editions may be easier to find. Hard-to-find or out-of-print titles often are available through inter-library loan services or through Internet booksellers.

Bainbridge, Beryl. *Every Man For Himself*. New York: Carroll & Graf Publishers, 1997.

Beach, Edward L. *Run Silent, Run Deep*. New York: Henry Holt & Company, 1967.

Crane, Stephen. *Stephen Crane: Stories and Tales*. New York: Vintage Books, 1955.

Esquire. July 2000. (For "Everest at the Bottom of the Sea" by Bucky MacMahon.)

Golding, William. *Pincher Martin*. Orlando, FL: Harcourt Brace, 1984.

Kent, Rockwell. *N by E*. Hanover, NH: University Press of New England, 1996.

Melville, Herman. *Moby Dick*. New York: Random House, 1930.

Mowat, Farley. *The Boat Who Wouldn't Float*. New York: Bantam Books, 1981.

Neider, Charles. *Great Shipwrecks and Castaways*. New York: Harpers, 1952. (For "Philip Ashton's Own Account" by Philip Ashton.)

O'Brian, Patrick. *The Nutmeg of Consolation*. New York: W.W. Norton & Company, 1991.

Philbrick, Nathaniel. *In the Heart of the Sea*. New York: Penguin Books, 2000.

Simon, Alvah. *North To the Night*. New York: Broadway Books, 1998.

Stevenson, Robert Louis. *Treasure Island*. New York: Penguin Books, 1981.